Contents

CONTENTS

100 Maths Framework Lessons

About the series

100 Maths Framework Lessons is designed to support you with the implementation of the renewed *Primary Framework for Mathematics*. Each title in the series provides clear teaching and appropriate learning challenges for all children within the structure of the renewed Framework. By using the titles in this series, a teacher or school can be sure that they are following the structure and, crucially, embedding the principles and practice identified by the Framework.

About the renewed Framework

The renewed *Primary Framework for Mathematics* has reduced the number of objectives from the original 1999 Framework. Mathematics is divided into seven strands:
- Using and applying mathematics
- Counting and understanding number
- Knowing and using number facts
- Calculating
- Understanding shape
- Measuring
- Handling data.

The focus for teaching is using and applying mathematics, and these objectives are seen as central to success for the children's learning. While the number of objectives is reduced, the teaching programme retains the range of learning contained in the 1999 Framework. There are, though, significant changes in both the structure and content of the objectives in the new Framework and this series of books is designed to help teachers to manage these changes of emphasis in their teaching.

About this book

This book is set out in the five blocks that form the renewed *Primary Framework for Mathematics*. Each block consists of three units. Each unit within a block contains:
- a guide to the objective focus for each lesson within the unit
- links with the objectives from the 1999 objectives
- the 'speaking and listening' objective for the unit
- a list of key aspects of learning, such as problem solving, communication, etc.
- the vocabulary relevant to a group of lessons.

Within each unit the 'using and applying' objectives are clearly stated. They are incorporated within the individual lessons through the teaching and learning approach taken. Sometimes they may be the only focus for a lesson.

Lessons

Each lesson contains:
- A guide to the type of teaching and learning within the lesson, such as Review, Teach, Practise or Apply.
- A starter activity, with a guide to its type, such as Rehearse, Reason, Recall, Read, Refine, Refine and rehearse, or Revisit.
- A main activity, which concentrates on the teaching of the objective(s) for this lesson.
- Group, paired or individual work, which may include the use of an activity sheet from the CD-ROM.
- Clear differentiation, to help you to decide how to help the less confident learners in your group, or how to extend the learning for the more confident. This may also include reference to the differentiated activity sheets found on the CD-ROM.
- Review of the lesson, with guidance for asking questions to assess the children's understanding.

You can choose individual lessons as part of your planning, or whole units as you require.

MSCHOLASTIC

What's on the CD-ROM?

Each CD-ROM contains a range of printable sheets as follows:
- **Core activity sheets** with answers, where appropriate, that can be toggled by clicking on the 'show' or 'hide' buttons at the bottom of the screen.
- **Differentiated activity sheets** for more or less confident learners where appropriate.
- Blank core activity sheets or **templates** to allow you to make your own differentiated sheets by printing and annotating.

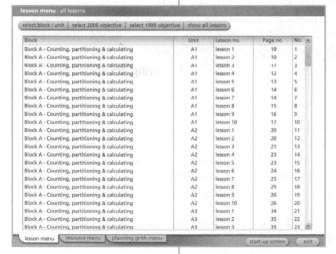

- **General resource sheets** (such as number grids) designed to support a number of lessons.
- **Editable curriculum grids** (in Word format) to enable you to integrate the lessons into your planning.
   In addition, the CD-ROM contains:
- **Interactive whiteboard resources** – a set of supporting resources to be used with the whole class on any interactive whiteboard or on a PC for small group work. These include number grids, money, clocks and so on.
- **Interactive Teaching Programs** – specific ITPs, originally developed for the National Numeracy Strategy, have been included on each CD-ROM.
- **Whiteboard tools** – a set of tools including a 'Pen', 'Highlighter' and 'Eraser', have been included to help you to annotate activity sheets for whole-class lessons. These tools will work on any interactive whiteboard.
- **Diagrams** – copies of all the diagrams included on the lesson pages.

How to use the CD-ROM
System requirements

Minimum specification:
- PC with a CD-ROM drive and 512 Mb RAM (recommended)
- Windows 98SE or above/Mac OSX.1 or above
- Recommended minimum processor speed: 1 GHz

Getting started

The *100 Maths Framework Lessons* CD-ROM should auto run when you insert the CD-ROM into your CD drive. If it does not, use **My Computer** to browse the contents of the CD-ROM and click on the '100 Maths Framework Lessons' icon.

From the start-up screen there are four options: click on **Credits & acknowledgements** to view a list of acknowledgements. You should also view the **Terms and conditions** of use and register the product to receive product updates and special offers. Finally, you can access extensive **How to use this CD-ROM** support notes and (if you agree to the 'Terms and conditions') click on **Start** to move to the main menu.

Each CD-ROM allows you to search for resources by block, unit or lesson. You can also search by Framework objective (both 2006 and 1999 versions) or by resource type (for example, activity sheet, interactive resource or ITP).

Planning

The renewed Framework planning guidance sets out the learning objectives in blocks, and then subdivides these into units. The blocks are entitled:
- **Block A:** Counting, partitioning and calculating
- **Block B:** Securing number facts, understanding shape
- **Block C:** Handling data and measures
- **Block D:** Calculating, measuring and understanding shape
- **Block E:** Securing number facts, relationships and calculating.

Within each block there are three progressive units, which set out the learning objectives for a two- or three-week teaching period. Because of the interrelated nature of learning in mathematics, some of the same learning objectives appear in different blocks so that the children have the opportunity to practise and apply their mathematics.

	Block A: Counting, partitioning and calculating (6 weeks)	Block B: Securing number facts, understanding shape (9 weeks)	Block C: Handling data and measures (6 weeks)	Block D: Calculating, measuring and understanding shape (6 weeks)	Block E: Securing number facts, relationships and calculating (9 weeks)
Autumn	Unit A1	Unit B1	Unit C1	Unit D1	Unit E1
Spring	Unit A2	Unit B2	Unit C2	Unit D2	Unit E2
Summer	Unit A3	Unit B3	Unit C3	Unit D3	Unit E3

It is recommended that planning for the year takes the blocks and units in the following order:
However, the book has been structured in block order (Block A1, A2, A3 and so on), so that teachers can plan progression across units more effectively, and plan other configurations of lessons where required. You can use the different menus on the CD-ROM to find suitable teaching and learning material to match your planning needs.

In each unit in this book, the 1999 Framework objectives are listed, so that it is possible to use materials from previous planning alongside these lessons. The CD-ROM has a facility that allows for filtering by 2006 and 1999 learning objectives in order to find suitable lessons.

The blocks and units, taught in the order above, make a comprehensive teaching package which will effectively cover the teaching and learning for this year group.

Differentiation

Each lesson contains three levels of differentiation in order to meet the wide variety of needs within a group of children. There are differentiated activity sheets for many lessons that can be accessed on the CD-ROM (see 'What's on the CD-ROM', above). The units within a block are placed together within this book. This is in order to enable you to make choices about what to teach, when and to which children, in order to encourage more personalised learning.

Assessment

Within this book the guidelines for 'Assessment for learning' from the Framework are followed:
● Assessment questions are provided within each lesson in order to identify children's learning and to provide the children with effective feedback.
● The questions encourage children to be actively involved in their own learning.
● Many activities are undertaken in groups or pairs so that children have the opportunity to plan together and assess the effectiveness of what they have undertaken.
● The assessment outcomes give the teacher the opportunity to adjust teaching to take account of the results of assessment.
● The crucial importance of assessment is recognised, and the profound influence it has on the motivation and self-esteem of children, both of which are essential for learning.
● The assessment questions offer children the opportunity to understand what they know, use and understand and also to understand how to improve.

Counting, partitioning and calculating

Key aspects of learning
- Problem solving
- Reasoning
- Social skills
- Communication

Expected prior learning
Check that children can already:
- count from any given number in whole-number steps
- use positive and negative numbers in practical contexts; position them on a number line
- add or subtract mentally pairs of two-digit whole numbers, eg 47 + 58, 91 – 35
- use efficient written methods to add and subtract two- and three-digit whole numbers and £.p
- recall multiplication and division facts to 10 ×10
- multiply or divide numbers to 1000 by 10 and then 100 (whole-number answers)
- use written methods to multiply and divide TU × U, TU ÷ U
- use decimal notation for tenths and hundredths in the context of money and measurement
- order decimals to two places and position them on a number line
- use a calculator to carry out one- and two-step calculations involving all four operations; interpret the display correctly in the context of money
- use the relationship between m, cm and mm

Objectives overview
The text in this diagram identifies the focus of mathematics learning within the block.

Solving one- and two-step word problems involving numbers, money or measures

Ordering, partitioning and rounding whole numbers and decimals to two places

Explaining methods and reasoning, orally and on paper, using words, diagrams, graphs, symbols

Block A: Counting, partitioning and calculating

Addition and subtraction

Mental methods: special cases

Written methods: whole numbers and decimals

Multiplication and division

Tables to 10 × 10; multiplying multiples of 10 and 100; factors

Mental methods: TU × U and special cases

Written methods: HTU × U, TU × U, U.t × U, HTU/U

Using a calculator

Unit 1 ▭ **2 weeks**

Counting, partitioning and calculating

Lesson	Strands	Starter	Main teaching activities
1. Review	Counting	Count from any given number in whole number and decimal steps, extending beyond zero when counting backwards; relate the numbers to their position on a number line.	**Explain what each digit represents in whole numbers and decimals with up to two places, and partition, round and order these numbers.**
2. Teach	Counting	**Explain what each digit represents in whole numbers and decimals with up to two places, and partition, round and order these numbers.**	• Count from any given number in whole number and decimal steps, extending beyond zero when counting backwards; relate the numbers to their position on a number line. • **Explain what each digit represents in whole numbers and decimals with up to two places, and partition, round and order these numbers.**
3. Practise	Use/apply Knowledge	As for Lesson 2	• Explain reasoning using diagrams, graphs and text; refine ways of recording using images and symbols. • Use understanding of place value to multiply and divide whole numbers and decimals by 10, 100 or 1000.
4. Teach	Use/apply Calculate	• **Use knowledge of place value and addition and subtraction of two-digit numbers to derive sums and differences, doubles and halves of decimals, eg 6.5 ± 2.7, halve 5.6, double 0.34.** • Extend mental methods for whole-number calculations, eg to multiply a two-digit by one-digit number (eg 12 × 9), to multiply by 25 (eg 16 × 25), to subtract one near multiple of 1000 from another (eg 6070 – 4097).	• Explain reasoning using diagrams, graphs and text; refine ways of recording using images and symbols. • Extend mental methods for whole-number calculations, eg to multiply a two-digit by one-digit number (eg 12 × 9), to multiply by 25 (eg 16 × 25), to subtract one near multiple of 1000 from another (eg 6070 – 4097).
5. Teach and practise	Calculate	Extend mental methods for whole-number calculations, eg to multiply a two-digit by one-digit number (eg 12 × 9), to multiply by 25 (eg 16 × 25), to subtract one near multiple of 1000 from another (eg 6070 – 4097).	Extend mental methods for whole-number calculations, eg to multiply a two-digit by one-digit number (eg 12 × 9), to multiply by 25 (eg 16 × 25), to subtract one near multiple of 1000 from another (eg 6070 – 4097).
6. Teach	Calculate	As for Lesson 5	**Use efficient written methods to add and subtract whole numbers and decimals with up to two places.**
7. Practise	Calculate	Recall quickly multiplication facts up to 10 × 10, use to multiply pairs of multiples of 10 and 100 and derive quickly corresponding division facts.	• **Use efficient written methods to add and subtract whole numbers and decimals with up to two places.** • Extend mental methods for whole-number calculations, eg to multiply a two-digit by one-digit number (eg 12 × 9), to multiply by 25 (eg 16 × 25), to subtract one near multiple of 1000 from another (eg 6070 – 4097).
8. Apply	Calculate Knowledge	As for Lesson 7	• **Use efficient written methods to add and subtract whole numbers and decimals with up to two places.** • Use knowledge of rounding, place value, number facts and inverse operations to estimate and check calculations.
9. Apply	Use/apply	• Recall quickly multiplication facts up to 10 × 10, use to multiply pairs of multiples of 10 and 100 and derive quickly corresponding division facts. • Use understanding of place value to multiply and divide whole numbers and decimals by 10, 100 or 1000.	Explain reasoning using diagrams, graphs and text; refine ways of recording using images and symbols.
10. Teach and practise	Use/apply Knowledge	Count from any given number in whole number and decimal steps, extending beyond zero when counting backwards; relate the numbers to their position on a number line.	• Explain reasoning using diagrams, graphs and text; refine ways of recording using images and symbols. • Identify pairs of factors of two-digit whole numbers and find common multiples, eg for 6 and 9.

Unit 1 ▭ 2 weeks

- Present a spoken argument, sequencing points logically, defending views with evidence and making use of persuasive language.

Introduction

Lessons 1 to 3 of this unit revisit ordering and partitioning numbers in order to ensure confidence with place value, which underpins much of the Year 5 framework. Children are asked to explain what they know about place value and the decisions that they have to make in order to decide how to order numbers correctly. Lessons 4 to 10 focus on written methods of subtraction and addition. Emphasis is placed on choosing the most efficient method, whether mental, informal jottings or a written calculation, to solve a problem. Throughout this unit, children are encouraged to reason and explain verbally in order to consolidate their own understanding and also to present their thinking to others.

Use and apply mathematics

Explain reasoning using diagrams, graphs and text; refine ways of recording using images and symbols.

Lessons 1-3

Preparation

Make the digit cards, arrow cards and symbol cards. For the arrow cards, it will be helpful if the units, tens, hundreds and so on are on different colours to assist with selection and recombining.
Lesson 1: Photocopy 'Place value chart' onto A3.

You will need

Photocopiable pages
'Number line shuffle' (page 18) and 'Multiplication bingo (page 19), one per child.
CD resources
Support and extension versions of 'Number line shuffle' and 'Multiplication bingo'; 'Multiplication bingo' template. General resource sheets: 'Place value arrow cards', one set per pair; 'Place value chart', copied to A3; '0-9 digit cards', one set for teacher/LSA and one set per pair; 'Symbol cards' (< and >).
Equipment
Calculators.

Learning objectives

Starter

- Count from any given number in whole number and decimal steps, extending beyond zero when counting backwards; relate the numbers to their position on a number line.
- Explain what each digit represents in whole numbers and decimals with up to two places, and partition, round and order these numbers.

Main teaching activities

2006
- Explain reasoning using diagrams, graphs and text; refine ways of recording using images and symbols.
- Count from any given number in whole number and decimal steps, extending beyond zero when counting backwards; relate the numbers to their position on a number line.
- Explain what each digit represents in whole numbers and decimals with up to two places, and partition, round and order these numbers.
- Use understanding of place value to multiply and divide whole numbers and decimals by 10, 100 or 1000.

1999
- Explain methods and reasoning, orally and in writing.
- Recognise and extend number sequences formed by counting from any number in steps of constant size, extending beyond zero when counting back, eg count on in steps of 25 to 1000, and then back; count on or back in steps of 0.1, 0.2, 0.3, ...
- Read and write whole numbers in figures and words, and know what each digit represents.
- Know what each digit represents in a number with up to two decimal places.
- Multiply and divide decimals by 10 or 100 and integers by 1000 and explain the effect (Year 6).

Vocabulary

units, tens, hundreds, thousands, ten thousand, hundred thousand, million, tenths, hundredths, decimal point, decimal place, digit, numeral, partition, place value, between, ascending, descending, greater than (>), less than (<), pattern, sequence, multiply, divide

▷

Unit 1 ▢ 2 weeks

Lesson 1 (Review)

Starter

Rehearse: Challenge the children to spot and continue number patterns, for example: *75, 100, 125, what comes next? 45, 60, 75... 440, 420, 400...* Once the pattern has been spotted, let the children continue each sequence by 'passing it on' around the room.

Main teaching activities

Whole class: Display the 'Place value chart' and indicate how the place value of each digit moves one place to the left as you move up the chart. Revise the vocabulary of place value to ensure that everyone is clear about it. For example, point to 300 and ask the children to identify the names of all the numbers in that row, then repeat for 30,000 or 3000.

Talk about how digits can be combined to build up any number. Use the arrow cards to build a number. Start with a four-digit number and invite four children to hold up the correct arrow cards (for example 2000, 400, 30 and 1 to make 2431). Ask these children to read out each digit individually, then combine the arrows to make the number and read out the whole number together. Invite someone to write it in words on the board. Repeat, choosing different digits. Try a five-digit number. For each example, pick a digit and ask: *What is the value of the 7 in 37,306? Identify the value of the first digit. ...last digit.*

Paired work: Give each pair a set of arrow cards. Ask them to select one card from each place value set at random, then record them as, for example: 60,000 + 4000 + 200 + 10 = 64,210 = sixty-four thousand, two hundred and ten.

Review

Give out calculators and ask the children to put in the number 1024 (say one thousand and twenty-four). Ask them what they have displayed. Ask: *How did you get the 1 into the thousands column? What did you have to remember to put in?* (The 0 for no hundreds.) *What would the display have read if you had forgotten the 0?* (One hundred and twenty-four.) Ask the children to clear the display and repeat with 10,046.

Differentiation

Less confident learners: These children should make four-digit, or possibly three-digit, numbers.
More confident learners: These children should make six-digit numbers.

Lesson 2 (Teach)

Starter

Reason: Write a five-digit number (such as 65,213) on a piece of paper and hide it from the children. Write the digits of your number on the board in a random order. Tell the children to ask you questions to which the answer may be Yes/No or higher/lower. For example: *Is the 5 digit in the tens column?* (No, higher.) Explain that they have 20 questions to work out the position and place value of each digit in order to find the number.

Main teaching activities

Whole class: Play 'Human digit cards'. Draw a number line on the board. Invite four children to select a digit card each. Ask the rest of the class to arrange these children so as to make the smallest possible number. Write this number on the left of the number line. *What is the largest number possible from the same digits? What do you notice?* (The order is reversed.) Write this number on the right of the number line.

Ask the children to make two more numbers with the same digits. Together, estimate the position of each number on the line by discussing halfway points. Record both numbers on the line.

Finally, using the relevant cards from the 'Symbol cards' set, introduce or revise the symbols < (less than) and > (greater than), and put them between the numbers on the line:

2479_<__2497_____<_____4297_____<_____9742

Paired work: Give each pair a set of digit cards and ask them to generate four- or five-digit numbers, then record the smallest and greatest possible numbers at either end of the number lines provided on the 'Number line shuffle' activity sheet. They then make two more numbers from the same set and estimate their positions. They should use the < symbol to write a number sentence as above.

Review
Draw a number line:

1459 _____ 9531

Ask: *How can we find the midpoint of this number line by rounding and estimating?* (From 1500 to 9500 is 8000, so the midpoint is 4000 + 1500 = 5500.) *How could this help us to divide the line into quarters?* (Half of 4000 is 2000, so the quarters are at 3500 and 7500.) Repeat for 2422 and 9470 or for 12,321 and 20,854.

Lesson 3 (Practise)

Starter
Reason/recall: Repeat the starter from Lesson 2 but this time introduce decimal numbers into the game. Ensure that the children are clear about the relative size of decimal numbers and remind them that decimals are all fractions, less than one whole integer.

Main teaching activities
Whole class: Distribute calculators. Ask the children to key in 24 × 10 and note the answer. Ask them to clear the display, then key in 24 × 100. *What is happening?* (The place value is moving to the left, with the spaces filled by 0.)
Independent work: Introduce the 'Multiplication bingo' activity sheet. Check that the children understand the rules. Discuss strategies, including doing approximate mental calculations to help in choosing numbers.

Review
Ask: *If we multiply a decimal number by 10 or 100, does the same place value rule apply as for a whole number?* (Yes.) Demonstrate: 0.5 × 10 is 5; 0.2 × 100 is 20. Show why 'add a zero' is not a good rule here: 0.5 × 10 is 5, not 0.50. *Does the same theory apply when we divide a number by 10 or 100? For example, what is 640 divided by 10? Can anybody describe what has happened to the digits this time? What about if we divided by 100? Can we suggest a rule that we could always apply when multiplying and dividing by 10 or 100?* (The digits stay the same, but the place value moves to the left when multiplying and to the right when dividing.) Chant this as a class.

Differentiation
Less confident learners:
Provide the support version of the sheet, which gives sets of three digits. They must complete the number sentences provided.
More confident learners:
Provide the extension version, which involves making six-digit numbers. Complete the follow-up challenge (answers: 2 numbers with 2 digits, 6 with 3 digits, 24 with 4 digits).

Differentiation
Less confident learners: Use the support version of the activity sheet, which uses single digits, 10 and 100.
More confident learners: Use the extension version, which includes decimal numbers.

Lessons 4-10

Preparation
Write questions on the board for **Lesson 4** starter and main activity, **Lesson 5** main activity, **Lesson 6** main activity, **Lesson 8** main activity.

You will need
CD resources
Support and extension versions of 'Work it out'; 'Word problems', 'Investigating factors' and 'Find the difference'. General resource sheets: '0-9 digit cards'; 'Number cards 1-100' (even-numbered cards from the range 50-100); 'Number fan cards 0-9'; 'Blank multiplication grid'; 'Multiplication square', one each for less confident learners, 'Number lines' (optional). 'Multiplication square' interactive resource.

Learning objectives

Starter
● Count from any given number in whole number and decimal steps, extending beyond zero when counting backwards; relate the numbers to their position on a number line.
● Use knowledge of place value and addition and subtraction of two-digit numbers to derive sums and differences, doubles and halves of decimals, eg 6.5 ± 2.7, halve 5.6, double 0.34.
● Recall quickly multiplication facts up to 10×10, use to multiply pairs of multiples of 10 and 100 and derive quickly corresponding division facts.
● Use understanding of place value to multiply and divide whole numbers and decimals by 10, 100 or 1000.
● Extend mental methods for whole-number calculations, eg to multiply a two-digit by one-digit number (eg 12×9), to multiply by 25 (eg 16×25), to subtract one near multiple of 1000 from another (eg 6070 - 4097).

Main teaching activities
2006
● Explain reasoning using diagrams, graphs and text; refine ways of recording using images and symbols.
● Use efficient written methods to add and subtract whole numbers and decimals with up to two places.
● Identify pairs of factors of two-digit whole numbers and find common multiples, eg for 6 and 9.
● Extend mental methods for whole-number calculations, eg to multiply a two-digit by one-digit number (eg 12×9), to multiply by 25 (eg 16×25), to subtract one near multiple of 1000 from another (eg 6070 - 4097).
● Use knowledge of rounding, place value, number facts and inverse operations to estimate and check calculations.
1999
● Explain methods and reasoning, orally and in writing.
● Extend written methods to: addition of more than two integers; addition or subtraction of a pair of decimal fractions (eg £29.78 + £53.34).
● Find all the pairs of factors of any number up to 100.
● Use mental calculation strategies –several objectives, including: partitioning; find a difference by counting up (eg 5003 - 4996); use related facts, eg to multiply by 25, multiply by 100 then divide by 4.
● Check results of calculations.

Vocabulary
add, sum, total, odd, even, multiple, factor, prime, significant digit, bridging next 10/100, inverse, subtract, take away, difference between, counting on/back, consecutive, predict, relationship, problem, solution, calculate, calculation, operation, answer, method, explain, reasoning, reason, rule, pattern, sequence, partition, redistribute

Lesson 4 (Teach)

Starter
Refine and rehearse: Prepare a number of two-digit sums and difference questions, including some with decimals, eg 5.7 + 3.9; 6.4 - 5.3; 27 + 43. Ask the children to look at each and explain to you how they could be calculated in their heads. Ask: *Do the same strategies apply to decimal numbers as whole two-digit numbers?* (Yes.)

Main teaching activities
Whole class: Write on the board the question 3001 - 2785. Ask the children

to suggest ways to solve it. They may suggest a written calculation or a number line. Some may suggest counting on. Explain that although these numbers look fairly big, they are not very far apart and so can be calculated by counting on. Explain that subtracting by counting on is easier in many cases than calculating, and should be tried first where appropriate (that is, where the numbers do not have too great a difference).

Draw a number line and demonstrate counting on in 'jumps':

Repeat this method for 4005 - 3826 and 3012 - 2699. Ask the children whether they think these calculations could be done mentally with practice.
Independent work: Ask the children to work out the following calculations, which are written up on the board: 3004 - 2891; 4003 - 3728; 4011 - 3883; 5001 - 4569; 8002 - 7695; 7003 - 5991. They should use the counting on method, drawing a number line to demonstrate their understanding (use the 'Number lines' resource sheet if appropriate).

Review

Ask individuals to demonstrate on the board how they found some of the differences. Ask: *What clues did you look for when deciding whether you could solve a problem mentally? Were the 'jumps' or steps the same for everybody? Did some children put different 'jumps' together?* For example: 3001 - 2785 = 200 + 15 + 1 = 216. *Could you use this method to find larger differences?* Ask the children when the method might become too cumbersome. (When the difference to be calculated is very big, and the steps would be difficult to remember.)

Lesson 5 (Teach and practise)

Starter
Rehearse: Give one table group a single-digit number, which they must double before passing it on to the next group. The next group doubles that, and so on until 100 is bridged. The group that bridges 100 receives a point and is given another single-digit number to start again. The group with the most points at the end wins.

Main teaching activities
Whole class: Remind the children that we can calculate some differences mentally (such as 50 - 17, 100 - 56 or 1008 - 12) and find others by using informal jottings, either with or without a number line (such as 3004 - 2894, 294 - 177 or 9003 - 8895). Write some similar calculations on the board and ask the children to choose the most efficient method to solve each one. Solve them together, either by counting on out loud, or with a volunteer using a number line on the board. If they suggest that a mental method is best ask: *Why is it possible to solve this one mentally? What clues did you look for?*

Write 751 - 239 on the board. Ask whether the children think this might be too difficult to count on. What about 6383 - 2846? Explain that at some point we need a written method to support our calculations, because errors are otherwise too likely. Some individuals will still want to calculate mentally, and may be able to do so; but you need to point out that if the risk of error is high, we need a more 'secure', efficient method to check with.
Independent work: Provide the 'Find the difference' activity sheet. Explain that the children have to decide which method to use to find each of the differences – either just mentally or with informal jottings to support accuracy. Stress that number lines may be used if they are helpful (you could provide the 'Number lines' general resource sheet), but none of the

Differentiation

Less confident learners: Provide the support version of the activity sheet, which uses numbers up to three digits. They can use number lines for support.

More confident learners: Provide the extension version of the activity sheet, which uses numbers up to five digits and some negative and decimal numbers.

subtractions should require a full written method. The puzzle at the end of the sheet will help them to revise the vocabulary of subtraction (answers: minus, difference, subtract, take away).

Review

Ask some of the children to explain their methods, for example with 73 - 38: 'In my head I counted on 2 from 38 to 40, then in tens to 50, 60, 70, then the extra 3, so the difference is 2 + 30 + 3 = 35.' From these explanations, you will be able to judge the children's understanding of informal calculation methods.

Lesson 6 (Teach)

Starter

Rehearse: Play 'Doubles bingo'. Give six even-number cards from the range 50-100 to each group. Call out doubles. For example, if you call out double 28, the group with the 56 card must turn it face down. The game progresses until one group has turned over all of its cards.

Main teaching activities

Whole class: Explain to the class that they are going to look at how we can use written calculation methods to work out subtraction problems with more complex numbers. Using demonstration and asking volunteers to help, go through the expanded method without decomposition and then the expanded method with decomposition. Finally, work towards the standard vertical method. You will have to decide the rate at which your pupils progress through these written methods, according to your school's policy on calculation skills.

Independent work: Ask the children to use the expanded subtraction method to work out the calculations written on the board: 578 - 243; 659 - 318; 4261 - 2110; 351 - 138; 2422 - 1375.

Differentiation

Less confident learners: The children should practise the expanded method without having to redistribute the numbers. It is important that they are able to partition numbers and understand how this can be used for subtraction. They should try 295 - 123; 379 - 245; 664 - 243; 748 - 326; 754 - 513.

More confident learners: Teach this group the standard method of vertical subtraction.

Review

Ask the children to redistribute the number 342 in a variety of ways. Record each way on the board and ask another child to check that it produces the correct number. For example, the children might suggest: 300 + 40 + 2; 300 + 30 + 12; 200 + 130 + 12.

Write the following calculation on the whiteboard and ask what is wrong with it:

$$
\begin{array}{r}
631 \\
- \underline{342} \\
311
\end{array}
$$

Establish that the smaller digit has been taken away from the larger one in each column, whereas the correct method would be to take the digit below from the one above.

Lesson 7 (Practise)

Starter

Rehearse: Call out a range of multiplication facts (2-, 3-, 5- and 10- times tables) using a variety of vocabulary: *5 × 3... 6 lots of 2... multiply 4 by 10... what is 10 times bigger than 8?...* Ask the children to show you the answer with their number fans when you say Show me.

Main teaching activities

Whole class: Distribute the 'Work it out' activity sheet. Discuss which of the questions might be calculated mentally, which need informal jottings and which need a written method. Read some of the word questions together and decide how to convert them to calculations, asking questions such as:

Is it an addition or a subtraction problem? Does the calculation require a written method? Revise vertical addition, both the expanded method and, for those you feel are ready, the standard method.

Independent work: Ask the children to work through the mixed addition and subtraction questions on the 'Work it out' sheet, using the most appropriate method. Where the children use informal jottings, ask them to explain how they worked out the answer.

Review
Hear some of the children's answers and explanations. Iron out any misconceptions.

Write the following calculations on the board.

```
  H  T  U
  2  1  8
+ 1  3  5
  3  0  0
     4  0
        1  7
  3  5  7
```

```
     H  T  U
     4  2  6
  +  2  3  7
     6  1  3
           1
```

Ask the children: *Is this correct? How can you check? Can you tell me what this person has done wrong? Can you correct the mistakes? How can you advise this person not to make the same mistakes again?*

In the first calculation, the decomposition is correct, but the numbers in the units column have been added incorrectly. In the second calculation, an upper digit has been taken away from a lower one.

Differentiation

Less confident learners: The children can use the support version of the activity sheet, with smaller numbers and easier calculations, which require no carrying or redistribution in the written methods.
More confident learners: The children should use standard written methods of addition and subtraction.

Lesson 8 (Apply)

Starter
Review and rehearse: Display the 'Multiplication square' interactive resource. Remind the children what a multiple is: a multiple of 5 is a number in the 5- times table, or several lots of 5. Say, *Where would the number 15 go on the grid?* Demonstrate by clicking in the square that intersects the 3 row and the 5 column, and vice versa, saying that *15 is a multiple of 3 and a multiple of 5.* Invite suggestions of other multiples and click to reveal them. If an incorrect answer is offered, ask the class to count up in the appropriate times table.

Alternatively do this using the 'Blank multiplication grid' general resource sheet on OHP.

Main teaching activities
Whole class: Write this question on the board: *There were 5019 people at a rock concert. Because it was late, 2476 people left before the encore. How many were still there at the end?* Ask the children to suggest a method for solving this problem. Work through each method on the board. They may suggest:
- Counting on (using informal jottings):
- 2476 + 24 makes 2500, another 2500 makes 5000, add 19. Answer is 2543 people.
- Written subtraction, both methods:

```
TH H  T  U
   4  9  1
   5  0  1  9
 - 2  4  7  6
   2  5  4  3
```

or:

```
TH  H   T   U
 5  0   1   9   =   5000 + 0 + 10 + 9   =   4000 + 900 + 110 + 9
−2  4   7   6   =   2000 + 400 + 70 + 6 =   2000 + 400 +  70 + 6
 2  5   4   3                                2000 + 500 +  40 + 3
```

Encourage the children to check their answer using the inverse operation (addition).

Independent work: Distribute the 'Word problems' activity sheet. These problems require a mixture of addition and subtraction methods. Ask the children to read through the questions first and decide which method will be best for each problem.

Review

Hear some of the children's answers and explanations. Iron out any misconceptions. Write up a new calculation, such as:

```
TH  H   T   U
 2  3   2   0
−1  4   7   2
```

Ask for two brave volunteers to demonstrate how to solve this, using their own choice of method, explaining each step that they take. Choose one child to demonstrate the standard method and one to demonstrate the expanded method. If the children find the calculation difficult, ask the rest of the class to advise them. Compare the decomposition processes used, and look for and emphasise the similarities between them.

Discuss some common errors when subtracting, for example taking the top number from the bottom, not checking that the same number remains after redistributing the digits, and so on.

Differentiation

Less confident learners: Provide the support version of the activity sheet, which provides simpler numbers and calculations.
More confident learners: Provide the extension version, using more complex numbers and calculations. Encourage the use of standard written methods.

Lesson 9 (Apply)

Starter

Rehearse: Write a multiple of 10 on the board, such as 560. Ask the children to double it. Repeat with 430, 80, 120, 440, 370, 270 and 190. Discuss the strategy they are using: if they can double a two-digit number such as 43, then doubling 430 involves moving the same digits one place value to the left (making the double 10 times bigger).

Main teaching activities

Whole class: Explain that the children are going to investigate number pyramids. Using the digit cards 1–9, put three different digits in a row. Find the differences between each pair of digits and put these in the second row, then find the difference between these to give the top number. For example:

```
          0                                    4
      1       1                            2       6
   3     4       5                      1       3       9
```

Ask the children to investigate these questions:
● *What is the highest number you can get at the top of the pyramid?*
● *Is there a systematic way of finding the answer?*
Independent work: The children should investigate the pyramid questions, using reasoning and trial and error.

Review

Ask the children for a progress report on their investigation. *What is the*

Differentiation

Less confident learners: The children may find it helpful to use digit cards to make the pyramids.
More confident learners: Look for independent work and a systematic approach. Extend the investigation by allowing two-digit numbers (up to 20) along the bottom row. Does this change the range of possible numbers at the top of the pyramid?

▷ *highest top number anyone has found? Can you describe your strategy? What would happen if you used the same digit in all three bottom spaces? What would be the result? Would it be the same no matter which digit you used? Would it be easier or harder if I said that you had to use three different digits in the bottom row?*

Lesson 10 (Teach and practise)

Starter
Rehearse: Start chanting number patterns, inviting the children to join in when they recognise the pattern. Clap your hands to change the direction from counting on to counting back or vice versa. Say: *1, 3, 5, 7, 9... 25, 20, 15, 10, 5, 0 , -5, -10... 4, 8, 12, 16, 20... 24, 21, 18, 15, 12, 9, 6, 3, 0 , -3...*

Main teaching activities
Whole class: Explain that this lesson is about factors. Ask: *What is a factor? What are the factors of 12?* (1, 2, 3, 4, 6, 12.) *Do some numbers have more than two factors?* (Yes.) *What do we call numbers that are only divisible by themselves and 1?* (Prime numbers.) Explain that the children are going to make a list of the factors of various numbers. They have to work out all the factors for the numbers given, then circle the prime numbers.
Independent work: Distribute the activity sheet 'Investigating factors'. Explain that a table has been started on the sheet to list the factors of all numbers from 1 to 50. The children must complete the list.

Review
Ask: *What is a prime number? What are the prime numbers from 1 to 50?* (1, 2, 3, 5, 7, 11, 13, 17, 19, 23, 29, 31, 37, 41, 43, 47.) *Can we make any generalisations about them?* (They are all odd numbers apart from 2.) *What are the factors of 42?... 49?... 36?...*

Play 'Goose'. Ask the children to sit in a circle, and one person starts the count. Explain that they have to count in ones around the circle from 1 to 50, but every time they come to a prime number, they have to say 'Goose' instead of the number. Play continues until someone makes an error - then the direction of play is reversed. This can be played as a knockout game, where a player is 'out' if he or she makes an error.

Differentiation
Less confident learners: The children can use the support version of the activity sheet, which involves finding the factors of the numbers 1-20. They can use the multiplication square to help them.
More confident learners: The children can use the extension version, which has a further challenge. Ask: *From the factors you have found, can you think of a quick and easy way to find the factors for the even numbers from 50 to 100?* (Halve each number, list the factors of the half, then double these.)

Name _____ Date _____

Number line shuffle

1. Take four digit cards. Arrange them to make the smallest possible number. Write it at the left-hand end of the number line below.
2. Rearrange the cards to make the largest possible number. Write it at the right-hand end of the number line.
3. Can you make two more numbers from the digits and estimate their positions on the number line?
4. Complete a number sentence using either < or > symbols.

_____

Number sentence: _____

_____

Number sentence: _____

_____

Number sentence: _____

5. Now try making some five-digit numbers with the digit cards.

_____

Number sentence: _____

_____

Number sentence: _____

Challenge: Draw some more number lines on the back of the sheet, using a ruler, and use them to create some more number sentences.

Name _____   Date _____

Multiplication bingo

A game for two players.

You need a calculator between you
and several counters each (choose a
different colour from your partner).

Take turns to choose two numbers from:

200	100	40	30	20	10	5	4	3	2	1

Multiply your two chosen numbers together on the calculator. If the answer is one of the numbers
in the grid, cover it with one of your counters.

The winner is the first player to cover four numbers in a straight line (in any direction) with
their counters.

5	80	40	6	40	20 000
4000	1000	30	160	2	20
60	10	150	2000	600	300
90	3000	6000	500	300	15
200	120	12	80	50	800
8	100	1200	400	3	8000

Unit 2 ▢ 2 weeks

Counting, partitioning and calculating

Lesson	Strands	Starter	Main teaching activities
1. Review and teach	Use/apply Counting Calculate	Identify pairs of factors of two-digit whole numbers and find common multiples, eg for 6 and 9.	• Explain reasoning using diagrams, graphs and text; refine ways of recording using images and symbols. • **Explain what each digit represents in whole numbers and decimals with up to two places, and partition, round and order these numbers.** • Use a calculator to solve problems, including those involving decimals or fractions, eg to find ¾ of 150g; interpret the display correctly in the context of measurement.
2. Teach and practise	Counting	Use understanding of place value to multiply and divide whole numbers and decimals by 10, 100 or 1000.	**Explain what each digit represents in whole numbers and decimals with up to two places, and partition, round and order these numbers.**
3. Teach and practise	Counting	As for Lesson 2	Count from any given number in whole number and decimal steps, extending beyond zero when counting backwards; relate the numbers to their position on a number line.
4. Review and teach	Calculate Knowledge	• Explain reasoning using diagrams, graphs and text; refine ways of recording using images and symbols. • Identify pairs of factors of two-digit whole numbers and find common multiples, eg for 6 and 9.	• **Use efficient written methods to add and subtract whole numbers and decimals with up to two places.** • Use knowledge of rounding, place value, number facts and inverse operations to estimate and check calculations.
5. Teach	Use/apply Knowledge Calculate	As for Lesson 4	• Solve one- and two-step problems involving whole numbers and decimals and all four operations, choosing and using appropriate calculation strategies, including calculator use. • **Use knowledge of place value and addition and subtraction of two-digit numbers to derive sums and differences, doubles and halves of decimals, eg 6.5 ± 2.7, halve 5.6, double 0.34.** • Use knowledge of rounding, place value, number facts and inverse operations to estimate and check calculations.
6. Practise and apply	Use/apply Calculate	Extend mental methods for whole-number calculations, eg to multiply a two-digit by one-digit number (eg 12 × 9), to multiply by 25 (eg 16 × 25), to subtract one near multiple of 1000 from another (eg 6070 – 4097).	• Solve one- and two-step problems involving whole numbers and decimals and all four operations, choosing and using appropriate calculation strategies, including calculator use. • **Use efficient written methods to add and subtract whole numbers and decimals with up to two places.**
7. Apply	Use/apply Calculate	Solve one- and two-step problems involving whole numbers and decimals and all four operations, choosing and using appropriate calculation strategies, including calculator use.	As for Lesson 6
8. Teach	Use/apply Calculate	As for Lesson 7	• Explain reasoning using diagrams, graphs and text; refine ways of recording using images and symbols. • Solve one- and two-step problems involving whole numbers and decimals and all four operations, choosing and using appropriate calculation strategies, including calculator use. • Use a calculator to solve problems, including those involving decimals or fractions, eg to find ¾ of 150g; interpret the display correctly in the context of measurement.
9. Practise	Use/apply Calculate Knowledge	As for Lesson 7	• Explain reasoning using diagrams, graphs and text; refine ways of recording using images and symbols. • Use a calculator to solve problems, including those involving decimals or fractions, eg to find ¾ of 150g; interpret the display correctly in the context of measurement. • Use knowledge of rounding, place value, number facts and inverse operations to estimate and check calculations.
10. Apply	Use/apply Calculate	• Recall quickly multiplication facts up to 10 × 10, use to multiply pairs of multiples of 10 and 100 and derive quickly corresponding division facts. • Extend mental methods for whole-number calculations, eg to multiply a two-digit by one-digit number (eg 12 × 9), to multiply by 25 (eg 16 × 25), to subtract one near multiple of 1000 from another (eg 6070 – 4097).	• Explain reasoning using diagrams, graphs and text; refine ways of recording using images and symbols. • Use a calculator to solve problems, including those involving decimals or fractions, eg to find ¾ of 150g; interpret the display correctly in the context of measurement.

Unit 2 — 2 weeks

Speaking and listening objectives
- Analyse the use of persuasive language.

Introduction
The first three lessons of this unit are designed to encourage children to use their knowledge of place value to order numbers, including both positive and negative integers. Lessons 4 to 10 focus on calculations to solve problems. Children are asked to make choices and to estimate and reason about the steps that they take to solve a problem. The speaking and listening objective asks children to try to persuade others of the suitability of their choices. The final three lessons present problems which may be solved by the use of a calculator to aid lateral thinking or by representing problems graphically to aid understanding.

Use and apply mathematics
- Explain reasoning using diagrams, graphs and text; refine ways of recording using images and symbols.
- Solve one- and two-step problems involving whole numbers and decimals and all four operations, choosing and using appropriate calculation strategies, including calculator use.

Lessons 1-3

Preparation
Make up the 'Negative digit cards'.

You will need
Photocopiable pages
'Greater or smaller?' (page 30) and 'Weather around the world', (page 31), one per child.
CD resources
Support and extension versions of 'Greater or smaller?' and 'Weather around the world'. General resource sheets: 'Number fan cards 0-9'; 'Number cards 1-100'; '0-9 digit cards'; 'Place value arrow cards'; 'Place value chart'; 'Number lines'; several sets of 'Symbol cards' (<, > and =), 'Negative digit cards'. 'Thermometer' ITP (optional).
Equipment
Calculators; Blu-Tack; dice.

Learning objectives

Starter
- Identify pairs of factors of two-digit whole numbers and find common multiples, eg for 6 and 9.
- Use understanding of place value to multiply and divide whole numbers and decimals by 10, 100 or 1000.

Main teaching activities
2006
- Explain reasoning using diagrams, graphs and text; refine ways of recording using images and symbols.
- Count from any given number in whole number and decimal steps, extending beyond zero when counting backwards; relate the numbers to their position on a number line.
- Explain what each digit represents in whole numbers and decimals with up to two places, and partition, round and order these numbers.
- Use a calculator to solve problems, including those involving decimals or fractions, eg to find $\frac{3}{4}$ of 150g; interpret the display correctly in the context of measurement.

1999
- Explain methods and reasoning, orally and in writing.
- Recognise and extend number sequences formed by counting from any number in steps of constant size, extending beyond zero when counting back, eg count on in steps of 25 to 1000, and then back; count on or back in steps of 0.1, 0.2, 0.3, ...
- Read and write whole numbers in figures and words, and know what each digit represents.
- Know what each digit represents in a number with up to two decimal places.
- Develop calculator skills and use a calculator effectively.

Vocabulary
place value, compare, order, size, ascending, descending, positive, negative, above/below zero, minus, integer, halfway between, midpoint, place value, digit, numeral, decimal point, decimal place, pattern, sequence, thousands, ten thousands, hundred thousands, million, tenths, hundredths, greater than (>), less than (<), round, estimate, approximately, factor, difference, multiply, significant digit

Lesson 1 (Review and teach)

Starter

Recall: Hold up number cards such as 42, 36, 8, 24, 12 and 15, saying: *Show me the factors of...* Children should work in pairs, with each pair using number fans to display a pair of factors for the number.

Main teaching activities

Whole class: Put the number 4507 on the board and ask: *What is the value of the 7? ...the 5?...* Select four digits randomly from the digit card pack. Display them on the board using sticky tack. Ask the children to rearrange these digits into the smallest number possible. Write this up on the board.

Now ask the children to rearrange the digits to make the largest number they can. Draw a blank number line on the board and write these two numbers at either end. Now ask the children to round each number to the nearest 100, then estimate the difference between them and work out the midpoint. Difference is 9500 – 1400 = 8100. Half of this is 8100 ÷ 2 = 4050. So midpoint is 1400 + 4050 = 5450. Mark this on the number line.

Now ask the children to use a calculator to follow this process and find the exact midpoint of the original numbers. Explain that it would be incorrect to simply halve the difference, because this would give only the midpoint of the difference without taking account of the starting number. Mark the exact midpoint on the original number line.

Independent work: Ask the children to repeat this activity, drawing their own number lines with a ruler (or using the 'Number lines' general resource sheet). Give them some sets of four-digit numbers to use. Ask them to estimate the difference by rounding and so find the approximate midpoint, then check using a calculator and add the exact midpoint to the number line.

Differentiation

Less confident learners: The children can use three-digit or even two-digit numbers until their confidence in finding the difference and the midpoint grows.
More confident learners: Extend the exercise to using five-digit numbers and attempting to find the quarter-point and three-quarter point by halving and halving again.

Review

Draw a number line on the board with 5921 at one end and 6844 at the other. Say: *Tell me a number between these integers.* (Write it on the line.) *Which integer is it nearer to? How do you know? What do you estimate is the midpoint? How did you work that out?* Repeat this with another pair of four-digit integers.

Discuss the importance of considering the most significant digit first when ordering numbers. Write 6473, 6492 and 6880 on the board. Ask the children to order these, smallest first. *Which digits were most important when you decided the order?* Repeat this for other four-digit sets.

Lesson 2 (Teach and practise)

Starter

Refine and rehearse: Ask the children: *Think of the number 3. Multiply it by 10. What does it become? Now multiply it by 10 again... and again.* Ask the children to suggest another way we could have got from 3 to 3000 (such as 3 × 1000 or 3 × 100 × 10). Show how the number 3 grew to 3000 using arrow cards. Ask the children to notice how the place value moved up one space each time the number was multiplied by 10. Repeat the process, starting at 5, then 8. Each time, ask the children to record the number pattern.

Main teaching activities

Whole class: Show children the symbol cards =, < and >. Invite children to choose one card and explain what it means. Remind them that the smaller number always goes at the sharp end. Write some number sentences such as: 7.26 > 2.90; 3542 < 4687; 0.23 > 0.12.

Explain that these symbols can be useful when ordering numbers. Ask for a volunteer to write the numbers 256, 187, 387, 342 and 196 in ascending order, sticking a < symbol card in between each number with Blu-Tack. Ask another child to rearrange these numbers in descending order, using the >

symbol card. Now ask for a third child to use the integers and a mixture of < and > symbol cards to write an accurate number sentence using the numbers in the original order (for example, 256 > 187 < 387 > 342 > 196).

Paired work: Distribute the 'Greater or smaller?' activity sheet, explaining that the children should generate numbers using dice and order them using the < and > symbols.

Review

Write some pairs of numbers on the board. Invite children to write symbols between them. Include some decimal numbers, negative numbers and some numbers that are equal. For example: 25.6 < 45.6; 0.05 < 0.1; 3809 > 3807; 12,084 > 12,083; 0.3 > 0.03; 3.4 = 3.40; 1.77 < 1.78; –6 < 6; 8 > –2; –1 < 0; 112 = 112.0. Ask the child as he or she completes each example: *What part of the number are you using to help you decide which number is larger? Is it the same digit in every example? What must we consider when we are looking at negative numbers?* Discuss the fact that the minus sign in front of a negative number tells us that we are counting back from zero – the bigger the number size, the further below zero it is.

Write up some pairs of negative numbers to order using symbol cards.

Lesson 3 (Teach and practise)

Starter

Refine and review: Repeat the Starter from Lesson 2, but this time divide repeatedly by 10. Start with 10,000, then 9000. Now try 8750 and 7945, going on to at least one decimal place.

Main teaching activities

Whole class: Draw a number line from –10 to +10. Display the positive and negative digit cards, including zero. Ask the children to estimate each card's place on the line. Discuss the minus sign as meaning an amount less than zero or a distance from zero. The larger the number, the further from zero. Link this to temperatures below zero. *Which is colder, -1°C or -10°C?* (-10°C.) Use the number line to count on and back, crossing zero, in intervals of ones and twos to familiarise the children with negative numbers.

Now ask the children to calculate differences in temperature. For example, *What is the difference between -6°C and 2°C?* You cannot take the 2 from the –6 because 2 is the bigger number. It is better to count on from -6°C to zero and then on to 2°C (making a difference of 8°C). Repeat with some more examples.

Alternatively you could use the 'Thermometer' ITP on the CD-ROM for this activity.

Independent work: Distribute the 'Weather around the world' activity sheet. The children have to place temperatures on the number line and calculate some differences.

Review

Write on the board a list of 12 random positive and negative integers within the range –20 to +20. Ask the children to say the coldest temperature (the lowest number), the next coldest and so on. Say: *Tell me two numbers that fall between 0 and -6; -8 and -15; -4 and -11.* For each answer, ask: *Which temperature is warmer?* Ask the children to calculate the differences. Remind them that counting on from the 'coldest' to the 'warmest' is the best method. Draw a vertical number line and mark on zero to help the children with counting through zero. Ask: *Tell me the difference between -3.5 and -8.5; 4.5 and -3.5; 8 and -15.* Pose word problems such as: *If the temperature is -5°C at 02:00 and rises by 8 degrees by midday, what is the temperature then?* Invite children to pose similar questions to the class.

Differentiation

Less confident learners: Provide the support version of the activity sheet, which uses two- and three-digit numbers.
More confident learners: Provide the extension version, which uses four- and five-digit numbers.

Differentiation

Less confident learners: Provide the support version of the activity sheet, which uses numbers closer to zero.
More confident learners: Provide the extension version, which has more challenging differences to calculate.

Lessons 4-10

Preparation

Lessons 6 and 7: Supplementary planning sheet.
Lesson 7: Write up word problems for starter.
Lesson 8: Prepare some sets of numbers for the paired work.
Lesson 10: Make up some fractions of measures and money questions.

You will need

Photocopiable pages
'Sid's Snowy Sports shop' (page 32), 'Maths Theme Park' (page 33), one per child.
CD resources
Support version of 'Sid's Snowy Sports shop'; support and extension versions of 'What's the question?'. General resource sheets: 'Number fan cards 0-9' and '0-9 digit cards'.
Equipment
Calculators; OHP or whiteboard calculator.

Learning objectives

Starter

● Explain reasoning using diagrams, graphs and text; refine ways of recording using images and symbols.
● Solve one- and two-step problems involving whole numbers and decimals and all four operations, choosing and using appropriate calculation strategies, including calculator use.
● Recall quickly multiplication facts up to 10 × 10, use to multiply pairs of multiples of 10 and 100 and derive quickly corresponding division facts.
● Identify pairs of factors of two-digit whole numbers and find common multiples, eg for 6 and 9.
● Extend mental methods for whole-number calculations, e.g. to multiply a two-digit by one-digit number (eg 12 × 9), to multiply by 25 (eg 16 × 25), to subtract one near multiple of 1000 from another (eg 6070 - 4097).

Main teaching activities

2006

● Explain reasoning using diagrams, graphs and text; refine ways of recording using images and symbols.
● Solve one- and two-step problems involving whole numbers and decimals and all four operations, choosing and using appropriate calculation strategies, including calculator use.
● Use knowledge of place value and addition and subtraction of two-digit numbers to derive sums and differences, doubles and halves of decimals, eg 6.5 ± 2.7, halve 5.6, double 0.34.
● Use efficient written methods to add and subtract whole numbers and decimals with up to two places.
● Use a calculator to solve problems, including those involving decimals or fractions, eg to find $3/4$ of 150g; interpret the display correctly in the context of measurement.
● Use knowledge of rounding, place value, number facts and inverse operations to estimate and check calculations.

1999

● Explain methods and reasoning, orally and in writing.
● Use all four operations to solve simple word problems involving numbers and quantities based on 'real life', money and measures (including time), using one or more steps, including finding simple percentages.
● Choose and use appropriate number operations to solve problems, and appropriate ways of calculating: mental, mental with jottings, written methods, calculator.
● Derive quickly pairs of decimals that total 1 (eg 0.2 + 0.8) or 10 (eg 6.2 + 3.8).
● Use known number facts and place value for mental addition and subtraction (eg 7.4 + 9.8, 9.2 - 8.6).
● Derive quickly doubles of two-digit decimals (eg 3.8 × 2, 0.76 × 2), and the corresponding halves. (Year 6)
● Extend written methods to: addition of more than two integers; addition or subtraction of a pair of decimal fractions (eg £29.78 + £53.34).
● Develop calculator skills and use a calculator effectively.
● Check results of calculations.

Vocabulary

sign, operation, inverse, symbol, method, strategy, jotting, answer, calculate, calculation, explain, reasoning, decimal point, decimal place, significant digit, multiple, add, sum, total, subtract, difference, problem, solution

▷

SCHOLASTIC

Lesson 4 (Review and teach)

Starter

Recall and reason: Draw a Venn diagram of two overlapping set rings on the board, labelling one ring '24' and the other '18'. Ask the children to supply number facts to fit into the diagram, such as 6 × 4 = 24 or 12 + 6 = 18. Ask the children whether any number facts will fit into the intersection. (No.) Repeat using two different numbers.

Main teaching activities

Whole class: Explain that today's activities will include adding more than two items. Revise how to do this, including 'carrying'. Remind the children of familiar addition strategies, such as looking for opportunities to make 10 or using near doubles. Also demonstrate how we can check an addition by adding the numbers in a different order, perhaps adding the most significant digits first (as in the expanded method).

Independent work: Distribute the 'Sid's Snowy Sports shop' activity sheet. Ask the children to calculate the given shopping bills from the price list. The last question is relatively 'open'.

Review

Write a list of three of the items from Sid's Snowy Sports shop on the board. Ask: *Why is it not advisable to try to add more than two of these numbers mentally? What advice would you give to someone who is adding a list of numbers, especially decimal numbers such as amounts of money?* Listen to reasons for the choice of various methods. Make a class checklist of suggestions. This should include: line up the place values exactly; write the carried-over number below the calculation, but in the correct place value space; look for easy addition strategies; check with an alternative calculation. Share some of the children's answers to the activity sheet. Ask the children to use the class checklist to find out where they have made errors, and to correct some of the calculations together on the board. Use this to establish any problem areas.

Differentiation

Less confident learners: Provide the support version of the activity sheet, which uses a simplified price list.
More confident learners: Encourage the children to use the standard compact method for their calculations, and to check their answers by adding in a different order (using informal jottings).

Lesson 5 (Teach)

Starter

Reason: Repeat the Venn diagram activity from Lesson 4, labelling one ring 'multiples of 6' and the other 'multiples of 8'. This time there will be numbers in the section where the two rings overlap. Discuss why. Repeat with rings labelled 'even numbers' and 'multiples of 3'. Ask the children to predict the numbers in the overlap.

Main teaching activities

Whole class: Explain that today's activity continues with the theme of Sid's Snowy Sports Shop, but involves problems with more than one step. For example: *If I buy my nephew a pair of skates, socks, gloves and a hat, how much change will I get from £100?* Work through this problem together, pointing out that the first step is to work out how much was spent and the second step is to subtract that from £100. Ask for volunteers to work through the steps on the board. Ask: *Do we need written subtraction to work out the change?* Help the children to see that it is easier to count on to £100, since this is a relatively small difference.

Independent work: Set a budget and ask the children to calculate the change for five sets of two items, using the price list on 'Sid's Snowy Sports shop'.

Review

Ask the class: *What is an inverse operation? How can using the inverse operation help us to check this work?* Remind the children that the inverse is the opposite of a given operation, reversing the effect – for example, adding

Differentiation

Less confident learners: The children should use the support version of the price list (see Lesson 4), which uses more manageable numbers.
More confident learners: Offer an additional challenge: *Imagine you have £200 to spend on sports equipment. You cannot go over this limit. Try to spend as much money as possible. What is the smallest amount of change you could receive?*

Unit 2 ▭ 2 weeks

after subtracting or multiplying after dividing. Explain that this is helpful for checking an answer: for example, we can check a subtraction by adding back the answer and the lower number to get the higher number. Demonstrate this, using some of the sports shop examples. Ask one child to provide a back-up by checking these examples on the board, using the expanded method of addition with informal jottings.

Lesson 6 (Practise and apply)

Starter
Recall: Multiplying by 4. Demonstrate that 16 × 4 is 16 doubled twice; double 16 = 32 and double 32 = 64. Repeat using different numbers. Ask: *Can we use a similar method for dividing by 4?* (Yes: halving and halving again.) Demonstrate that 52 ÷ 4 is 52 halved twice; half 52 = 26 and half 26 = 13. Repeat using 64 ÷ 4; 72 ÷ 4; 68 ÷ 4. The children can use their number fans to show the answers. Now try 26 ÷ 4; 26 halved twice = half 13 = 6.5.

Main teaching activities
Whole class: Explain to the children that during the next two days, they are going to use all of their problem-solving, addition and subtraction skills. They have to use the information on the 'Maths Theme Park' sheet to plan a seven-day holiday for two people. They will need to plan visits and activities over the seven days, and everything spent must be kept as a running budget. Their holiday spending money is €1000 for the week, and this must pay for everything including fares, drinks, food and so on.

Model an example that might represent Day 1, such as:

Visit to the Maths Theme Park

Entry fees	2 × €16.00	= €32.00
Tricky Tractors	2 × €1.50	= € 3.00
Wacky Walrus	2 × €4.00	= € 8.00
Skyrider	2 × €3.00	= € 6.00
Ice cream	2 × €1.00	= € 2.00
Creepy Cinema	2 × €7.00	= €14.00
Total for the day		= €65.00
Money left over €1000 – €65		= €935.00

Paired work: Ask the children to use the theme park holiday tariff on the 'Maths Theme Park' activity sheet to plan holiday activities for two people for seven days, keeping within the €1000 overall budget. Allow the children to work in pairs at their own pace. Some may manage only a few days' planning; others may complete the week.

Review
Use this time to check the children's progress and troubleshoot difficulties. Remind the children that there are two people and everything has to be paid for per person, so some doubling will be needed.

Ask: *What method are you using to keep track of your running total?* Some children may prefer to draw a number line and count on each day's spending; others will be subtracting as they go, using the compact written method. Ask: *If I spent €379 in the first two days, how much will I have left for the rest of the week?* Ask for volunteers to demonstrate their methods of finding the answer, one of which is shown below.

$$
\begin{array}{r}
\cancel{1}\ {}^{9}\cancel{0}\ {}^{9}\cancel{0}\ {}^{1}0 \\
-\quad 3\ \ 7\ \ 9 \\
\hline
6\ \ 2\ \ 1 \\
\hline
\end{array}
$$

Differentiation
Less confident learners: The children can use a prepared supplementary planning sheet as a framework for planning activities and calculating costs, and use a calculator to keep track of their budgeting.
More confident learners: Differentiate the activity by outcome. Look for more adventurous choices.

■ SCHOLASTIC

Lesson 7 (Apply)

Starter

Refine and reason: Indicate the following word problems written on the board. Ask the children to solve them and use their number fans to show the answer. Encourage them to explain the operations and methods they have used.

● A man cycles 5 miles to work and the same on his return. He works 5 days a week. How far does he cycle each week?

● Joe has collected 45 football stickers. He buys 19 more. How many stickers does he have in total?

● Felicity decides that she has far too many hair clips, and gives half of them to her sister. If she started with 52 hair clips, how many does Felicity have left?

● Fruity chews are sold in bags of 84. Each bag has equal numbers of the 4 different flavours. How many of each flavour are there?

Main teaching activities

Paired work: Continue from the previous lesson. Allow the children to add to the tariff list with their own ideas of holiday fun. An extension challenge, for children who have finished the main task, might be to plan an alternative day out: the budget is €100, and all expenses must be fully accounted for. They can invent places to visit and think of likely costs.

Review

Ask questions to assess the children's ability in computation, estimation and decision-making. *What skills have you employed to solve this problem?* (The children should be able to identify decision-making, doubling, adding, subtracting and so on.) *How did you decide which part to do first? Did you plan how much to spend each day? How did you calculate the cost of that excursion? Can you persuade us that this is the most suitable method to use? Are your strategies most suited to these particular numbers? Which operation did you use? Did anybody run out of money?*

Differentiation

Less confident learners: Provide a modelled supplementary planning sheet with the activity sheet as a framework for planning activities and calculating costs. Children can use a calculator to keep track of their budgeting.

More confident learners: Differentiate the activity by outcome. Look for more adventurous choices. The children should move on to the extension activity.

Lesson 8 (Teach)

Starter

Rehearse and reason: Ask the children to think of word problems involving mental calculations, such as: 'I picked 28 plums from my aunt's tree. She gave me half of them to take home. How many plums did I have?' Take suggestions. Write good examples on the board and ask the class to solve them, explaining their methods.

Main teaching activities

Whole class: Explain to the children that this lesson is going to be about the efficient use of a calculator. They will learn how calculators can help to solve problems that require multiple calculations. Write up on the board: 6, 2.5, 10, 2. Say: *These digits can be combined to make 300. Can anybody use their calculator to work out how I did it? You must be able to explain the stages.* The process is $(2.5 \times 2) = 5$; $5 \times 6 = 30$; $30 \times 10 = 300$. Model the calculation on the calculator and the way in which you record the buttons to be pressed for each stage. Now challenge the children to use their calculators to use the same numerals but this time use all four operations to create a calculation. They must record their processes on a whiteboard or rough paper. Invite the children to share their calculations. How many different answers have they achieved? Look at a variety of operations and recording methods. Ask individuals to explain to the class what they were thinking and how the calculator supported their calculations. Remind them to read the display accurately when combining whole numbers and decimals.

Paired work: Write up on the board several sets of four numbers, eg 20, 4, 3.5, 12; 25, 3.2, 10, 15; 45, 2, 1.6, 10. Ask each pair to find as many different combinations of calculations as they can. They can use each number and each of the four operations once, with a calculator to help them. Stress that it is very important that they record their thinking in whatever way helps them to explain it to others.

Review
Ask for pairs of children to demonstrate to the others the combinations achieved and their recording methods. Ask: *How do you know that you have covered all the combinations? Have you developed a methodical way of working? Can you recommend it and explain it to the others?*

Lesson 9 (Practise)

Starter
Recall: Write a number on the board, such as 24. Ask the children to suggest number sentences that give that answer, such as 6 × 4, 12 + 12, 25 – 1, 48 ÷ 2, and so on. Record this as a web, with the number in the centre and lines radiating from it leading to number sentences. Repeat with 36, 18 and 32.

Main teaching activities
Whole class: Put up on the board the number 117.4. Say: *If this is the answer, what could the question be?* Ask the children to use their calculators to find a one- or two-step calculation and to explain how they got there. Discuss the use of the inverse when starting with an answer. Some children may have done this but then forgot to reverse it when describing their calculation. Other children may have used estimation of the relative size of the number and yet others may have used trial and error. Discuss the relative merits or difficulties of each method.
Independent work: Introduce the 'What's the question?' activity sheet. Explain that for each example they have been given an answer and four numbers. Using a calculator they must create a calculation with that answer. They can use any of the four operations. In the spaces provided it is very important that they record their thinking steps, describing how they reached their calculation as well as the calculation itself, since they will be asked to explain their methods in the review part of the lesson.

Review
Share answers and working practices from each ability group. Spend time discussing ways of working and asking children: *How did you decide what had to be keyed into your calculator? How does your working out differ from the actual final calculation that you identified? Did anyone find a different calculation for any of the answers?* Give five minutes for children to discuss their findings with 'talk partners' and report back.

Lesson 10 (Apply)

Starter
Rehearse: Holding up a digit card, go round the room asking each child to double the number until 100 is passed. Give that table a point. Repeat with other digit cards. The first table/group to score five points is the winner.

Main teaching activities
Whole class: Write up on the board the following word problem: A length of wood measuring 4.2 metres in length is cut into 6 equal pieces. How long is each piece? Ask the children to use their calculator to solve this problem. Take suggestions for answers (0.7m or 70cm) and discuss how the children need to be careful when interpreting the answer because of the decimal point. Repeat using the following question: *At a school concert, programmes were sold at 15p each and 20 programmes were sold. In pounds, how much money was made?* Revise the fact that numbers after the decimal point are tenths and then hundredths (10p and 1p for money). Show the children

Differentiation
Less confident learners: Provide these children with single-digit whole numbers to calculate in the first instance.
More confident learners: Provide these children with decimal numbers up to two decimal places.

Differentiation
Less confident learners: Use the support version of the activity sheet, which uses single whole numbers and lower totals.
More confident learners: Use the extension version of the sheet, which uses decimal numbers.

Unit 2 ▭ 2 weeks

Differentiation

Less confident learners: These children may need adult support to accurately key in the fraction and to read and interpret decimal answers. They may find it helpful to use digit cards on a whiteboard, marked in H T U . t h, to interpret their answers.

More confident learners: These children could begin to explore the use of the calculator to find multiple fractions such as $^2/_5$ and to combine answers to two-step problems. For example, if I give $^2/_5$ of £35 to charity and $^1/_5$ of what is left to my brother, how much money do I have left?

that fractions can be converted to decimal fractions by keying them into the calculator, ie $^1/_5$ keyed in as 1 divided by 5 gives the equivalent decimal fraction of 0.2. Give the children an opportunity to explore this using their calculator.

Independent work: Write up a number of fraction questions such as $^1/_5$ of £20; $^1/_4$ of 16.8m ; $^1/_3$ of 75kg; $^1/_5$ of 3.5m; $^1/_{10}$ of £2000 and ask children to solve them using the same method. Remind them again about taking care when reading a decimal answer.

Review

Go through some of the answers and ask children to help you to understand how they read the answers correctly. Ask: *How many grams is 0.5kg or how many pounds is 4000 pence?* Say: *Explain to me exactly what you would key into your calculator to find 25 lots of 60p. What would the answer look like? Can you convert the answer to pounds?*

Name _____ Date _____

Greater or smaller?

Throw a dice to make two three-digit numbers.

Write them on either side of the < or > symbol, in the correct places. Do this five times. An example has been done for you.

Numbers thrown		Numbers thrown	
421 and 645	645 > 421		>
	<		<
	<		>

Now use the dice to make some four-digit numbers and do the same thing.

Numbers thrown		Numbers thrown	
1235 and 6546	1235 < 6546		>
	>		<
	<		>

Write these numbers in ascending order, using the < symbol:

365   974   655   356   394

_____

Write these numbers in descending order, using the > symbol:

4675   7564   4665   7655   4567

_____

Write the < and > symbols into these number sentences so that they make sense.

834 ____ 945 ____ 756 ____ 757 ____ 576

2978 ____ 6457 ____ 2899 ____ 2795 ____ 2784

3967 ____ 4756 ____ 3987 ____ 3776 ____ 3765 ____ 3766

Name _____ Date _____

Weather around the world

°C

Here is a table of minimum temperatures, taken one November day all around the world.

Label the number line with arrows and the name of each place.

City	Min. temp. (°C)	City	Min. temp. (°C)
London	2	Washington	3
Reykjavik	−17	St Petersburg	−12
Moscow	−13	Oslo	−6
Copenhagen	−1	Barcelona	7
Paris	4	St Moritz	−5

What are the differences in temperature between...

London and Oslo? _____

Reykjavik and Paris? _____

St Petersburg and Oslo? _____

Washington and St Moritz? _____

Copenhagen and St Petersburg? _____

Which is the coldest place? _____

Which is the warmest place? _____

What is the temperature difference between these two places? _____

15 — 14 — 13 — 12 — 11 — 10 — 9 — 8 — 7 — 6 — 5 — 4 — 3 — 2 — 1 — 0 — −1 — −2 — −3 — −4 — −5 — −6 — −7 — −8 — −9 — −10 — −11 — −12 — −13 — −14 — −15 — −16 — −17 — −18 — −19 — −20

Name _____   Date _____

Sid's Snowy Sports shop

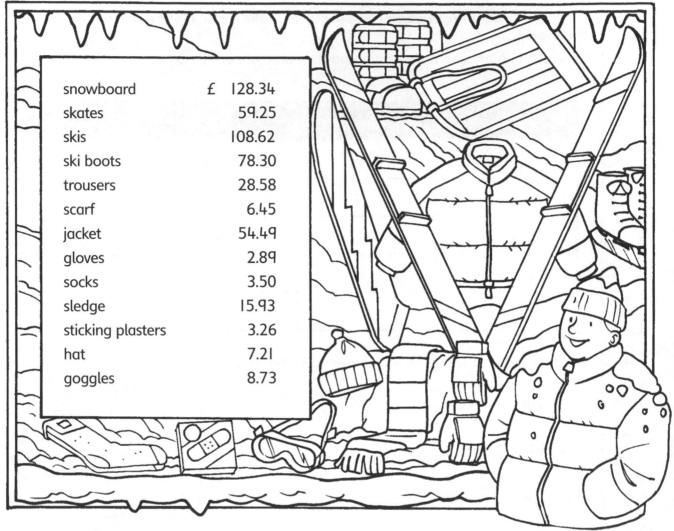

snowboard	£	128.34
skates		59.25
skis		108.62
ski boots		78.30
trousers		28.58
scarf		6.45
jacket		54.49
gloves		2.89
socks		3.50
sledge		15.93
sticking plasters		3.26
hat		7.21
goggles		8.73

On another sheet of paper, use Sid's price list to calculate the cost of...

a. skates and socks _____

b. ski boots, socks and trousers _____

c. hat, scarf and gloves _____

d. jacket, trousers, hat, scarf and gloves _____

e. sledge and sticking plasters _____

f. snowboard, goggles, hat and gloves _____

g. everything I might need for skiing _____

Name _____ Date _____

Maths Theme Park

THEME PARK ACTIVITIES

	€
Entry fee per person	16.00
Tricky Tractors	1.50
Wacky Walrus	4.00
Skyrider	3.00
Creepy Cinema	7.00
Numbskull Ride	3.80
Ice rink	6.50
Banana Boat	4.50

SNACKS AND DRINKS

	€
Ice cream	1.00
Fizzy orange	1.25
Cola	1.50
Hot dog	2.50
Burger	1.80
Veggie burger	1.60
Fruit juice	2.10
Doughnut	0.50
Coffee/Tea	1.00
Chips	1.20
Picnic	13.00 per person

DAY TRIPS

€ 2.00 per person for each km travelled

Sea	12km
Forest	30km
Mountains	35km
Diamond caves	48km
Pool	2km
Film set	3km
Play area	1km
Crazy golf	4km

ENTRY FEE PER PERSON

	€
Swimming pool	7.00
Crazy golf	3.50
Film set	18.00
Play area	4.00
Diamond caves	17.50
Ski lift (mountains)	12.50
Pedal boats (sea)	11.25
Water skiing (sea)	38.50
Paragliding (sea)	29.50

Unit 3 ▢ 2 weeks

Counting, partitioning and calculating

Lesson	Strands	Starter	Main teaching activities
1. Review and teach	Use/apply Knowledge	**Explain what each digit represents in whole numbers and decimals with up to two places, and partition, round and order these numbers.**	• Solve one- and two-step problems involving whole numbers and decimals and all four operations, choosing and using appropriate calculation strategies, including calculator use. • Recall quickly multiplication facts up to 10 × 10, use to multiply pairs of multiples of 10 and 100 and derive quickly corresponding division facts. • Identify pairs of factors of two-digit whole numbers and find common multiples, eg for 6 and 9. (Revision of Block A, Units 1 and 2)
2. Teach	Use/apply Knowledge	As for Lesson 1	As for Lesson 1
3. Teach	Knowledge	Solve one- and two-step problems involving whole numbers and decimals and all four operations, choosing and using appropriate calculation strategies, including calculator use.	Recall quickly multiplication facts up to 10 × 10, use to multiply pairs of multiples of 10 and 100 and derive quickly corresponding division facts.
4. Review, teach and practise	Calculate Knowledge	**Use knowledge of place value and addition and subtraction of two-digit numbers to derive sums and differences, doubles and halves of decimals, eg 6.5 ± 2.7, halve 5.6, double 0.34.**	• Refine and use efficient written methods to multiply and divide HTU × U, TU × TU, U.t × U, and HTU ÷ U. • Use knowledge of rounding, place value, number facts and inverse operations to estimate and check calculations.
5. Practise and apply	Calculate	Recall quickly multiplication facts up to 10 × 10, use to multiply pairs of multiples of 10 and 100 and derive quickly corresponding division facts.	Refine and use efficient written methods to multiply and divide HTU × U, TU × TU, U.t × U, and HTU ÷ U.
6. Teach and practise	Calculate	As for Lesson 5	As for Lesson 5
7. Practise	Calculate Knowledge	**Explain what each digit represents in whole numbers and decimals with up to two places, and partition, round and order these numbers.**	• Refine and use efficient written methods to multiply and divide HTU × U, TU × TU, U.t × U, and HTU ÷ U. • Use knowledge of rounding, place value, number facts and inverse operations to estimate and check calculations.
8. Apply	Use/apply Calculate	Count from any given number in whole number and decimal steps, extending beyond zero when counting backwards; relate the numbers to their position on a number line.	• Solve one- and two-step problems involving whole numbers and decimals and all four operations, choosing and using appropriate calculation strategies, including calculator use. • Refine and use efficient written methods to multiply and divide HTU × U, TU × TU, U.t × U, and HTU ÷ U.
9. Apply	Use/apply Calculate Knowledge	Use a calculator to solve problems, including those involving decimals or fractions, eg to find ¾ of 150g; interpret the display correctly in the context of measurement.	• Explain reasoning using diagrams, graphs and text; refine ways of recording using images and symbols. • Solve one- and two-step problems involving whole numbers and decimals and all four operations, choosing and using appropriate calculation strategies, including calculator use. • Refine and use efficient written methods to multiply and divide HTU × U, TU × TU, U.t × U, and HTU ÷ U. • Use knowledge of rounding, place value, number facts and inverse operations to estimate and check calculations.
10. Review	Use/apply Calculate Knowledge	**Use knowledge of place value and addition and subtraction of two-digit numbers to derive sums and differences, doubles and halves of decimals, eg 6.5 ± 2.7, halve 5.6, double 0.34.**	• Explain reasoning using diagrams, graphs and text; refine ways of recording using images and symbols. • Solve one- and two-step problems involving whole numbers and decimals and all four operations, choosing and using appropriate calculation strategies, including calculator use. • Refine and use efficient written methods to multiply and divide HTU × U, TU × TU, U.t × U, and HTU ÷ U. • Use knowledge of rounding, place value, number facts and inverse operations to estimate and check calculations.

SCHOLASTIC

Speaking and listening objectives
- Understand the process of decision making.

Introduction
This unit is all about multiplication and division, both mentally and using written methods. Children are required to move through the stages of multiplication at a rate that matches their ability and understanding. At each stage they need to estimate and understand the processes. The first three lessons build on previous work and introduce alternative methods for multiplying, given the knowledge that a set of numbers can be multiplied in any order. The remaining lessons of this unit build on experiences and use knowledge of partitioning numbers in order to use the grid method for multiplying, leading on, as appropriate, to standard methods of written multiplication. There are opportunities for making decisions about strategies and ways of working and throughout the unit runs the strand of problem solving.

Use and apply mathematics
- Explain reasoning using diagrams, graphs and text; refine ways of recording using images and symbols.
- Solve one- and two-step problems involving whole numbers and decimals and all four operations, choosing and using appropriate calculation strategies, including calculator use.

Lessons 1-10

Preparation
Lesson 1: Write on the board some four-digit and five-digit numbers. Provide each child with multiplication problems.
Lesson 2: Write on the board some four-digit and five-digit numbers in words.
Lesson 3: Prepare some problems using near multiples of 10.
Lesson 4: Write on the board some × problems to be solved using the grid method.
Lesson 5: Provide some ÷ questions.
Lessons 6 and 7: Prepare some ÷ questions.
Lesson 7: Write some jumbled sets of numbers both positive and negative, for ordering.
Lesson 8: Copy 'Multiply or divide' onto an OHT. Make up the 'Four operations vocabulary' cards and stick the × and ÷ ones randomly on the board.
Lesson 9: Write on the board the two-step problem. Copy 'Word problem frame' onto an OHT.
Lesson 10: Prepare some mixed × and ÷ questions, including word problems.

You will need
Photocopiable pages
'Find the X factor' (page 44), 'Trying times' (page 45), 'Multiplying matters' (page 46), one for each child.
CD resources
Support and extension versions of 'Find the X factor', 'Trying

Learning objectives

Starter
- Solve one- and two-step problems involving whole numbers and decimals and all four operations, choosing and using appropriate calculation strategies, including calculator use.
- Count from any given number in whole number and decimal steps, extending beyond zero when counting backwards; relate the numbers to their position on a number line.
- Explain what each digit represents in whole numbers and decimals with up to two places, and partition, round and order these numbers.
- Use knowledge of place value and addition and subtraction of two-digit numbers to derive sums and differences, doubles and halves of decimals, eg 6.5 ± 2.7, halve 5.6, double 0.34.
- Recall quickly multiplication facts up to 10×10, use to multiply pairs of multiples of 10 and 100 and derive quickly corresponding division facts.
- Use a calculator to solve problems, including those involving decimals or fractions, eg to find ¾ of 150g; interpret the display correctly in the context of measurement.

Main teaching activities
2006
- Explain reasoning using diagrams, graphs and text; refine ways of recording using images and symbols.
- Solve one- and two-step problems involving whole numbers and decimals and all four operations, choosing and using appropriate calculation strategies, including calculator use.
- Recall quickly multiplication facts up to 10×10, use to multiply pairs of multiples of 10 and 100 and derive quickly corresponding division facts.
- Identify pairs of factors of two-digit whole numbers and find common multiples, eg for 6 and 9. (Revision of Block A, Units 1 and 2)
- Refine and use efficient written methods to multiply and divide HTU × U, TU × TU, U.t × U, and HTU ÷ U.
- Use knowledge of rounding, place value, number facts and inverse operations to estimate and check calculations.

Unit 3 ▢ 2 weeks

times' and 'Multiplying matters'.
General resource sheets: 'Number
cards 1–100', 'Multiplication
square', for support, 'Four
operations vocabulary cards', for
teacher's/LSA's use.
Equipment
Calculators; Blu-Tack.

1999
● Explain methods and reasoning, orally and in writing.
● Use all four operations to solve simple word problems involving numbers
and quantities based on 'real life', money and measures (including time),
using one or more steps, including finding simple percentages.
● Choose and use appropriate number operations to solve problems, and
appropriate ways of calculating: mental, mental with jottings, written
methods, calculator.
● Know by heart all multiplication facts up to 10 × 10; derive quickly division
facts.
● Use known facts and place value to multiply and divide mentally.
● Find all the pairs of factors of any number up to 100.
● Extend written methods to HTU or U.t by U; long multiplication of TU by
TU; HTU by U (integer remainder).
● Check results of calculations.

Vocabulary
problem, solution, calculate, calculation, operation, inverse, answer, methods,
explain, reasoning, reason, place value, digit, decimal point, decimal place,
pattern, sequence, thousands, ten thousands, hundred thousands, million,
tenths, hundredth, positive, negative, above/below zero, minus, integer,
compare, order, ascending, descending, greater than (>), less than (<), round,
estimate, approximately, factors, multiply, multiple, significant digit, divide

Lesson 1 (Review and teach)

Starter
Refine: Show the children some four-digit and five-digit numbers, such as
4368 and 52,912. Highlight individual digits and ask the children the value
of those digits.

Main teaching activities
Whole class: Revise factors. Ask: *If 3 and 4 are factors of 12, what are the
others?* (1 and 12; 2 and 6.) *Name the factors of 50.* (1 and 50; 2 and 25; 5
and 10.) Explain that we can use our knowledge of factors to multiply bigger
numbers. For example: 50 × 6 = 5 × 10 × 6 or (5 × 6) × 10 or (10 × 6) × 5
or (5 × 10) × 6. Write all the variations on the board and ask for volunteers
to come and calculate them, demonstrating that factors can be multiplied in
any order. Explain that we can rearrange the factors to choose the easiest
calculation, and that brackets make the order of multiplication clearer.
Repeat the process to solve 60 × 7 using factors. Ask: *What factors could I
use to help me?*
Independent work: Provide each child with multiplication problems using
multiples of 5 or 10 (eg 60 × 5) for one of the multiples. Explain that the
children will be using factors to multiply multiples of 5 and 10. Ask them to
explore possible arrangements of factors and choose the simplest order for
calculation. Encourage them to write down a variety of arrangements and not
just multiply the first order they think of. Use questions such as: 50 × 5; 60 ×
5; 50 × 7; 30 × 5; 20 × 5; 20 × 6

Differentiation
Less confident learners:
Provide simplified questions with
only multiples of 10 to be
factorised, eg 50 × 5; 60 × 5; 30
× 5; 20 × 5; 40 × 5, etc.
More confident learners:
Provide a version with multiples
of 2, 5 and 10 to be factorised,
eg 14 × 5; 18 × 5; 16 × 5; 22 × 5;
28 × 5, etc.

Review
Ask: *What are factors? How can they help us multiply?* (They break down
a larger number into more manageable 'chunks'.) Ask the more confident
learners: *Were all the numbers you tried to multiply easier when you
used factors?* Write an example on the board and explain that the first
factorisation may not simplify the calculation enough: the numbers may need
to be further broken down. For example: 25 × 18 = (5 × 5) × (2 × 9) = (5 ×
5) × (2 × 3 × 3). This gives (5 × 2) × (5 × 9) = 10 × 45 = 450. The important
thing is to know the times tables!

Lesson 2 (Teach)

Starter

Refine and rehearse: As for Lesson 1, but write the numbers up in words (for example: eight thousand, nine hundred and fifty-two). Ask for a volunteer to come and write each number in digits. Then ask: *How many more would I need to add to this number to make the next whole thousand? How many more would I need to add to make 10,000?* Repeat with other word examples up to ten thousand.

Main teaching activities

Whole class: Follow on from Lesson 1. Explain that today, the children are going to use factors to multiply any numbers less than 100. They may have to factorise numbers more than once in order to find a manageable calculation. Ask the class to find factors to help solve 32×15, using brackets to keep the calculation order clear. For example: $(16 \times 2) \times (3 \times 5) = (8 \times 4) \times (3 \times 5)$ or $(2 \times 4) \times (3 \times 5) \times 4$. Discuss which combination would be easiest to multiply. Demonstrate multiplying the different combinations, and emphasise that the factors may be multiplied in any order.

It may be easier to use multiples of 10 than multiples of 5, so $(16 \times 5) \times (3 \times 2) = (8 \times 5) \times (3 \times 4) = 40 \times 12 = 480$. Or $(4 \times 5) \times 3 \times 4 \times 2 = 20 \times 3 \times 4 \times 2 = 480$. Repeat this process for several more examples.

Independent work: Provide the activity sheet 'Find the X factor' of multiplication problems with different factors for one multiple.

Review

Write the following calculations on the board: 17×23; 19×9; 12×24. Ask the children: *Which of these calculations is the easiest to break into factors? Are some numbers less helpful to factorise than others? Why?* Discuss why prime numbers and square numbers offer a limited choice of factors. Remind the children that larger numbers may have factors that need to be simplified further. Ask for a volunteer to factorise and work out 15×48. Encourage a method such as: $15 \times 48 = (3 \times 5) \times (6 \times 8) = (15 \times 4) \times 6 \times 2 = 60 \times 6 \times 2 = 360 \times 2 = 720$. Repeat with several more examples.

Differentiation
Less confident learners: Provide the version with simple multiples of 2, 5 and 10.
More confident learners: Provide the version with more challenging numbers that require further factorisation.

Lesson 3 (Teach)

Starter

Revisit: Distribute number cards randomly, one per person. Explain that you are going to ask three children to stand up and they must race each other to give the total of the three numbers they are holding. Award a point for the correct answer and choose three more children. Only the people who are standing are allowed to answer. Reward the winning group or table.

Main teaching activities

Whole class: Explain that the children are going to explore multiplying by numbers close to multiples of 10, such as 19 or 21. Say: *We can use what we know about place value and factors to help us multiply by multiples of 10.* Demonstrate that $15 \times 20 = (15 \times 2) \times 10 = 30 \times 10 = 300$. *We can use this skill to multiply a number like 19 or 21 by rounding it to 20, then adjusting the answer by adding or subtracting the missing amount.*

Demonstrate that:
$$15 \times 21 = ((15 \times 2) \times 10) + 15 = 300 + 15 = 315$$
and $15 \times 19 = ((15 \times 2) \times 10) - 15 = 300 - 15 = 285$

Repeat using 18×21; 18×19; 24×19; 24×21. Emphasise the importance of the final adjustment: *Is it one more 'lot of', or one less?*

Independent work: Ask the children to solve problems of near multiples of 10, such as 22×19 or 12×21, using the method they have learned.

Unit 3 ◗ 2 weeks

Review

Write up 23 × 31 on the board. Ask: *Which of these numbers is the near multiple of 10? Would you try to round both of the numbers?* Agree that it is only practical to round and adjust using one multiple, as using both would lead to confusion. Ask for a volunteer to come and demonstrate how they worked it out, talking through their method: 23 × 3 × 10 = 69 × 10 = 690. Then add on the extra 'one lot of' 23 = 713.

Now ask: *If we can do this with near multiples of 10, is it possible to do it with near multiples of 100?* Ask for a volunteer to work out 13 × 201 on the board: 13 × 201 = (13 × 2) × 100 = 2600. Then add one extra 13 = 2613. Use several more examples to consolidate these ideas.

Lesson 4 (Review, teach and practise)

Starter

Revisit and rehearse: Explain that the children must make target numbers that you will give them by writing 'How many more'. Start by holding up the 20 card from the set of number cards and saying, *The target number is 20. If I have 3.6, how many more to make 20?* Ask for a volunteer to give the answer. Repeat several times and then change the target number.

Main teaching activities

Whole class: Revise partitioning and the grid method of multiplying. Ask children to solve some multiplication problems. Three examples are shown below. Remind the children to estimate the answer first, so they know its approximate size.

X	H	T	U
			8
30			
4			

X	H	T	U
			9
40			
7			

X	Th	H	T	U
				5
100				
20				
3				

If a group of your children are very confident with the grid method, you could make them your focus group for this session and teach them vertical multiplication, starting with the most significant digit. The progression you adopt will depend on your individual school calculating policy.

```
  H T U
  1 2 4
×     6
  6 0 0
  1 2 0
    2 4
  7 4 4
```

Start with the most significant digit: the 100. Remind the children that they are multiplying 20 × 6, not 2 × 6. Add using the largest number first: 600... 700... 720... 744.

Independent work: Provide the children with activity sheet 'Trying times'. They must solve multiplication problems of three-digit numbers by one-digit numbers, using the multiplication method that each child is most comfortable with.

Review

Ask for two volunteers, one who is confident with the grid method and one who is confident with the vertical method, and ask them to find 206 × 4. Discuss what needs to be recorded when you multiply 0 tens by 4 (0). Demonstrate that both methods work. Ask: *How could we check the answer?* (Use the inverse operation, division.) Demonstrate the use of a calculator to divide the answer by 4.

Write up the calculation below and ask the children: *Is this correct? How do you know? Can you estimate what size the answer should be? Will the actual answer be bigger or smaller than that? Can you correct the errors in this calculation? What advice would you offer this person to help them avoid errors in the future?*

$$
\begin{array}{r}
3\;1\;6 \\
\times\qquad 5 \\
\hline
1\;5\;0\;0 \quad \text{Correct} \\
5 \quad \text{Incorrect place value} \\
3\;0 \quad \text{Poorly placed, inviting incorrect addition} \\
\hline
1\;8\;0\;5
\end{array}
$$

Differentiation
Less confident learners:
Provide the support version, which has multiplication problems with TU × U problems.
More confident learners:
Provide the extension version, which has more demanding numbers. Ask the children to use the vertical multiplication method throughout.

Lesson 5 (Practise and apply)

Starter
Recall: Play 'Division Lotto'. Give each group six number cards at random from a 1-10 set. Call out division questions such as *What is 35 ÷ 5?* or *How many lots of 3 in 18?* The children look for the answer among their cards and, if they find it, turn the card over. The first group to have turned all its cards over wins.

Main teaching activities
Whole class: Write the calculation 215 × 6 on the board. Ask for two volunteers to solve it in different ways. Check by using the inverse operation. Revise the 'chunking' method of division.

If you have a group who are confident with 'chunking' division, you could teach them short division or standard vertical multiplication with carrying. Provide a number of examples for the children to attempt. Talk them through each stage of the example shown:
● Multiply the units first (5 × 4 = 20). You cannot put 20 in the units column, so record the 0 and carry the 2 to be included with the tens.
● Multiply the tens (1 × 4 = 4 plus the carried over 2 = 6).
● Multiply the hundreds.

$$
\begin{array}{ccc}
H & T & U \\
1 & 1 & 5 \\
\times & & 4 \\
\hline
4 & 6 & 0 \\
& & \scriptstyle 2
\end{array}
\qquad
\begin{array}{r}
3\,\overline{)1\,{}^{1}2\,4} \\
0\;4\;1\;\text{r1}
\end{array}
$$

Ask: *What do you think is the most common mistake made when multiplying like this? Why is it important to carry across? What happens if you forget to count it in?*

Explain that when doing short division, you should think of the numbers as separate digits: the 1 is worth 100, but can be treated as a single digit. Careful placing of the numbers will give the correct place value. In the example shown:
● Divide, starting with the most significant digit (the 1 hundred). 1 ÷ 3 is impossible.
● Move the 1 across to join the tens. Now you have 12 ÷ 3 = 4. Record the 4 in the tens place.
● Move across to divide the units: 4 ÷ 3 = 1 remainder 1.

Ask: *What is the most common error made in short division? Why can you not afford to forget any numbers that you could not divide? What is the value of the 1 in this calculation?*

Repeat using a number of examples.

Independent work: Ask the children to complete the 'Multiplying matters' activity sheet, using their chosen method. They should check their answers using division.

Review

Ask for three volunteers to find 107 × 6 using different methods, explaining each step. Discuss and correct any discrepancies. Ask for a fourth volunteer to check the agreed answer using division, explaining each step. Ask:
● *Where do you think mistakes are most often made in each of these methods? What effect does this have on the answer?*
● *How can you quickly find the approximate size that the answer should be? What do you do first when estimating?*
● *Could you suggest any helpful tips for someone who is calculating using your chosen method?*

Differentiation
Less confident learners:
Provide the support version of the activity sheet, which uses TU × U problems.
More confident learners:
Provide the extension version, which includes word problems. Ask the children to use standard vertical multiplication, and to use standard short division for checking.

Lesson 6 (Teach and practise)

Starter
Recall: Play 'Division Lotto' as in Lesson 5. Keep a record of the division facts you ask in order to judge the children's accuracy at the end of the game.

Main teaching activities
Whole class: For progression in multiplication and division, refer to your own school calculating policy.

Introduce short division of HTU by U. Explain that we already know many TU × U facts from the times tables, but having a written method is useful for bigger numbers. Short division assumes that the child is confident with place value. Work through an example such as 3)369 = 123. Explain that we divide into each digit separately: instead of writing 300 ÷ 3 = 100, we only need to consider the 3 as a digit, then put the answer in the correct place value position.

Once the children have grasped this idea, move on to dividing into digits that leave a remainder to be 'transferred along':

$$3\overline{)1\ ^12\ 8}$$
$$\overline{0\ 4\ 2\ r2}$$

It is not possible to divide 1 by 3 using only whole numbers, so we can mark the place value with a 0 and transfer the 1 hundred across to the tens, so we now have 12 ÷ 3 = 4 and then 8 ÷ 3 = 2 remainder 2.

Repeat using 3)246 and 5)642. Emphasise that the remainders must be passed on to the next digit: they cannot be left behind or ignored. For example, discuss 3)172. Ask: *What should I put in the hundreds column? If I cannot divide 1 by 3 using whole numbers, what shall I do with the 1 hundred I have not used? Where should I put it so it can be divided? What value have I got in the tens column now? Can I divide it by 3? How much is the remainder? Where shall I put it so it can be divided? How many units are there now to be divided by 3?*

Independent work: Provide a variety of division questions. Ask the children to use the examples to practise short division. Use questions such as 264 ÷ 5; 163 ÷ 4; 257 ÷ 3; 288 ÷ 6; 534 ÷ 9.

Review
Write this calculation on the board and work through it with the children, asking: *What should I record for the tens column? Why is it important to place the 0 there? What should I do with the 2 tens that have not yet been divided? How many units are there now to be divided by 4?*

Differentiation
Less confident learners:
Provide some division questions that divide exactly, with no remainders to transfer (include a few remainders at the end if they are feeling more confident), for example: 552 ÷ 5; 843 ÷ 4 ; 964÷ 3; 882 ÷ 4 ;243 ÷2 Provide

$$\begin{array}{l}\text{H T U}\\ 4\overline{)4\ 2\ 6}\\ \overline{1\ 0\ 6\ r2}\end{array}$$

copies of the 'Multiplication square' to support division.
More confident learners:
Provide a variety of division questions and word problems with more challenging divisors, for example: 274 ÷ 9 ; 736 ÷ 8; 1933 ÷ 7; 1733 ÷ 6 ; 4733 ÷ 7; A farmer sowed 1846 bean seeds in 9 rows. How many were in each row? How many were left over?

Next, write up a number of examples with incorrect answers (three examples are shown below). Ask for individuals to come and explain where the calculations have gone wrong and why. Ask: *Is this correct? How do you know? How can we put it right? Can you think of some helpful hints to stop other people making the same mistakes?* Design and display a 'Division Health Warning', using the children's suggestions.

$$5\overline{)275} \qquad 6\overline{)709} \qquad 4\overline{)572}$$
$$011 \qquad 101\ r3 \qquad 118$$

Lesson 7 (Practise)

Starter
Recall: Indicate the sets of numbers you have written on the board, and ask for volunteers to help you write them in order of increasing size. Remind the children to look carefully, since some sets contain both positive and negative numbers.

Main teaching activities
Whole class: Continue with short division from Lesson 6. Encourage the children to round and estimate first in order to predict the size of the answer. This may help them to spot errors in their own calculations. For example, 5)138 is approximately 150 ÷ 5 = 30 (the exact answer is 27 r3). Demonstrate how to check the answer with the inverse operation, using a calculator. Key in 27 × 5 = 135 and then add on the remainder to make 138. (NB: Until the children understand remainders as fractions or decimals, they cannot put the exact answer into their calculators. This 'short cut' method serves as a check.)

Independent work: Provide further HTU ÷ U questions. Ask the children to round and estimate first, then calculate using short division, then check using the inverse operation. Examples: 372 ÷ 4; 927 ÷ 3; 637 ÷ 5; 779 ÷ 4; 218 ÷ 5; 602 ÷ 3.

Review
Write the incorrect calculation 4)398 = 22 on the board. Ask children to look at the answer to this calculation. *Is it the right size? How can rounding and estimating help you to spot an error in a calculation? Where has the person made the mistake? Can you put it right?* Provide several more division calculations for the children to estimate the answers, such as: 486 ÷ 5; 147 ÷ 5; 266 ÷ 6; 621 ÷ 3. Ask for volunteers to come and solve these. Ask: *What would you round this number to so that the answer is easy to estimate?*

Differentiation
Less confident learners:
Provide children with simpler TU ÷ U questions. Provide copies of the 'Multiplication square' to support division. Examples: 89 ÷ 3; 54 ÷ 5; 71÷ 2; 39 ÷ 4; 58 ÷ 3.
More confident learners:
Provide this group with division questions using more challenging divisors, such as 7, 8 and 9, rounding, estimating and checking as before. Examples: 286 ÷ 9; 635 ÷ 9; 2733 ÷ 9; 494 ÷ 7; 562.5 ÷ 8; 459.8 ÷ 8; 5288 ÷ 8.

Lesson 8 (Apply)

Starter
Recall: Ask the children to count out loud together in even steps, from various starting numbers. For example: *Count on from 10 in steps of 20 until we reach 150. Count back in twos from 20 to minus 20. Count on and back in fives from 5 to 100. Can you count in fives from 2? Count on in 10s from 1 until we reach 101, then count back.*

Main teaching activities
Whole class: Explain that this lesson is about the language of multiplication and division, and the clues we can look for when we try to solve a word problem. Indicate the multiplication and division vocabulary cards stuck randomly to the board. Ask the children to help you to sort these into lists, one for multiplication and one for division.
Independent work: Distribute the 'Multiply or divide?' activity sheet. Explain that for each question, the children need to underline the key word or phrase that gives a clue to the operation needed, then circle the important numbers. Warn them that sometimes questions contain redundant

Unit 3 ⬛ 2 weeks

information that has no bearing on the calculation needed. Ask the children to label each question with '×' or '÷', convert the words to a calculation and find the answer. On an OHP, go through question 1, which has been completed as an example. Please note that the answers given are not the only methods of working out. The children could use mental or short division, for instance.

Review
Start by discussing what clues the children looked for to help them decide which operation to use for each question. Invite them to share their ideas, and scribe some of the best ones onto a 'Helpful hints for solving word problems' sheet for display. Ask: *What words suggest division/multiplication to you? Are there any other hints you might look for?* (For example, the relative sizes of the numbers.)

Ask for volunteers to demonstrate some of the trickier questions they tackled, using your prepared OHT (or on a flipchart) and talking through their ideas. Discuss any misconceptions that arise.

Differentiation
Less confident learners: Provide the support version, which has simpler numbers.
More confident learners: Provide the extension version in which the problems include redundant information.

Lesson 9 (Apply)

Starter
Rehearse: Distribute calculators and demonstrate repeated addition or counting in 'lots of' using a calculator: key in 3 + 3 =. For some makes of calculator every time you press the = button it will add another 3. For others you need to key in 3 + 3 = + 3 = and thereafter the calculator will count on in threes every time you press the = button. Ask the children to key in 1.5 + 1.5 = and ask them to repeatedly press = and say out loud the steps. Repeat with other decimal steps to ensure confidence with this type of calculator use.

Main teaching activities
Whole class: Indicate this question written on the board:
A chocolate factory makes 246 chocolates per day. These are packed into gift boxes of six chocolates. How many boxes can the factory produce each day? The factory is open five days a week. How many boxes can it produce each week?

Explain that this is a two-step problem. To answer the second question, you need to have answered the first question. Look for clues such as *into gift boxes of 6*: putting a large number into lots of 6 must indicate a division. The numbers involved are big enough to require a written short division method. Now we can solve the second step. *Forty-one boxes are made in one day, so how many are made in five days?* This indicates a TU × U question. Most children should be able to do this mentally or by using jottings: 41 × 5 = (40 × 5) + 5 = 205. A few may need to use the grid method. The answer is 205 boxes of chocolates each week. Remind the children that a word question requires words in the answer, not just a number.
Independent work: Distribute the 'Word problem frame' activity sheet. Go through the questions, discussing the operations and calculating methods needed. Talk through the example on the sheet. Explain that the children need to identify the operation and method needed, isolate the number question and then estimate and calculate the answer.

Review
As in Lesson 8, use the prepared OHT (or flipchart) to help the children talk through their methods as they demonstrate how they solved some of the problems. Ask: *Roughly what answer do you expect to get? How did you make this estimate? Do you expect your answer to be greater or less than your estimate? Why? Talk me through your method of solving the problem. What were the clues that helped you decide which operation to use?*

Differentiation
Less confident learners: Provide the support version, with multiples from 2 to 6.
More confident learners: Provide the extension version, with two-step problems. Encourage the children to use a range of methods, including standard written multiplication and short division.

Lesson 10 (Review)

Starter

Refine and rehearse: Ask the children to imagine that they have £10.00 to spend. *How much change would you have if you spent 752p; 58p; £3.23; £1.45; 91p; £8.33; 17p; £6.29p; 67p?* The children should raise a hand to volunteer the answer.

Main teaching activities

Whole class: Use this session to 'troubleshoot' difficulties with solving multiplication and division word problems.

Independent work: Provide some mixed × and ÷ questions including word problems. Work with individual children, looking for errors in the choice of operation or the layout of the calculation, uncertain place value and answers that are far wide of the estimates.

Review

As in Lessons 8 and 9, ask for volunteers to demonstrate and talk through their decisions and calculations, using a prepared frame. Repeat the questions from the previous Review session.

Differentiation

Less confident learners:
Provide simple × and ÷ questions.

More confident learners:
Provide some challenging mixed × and ÷ problems, including word problems.

Name _____   Date _____

Find the X factor

Use factors to help solve these multiplication problems.
The first one has been done for you.

12 × 40
(6 × 2) × (4 × 10) can be rearranged as **(6 × 4) × 2 × 10 = 24 × 2 × 10 = 480** **or** **(3 × 4) × (4 × 10)**

1. 24 × 20	**2.** 32 × 15
3. 25 × 20	**4.** 35 × 20
5. 42 × 30	**6.** 27 × 30
7. 21 × 50	**8.** 21 × 15

Name _____   Date _____

Trying times

Use the written method of multiplication you have been working on to solve these sums.

1. 271 × 5	**2.** 128 × 6
3. 188 × 4	**4.** 321 × 3
5. 172 × 6	**6.** 316 × 8
7. 206 × 6	**8.** 413 × 4

Name _____   Date _____

Multiplying matters

1. Complete these calculations. Do an inverse calculation to check your answers.

Check 50 × 3 = 150 with 150 ÷ 3 = 50

312 × 3   423 × 3

_____   _____

352 × 5   371 × 6

_____   _____

263 × 7   216 × 9

_____   _____

2. There were 181 people at a meeting. The next week there were 3 times as many people. How many people were at the second meeting?

_____

3. Fred has 215 stamps in his collection; his brother has 4 times as many. How many stamps does his brother own?

_____

4. I have £18.34 in my money box. Dad says that if I work hard, I will have tripled this by Christmas. How much money will I have then?

_____

Securing number facts, understanding shape

BLOCK B

Securing number facts, understanding shape

Key aspects of learning

- Problem solving
- Social skills
- Self-awareness
- Creative thinking
- Managing feeling
- Empathy

Expected prior learning

Check that children can already:

- derive and recall multiplication facts up to 10 ×10 and the corresponding division facts
- multiply and divide numbers to 1000 by 10 and 100, understanding the effect
- add or subtract mentally pairs of two-digit whole numbers, eg 47 + 58, 91 – 35
- use decimal notation for tenths and hundredths, and partition decimals
- use efficient written methods to add and subtract two- and three-digit whole numbers and pounds (£) and pence (p)
- draw polygons and classify them by identifying their properties, including their line symmetry
- draw and complete shapes with reflective symmetry.

Objectives overview

The text in this diagram identifies the focus of mathematics learning within the block.

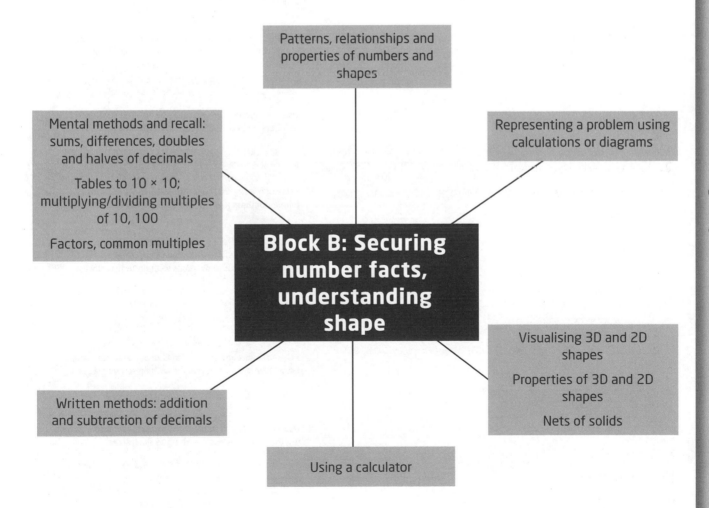

Patterns, relationships and properties of numbers and shapes

Mental methods and recall: sums, differences, doubles and halves of decimals

Tables to 10 × 10; multiplying/dividing multiples of 10, 100

Factors, common multiples

Representing a problem using calculations or diagrams

Block B: Securing number facts, understanding shape

Written methods: addition and subtraction of decimals

Visualising 3D and 2D shapes

Properties of 3D and 2D shapes

Nets of solids

Using a calculator

Securing number facts, understanding shape

Lesson	Strands	Starter	Main teaching activities
1. Review and teach	Shape	Recall quickly multiplication facts up to 10 × 10, use to multiply pairs of multiples of 10 and 100 and derive quickly corresponding division facts.	Identify, visualise and describe properties of rectangles, triangles, regular polygons and 3D solids; use knowledge of properties to draw 2D shapes and identify and draw nets of 3D shapes.
2. Practise	Shape	As for Lesson 1	As for Lesson 1
3. Review and teach	Use/apply Shape	As for Lesson 1	• Explore patterns, properties and relationships and propose a general statement involving numbers or shapes; identify examples for which the statement is true or false. • Identify, visualise and describe properties of rectangles, triangles, regular polygons and 3D solids; use knowledge of properties to draw 2D shapes and identify and draw nets of 3D shapes.
4. Teach	Use/apply Shape	• As for Lesson 1 • Use understanding of place value to multiply and divide whole numbers and decimals by 10, 100 or 1000. (Revision of Block A, Units 1 and 2)	As for Lesson 3
5. Practise	Use/apply Shape	As for Lesson 1	As for Lesson 3
6. Teach	Use/apply	As for Lesson 1	Explore patterns, properties and relationships and propose a general statement involving numbers or shapes; identify examples for which the statement is true or false.
7. Teach and practise	Calculate Use/apply	Identify pairs of factors of two-digit whole numbers and find common multiples, eg for 6 and 9.	• **Use efficient written methods to add and subtract whole numbers and decimals with up to two places.** • Explore patterns, properties and relationships and propose a general statement involving numbers or shapes; identify examples for which the statement is true or false.
8. Teach and practise	Calculate	As for Lesson 7	**Use efficient written methods to add and subtract whole numbers and decimals with up to two places.**
9. Practise	Use/apply Calculate	Explore patterns, properties and relationships and propose a general statement involving numbers or shapes; identify examples for which the statement is true or false.	• Explore patterns, properties and relationships and propose a general statement involving numbers or shapes; identify examples for which the statement is true or false. • **Use efficient written methods to add and subtract whole numbers and decimals with up to two places.**
10. Review and teach	Knowledge Calculate	Use knowledge of number facts, place value and rounding to estimate and check calculations.	• Use knowledge of rounding, place value, number facts and inverse operations to estimate and check calculations. • **Use efficient written methods to add and subtract whole numbers and decimals with up to two places.**
11. Teach and practise	Use/apply Knowledge Calculate	Identify, visualise and describe properties of rectangles, triangles, regular polygons and 3D solids; use knowledge of properties to draw 2D shapes and identify and draw nets of 3D shapes.	• Explore patterns, properties and relationships and propose a general statement involving numbers or shapes; identify examples for which the statement is true or false. • Use knowledge of rounding, place value, number facts and inverse operations to estimate and check calculations. • **Use efficient written methods to add and subtract whole numbers and decimals with up to two places.**
12. Review and teach	Use/apply Calculate	As for Lesson 11	As for Lesson 9
13. Teach and practise	Calculate	As for Lesson 1	**Use efficient written methods to add and subtract whole numbers and decimals with up to two places.**
14. Teach	Use/apply Knowledge	As for Lesson 1	• Explore patterns, properties and relationships and propose a general statement involving numbers or shapes; identify examples for which the statement is true or false. • Identify pairs of factors of two-digit whole numbers and find common multiples, eg for 6 and 9.
15. Practise and apply	Use/apply Knowledge	As for Lesson 1	As for Lesson 14

Unit 1 ▭ 3 weeks

Speaking and listening objectives

● Identify different question types and evaluate impact on audience.

Introduction

The first part of this unit gives opportunities to reason about both number and shape. Lessons 1 to 5 cover the classification and sorting of triangles and rectangles. Children are given opportunities to visualise, describe and to draw and measure. Lessons 6 to 13 deal with written addition and subtraction strategies. They are presented with a number of word problems and 'real life' situations in which they have to consider the most efficient way of solving the problems. This means that they have to identify different question types and make decisions. In the final two lessons, the children are asked to use their knowledge to explore patterns and relationships between numbers and to explain their thinking.

Use and apply mathematics

● Explore patterns, properties and relationships and propose a general statement involving numbers or shapes; identify examples for which the statement is true or false.

Lessons 1–5

Preparation

Lesson 1: Prepare some × questions for the starter. On the board, an equilateral triangle, an isosceles triangle, a scalene triangle and a right-angled triangle.

Lesson 2: On dotted paper, draw two different triangles. Display some enlarged blank dotted paper on the board or as an OHT or flipchart.

Lesson 3: Prepare a selection of rectangles.

Lessons 4–5: 'Blank axes' general resource sheet copied onto OHT or enlarged onto A3.

You will need

Photocopiable pages
'Drawing quadrilaterals' (page 61) and 'Quadrilateral battleships' (page 62), one per child.

CD resources
Extension version of 'Drawing quadrilaterals' and support version of 'Quadrilateral battleships'. General resource sheets: 'Number cards 1–100', '0–9 digit cards' (and extra zero cards), 'Symbol cards' (decimal point card), 'Blank axes' for display.

Equipment
A selection of different 2D triangle shapes; dotted paper; adhesive; scissors; rulers; protractors; a selection of 2D rectangles; coloured pencils.

Learning objectives

Starter

● Recall quickly multiplication facts up to 10 × 10, use to multiply pairs of multiples of 10 and 100 and derive quickly corresponding division facts.
● Use understanding of place value to multiply and divide whole numbers and decimals by 10, 100 or 1000. (Revision of Block A, Units 1 and 2)

Main teaching activities

2006
● Explore patterns, properties and relationships and propose a general statement involving numbers or shapes; identify examples for which the statement is true or false.
● Identify, visualise and describe properties of rectangles, triangles, regular polygons and 3D solids; use knowledge of properties to draw 2D shapes and identify and draw nets of 3D shapes.

1999
● Solve mathematical problems or puzzles, recognise and explain patterns and relationships, generalise and predict. Suggest extensions asking 'What if...?'
● Recognise and extend number sequences.
● Make and investigate a general statement about familiar numbers or shapes by finding examples that satisfy it; explain a generalised relationship (formula) in words.
● Recognise properties of rectangles; classify triangles (isosceles, equilateral, scalene), using criteria such as equal sides, equal angles, lines of symmetry.
● Make shapes with increasing accuracy; visualise 3D shapes from 2D drawings; identify different nets for an open cube.

Vocabulary

2D, two-dimensional, regular, irregular, polygon, side, diagonals, parallel, perpendicular, angle, degrees (°), acute, obtuse, protractor, names of shapes, including equilateral triangle, isosceles triangle, scalene triangle, right-angled triangle, quadrilateral, parallelogram, kite, rhombus, coordinates, *x*-coordinate, *y*-coordinate, symmetry, bisect

Lesson 1 (Review and teach)

Starter

Recall: Tell the children that you are going to set them a quick-fire multiplication quiz, with their table groups as teams. They have to volunteer the answer by being the first to raise a hand. Each correct answer wins a point. Children who have answered a question correctly may not answer again. This ensures that everybody has a try.

Main teaching activities

Whole class: Indicate the four triangles you have drawn on the board. Explain that these are all triangles because they are closed shapes with three straight sides. Tell the children that you want them to think of definitions that will separate these four triangles. They will have to consider the angles (acute, obtuse or right angles), length of sides (equal or not) and lines of symmetry (whether the halves would match exactly if we folded the triangle in half). Ask for observations and record appropriate ones on the board:

- Equilateral triangle: 3 sides of equal length; 3 equal angles, always acute; 3 lines of symmetry.
- Isosceles triangle: 2 sides of equal length, 1 of a different length; 2 equal angles (acute) and 1 different (can be obtuse or acute); 1 line of symmetry.
- Scalene triangle: 3 sides of different lengths; 3 different angles (1 may be obtuse), no lines of symmetry.
- Right-angled triangle: Can be either isosceles or scalene; 1 right angle; can have 1 line of symmetry.

Independent work: Ask the children to copy the definitions they have just created onto a sheet of paper under the headings: 'Equilateral triangle'; 'Isosceles triangle' and 'Scalene triangle'. Then, on a separate piece of paper, they should draw two examples of each triangle. They should exchange these with someone else and cut them out, then measure them carefully with a ruler and a protractor (you may need to revise the use of this) and stick them in the correct column.

Differentiation

Less confident learners: The children may need more support when measuring, and when discussing the criteria.
More confident learners: Ask the children to draw and classify more triangles of their own.

Review

Ask: *Why can't a right-angled triangle also be an equilateral triangle?* (Three equal angles of 90° wouldn't make a triangle.) Ask the children, in groups, to look around the room for right angles and angles that are greater or less than a right angle. They should note these on their whiteboards. Invite feedback. Ask: *What do you notice about the angles in buildings? Which angle did you observe most frequently? Why was that?*

Lesson 2 (Practise)

Starter

Recall: Play 'Division Lotto'. Give each group six number cards at random from a 1–10 set. Call out division questions such as *What is 35 ÷ 5?* or *How many lots of 3 in 18?* The children look for the answer among their cards and, if they find it, turn the card over. The first group to have turned all its cards over wins.

Main teaching activities

Whole class: Explain that you have drawn a triangle on some dotted paper, because it helps you draw accurately. Ask for a volunteer to come and draw the triangle from your description alone. For example: *My triangle has two sides that are four dots long and one that is three dots long. It has a right angle joining the two equal sides.* Or: *My triangle has three sides that are five dots long. One of the lines runs along the bottom of the page, so that one line of symmetry runs vertically down the page.* Show your original drawings to the class. Has the volunteer drawn the same shapes? Discuss how you might also have to describe which way up the triangle is and which way round it is. Ask the children to think about any differences from the original drawings. Can they explain these differences?

Paired work: Give each child a sheet of dotted paper. One child should draw a triangle and then describe it to their partner, who tries to draw it too; then the two swap roles. Under each triangle drawing, they should write the type of triangle (and how they know it is that type).

Review

Ask for some descriptions of triangles for you to draw. Ask: *Did anyone draw a triangle with an obtuse angle?* Play a triangle recognition game. You hold up or draw a triangle and the children, without speaking, perform an action to show what type of triangle it is. For scalene triangles, hands on heads; for isosceles triangles, fingers on noses; for equilateral triangles, fold their arms; for right-angled triangles, stand up. So for a right-angled isosceles triangle, the children would stand up with their fingers on their noses. Discuss any shapes that the children are getting wrong.

Lesson 3 (Review and teach)

Starter

Recall: Play 'Division Lotto' as in Lesson 2. This time, include 'time' questions such as: *The first maths puzzle I did took me 16 minutes. I did the second puzzle in half the time. How long did it take me?*

Main teaching activities

Whole class: Show the children the selection of 2D rectangle shapes. Ask them to define a rectangle in terms of sides, angles, diagonals and symmetry. Take suggestions from the class and write up a class definition. This should state that a rectangle must have: two pairs of parallel sides with each parallel pair the same length; four right angles; diagonals that bisect in the middle; two lines of symmetry.

Independent work: Ask the children to copy the definition of a rectangle onto a sheet of paper, then draw several examples of different rectangles and label their features.

Review

Explain that any four-sided shape is called a quadrilateral. Ask the children to visualise and then draw (on their whiteboards) a quadrilateral with one of the criteria for a rectangle present and the rest missing. For example, say: *Draw a quadrilateral with only one pair of parallel lines of the same length.* Ask: *Is it possible for this shape to have four right angles? How many right angles could it have? How many bisecting diagonals does your shape have? Do they bisect in the middle?* Hold up your shape to show the rest of the class. Repeat with another shape. Visualise and draw a quadrilateral with diagonals that bisect anywhere but in the middle. Compare and discuss the children's drawings.

Lesson 4 (Teach)

Starter

Refine and rehearse: Use a set of 0–9 digit cards (and some extra zero cards) to play 'Place Value Shuffle'. Give four different digits (not zero) to four children. They stand at the front of the class and hold up their cards. Ask the rest of the class to read the number displayed. Ask what the number would be if it was multiplied by 10. The children 'shuffle' to display this number, leaving a space. Ask what should fit into this space, and invite a volunteer to hold up that card (zero) in the line. Now ask what the number would be if divided by 100. The children 'shuffle' again. Ask what else we need now (a decimal point), and ask for a volunteer to represent it using the decimal point cards from the 'Symbol cards' set. Carry on multiplying and dividing and discussing the effect. Repeat with different digits and volunteers.

Differentiation

Less confident learners: Instead of drawing the triangles, the children could select one of the 2D triangle shapes and describe it to their partner, who has to find a matching one. They could then record by drawing around the shape and naming it.
More confident learners: The children could describe only the angles, not the lines, and write their observations about the type of triangle created.

Differentiation

Less confident learners: The children can draw around 2D rectangle shapes and label them.
More confident learners: The children can explain why a square is a special type of rectangle (it has four equal sides and four lines of symmetry).

Main teaching activities

Whole class: Display the 'Blank axes' resource sheet and demonstrate the use of coordinates in the first quadrant. Remind the children that the *x*-coordinate should be given first, then the *y*-coordinate. They are written in brackets with a comma between them: (2, 3). Mark some coordinates on the grid, using small crosses, and join them up with a ruler. (Do not use the coordinates given on the activity sheet.)

Independent work: Distribute copies of 'Drawing quadrilaterals' for the children to complete individually. Make sure they understand what to do.

Review

Call out a list of coordinates for children to mark with a small cross on the second grid on the activity sheet: (8, 10), (6, 10), (5, 9), (5, 7), (6, 6), (8, 6). Reinforce the importance of putting the *x*-coordinate first. Ask the children to join up these points. *What shape have you made?* Discuss what would happen if the coordinates were the wrong way round. (The shape would be turned on its side.) Check the children's shapes to inform your assessment.

Differentiation

Less confident learners: The children will need support from an adult to transfer from using alphanumeric coordinates to using numeric coordinates only.

More confident learners: The children can use the extension version, with coordinates across two quadrants, using negative numbers on the *x*-axis.

Lesson 5 (Practise)

Starter

Refine and rehearse: Play 'Place Value Shuffle' as in Lesson 4. Invite the class to create calculations for the human place value shufflers to carry out.

Main teaching activities

Whole class: Display the 'Blank axes' resource sheet and ask for a volunteer to follow your instructions for drawing a quadrilateral. Call out the coordinates (3, 5), (3, 8), (5, 5) and (5, 8). Explain that today, the children are playing a version of 'Battleships'. Distribute the 'Quadrilateral battleships' activity sheet and go through the instructions for the game.

Paired work: The children play the game in pairs.

Review

Revise the criteria for a rectangle. Ask: *Has anybody drawn another quadrilateral that has a name? Can somebody come and draw a parallelogram on the board? Can we use the definition of a rectangle as a model when we are describing this shape?* (Unless it is a rectangle, a parallelogram has: two pairs of parallel lines of different lengths, no right angles, no lines of symmetry, diagonals that bisect in the middle. Explain that a rectangle is a special kind of parallelogram that has only right angles.) Repeat for a rhombus (a parallelogram where all the lines are the same length) and a kite (two pairs of sides of equal length with each pair adjoining, two angles the same, diagonals cross at right angles).

Differentiation

Less confident learners: The children can use the support version of the sheet, with alphanumeric coordinates and only three quadrilaterals to find.

More confident learners: Ask the children to plot and find five more unusually shaped quadrilaterals.

Lessons 6-15

Preparation

Lesson 9: Write on the board the multiples of 50 from 50 to 950.
Lesson 11: Write the shopping lists on the board.
Lesson 12: Three square pieces of paper for the starter.
Lesson 14: Prepare some criteria labels for sorting numbers eg: Factors of 48; Multiples of 2; Even numbers; Odd numbers; Multiples of 5; Multiples of 3; Factors of 21; Prime numbers; square numbers; Factors of 30.
Lesson 15: Write up the task for paired work on the board.

You will need

Photocopiable pages
'Predict and estimate' (page 63), one per child.
CD resources
Support and extension versions of 'Predict and estimate'. 'Close to ten', 'Emma's Emporium', 'Written methods for addition' and 'Written methods for subtraction'. General resource sheets: 'Number cards 1-100' (for teacher use and for support); '0-9 digit cards' (for teacher and for each child).
Equipment
Sorting hoops; calculators (for support); dice (two for each pair); scissors.

Learning objectives

Starter

● Explore patterns, properties and relationships and propose a general statement involving numbers or shapes; identify examples for which the statement is true or false.
● Recall quickly multiplication facts up to 10 × 10, use to multiply pairs of multiples of 10 and 100 and derive quickly corresponding division facts.
● Identify pairs of factors of two-digit whole numbers and find common multiples, eg for 6 and 9.
● Use knowledge of rounding, place value, number facts and inverse operations to estimate and check calculations.
● Identify, visualise and describe properties of rectangles, triangles, regular polygons and 3D solids; use knowledge of properties to draw 2D shapes and identify and draw nets of 3D shapes.

Main teaching activities

2006
● Explore patterns, properties and relationships and propose a general statement involving numbers or shapes; identify examples for which the statement is true or false.
● Use efficient written methods to add and subtract whole numbers and decimals with up to two places.
● Use knowledge of number facts, place value and rounding to estimate and check calculations.
● Identify pairs of factors of two-digit whole numbers and find common multiples, eg for 6 and 9.

1999
● Solve mathematical problems or puzzles, recognise and explain patterns and relationships, generalise and predict. Suggest extensions asking 'What if...?'
● Recognise and extend number sequences.
● Make and investigate a general statement about familiar numbers or shapes by finding examples that satisfy it; explain a generalised relationship (formula) in words.
● Extend written methods to: addition of more than two integers; addition or subtraction of a pair of decimal fractions (eg £29.78 + £53.34).
● Check results of calculations.
● Find all the pairs of factors of any number up to 100.

Vocabulary

problem, solution, calculate, calculation, equation, method, explain, reason, reasoning, predict, pattern, relationship, formula, rule, classify, property, criterion/criteria, generalise, integer, square number, multiple, factor, divisor, divisible by, decimal, decimal point, decimal place, operation, inverse, add, subtract, multiply, divide, sum, total, difference, plus, minus, product, quotient, remainder, double, halve, round, estimate, approximate

Lesson 6 (Teach)

Starter

Refine and rehearse: Pick a number card 1-50 at random. Ask the class to call out its double. Try others. Ask: *Which ones are easy or well-known?* (20, 50...) *Which are more difficult? Why?* (16, 17, 18, 19, 26... because they cross the next ten and are harder to visualise.) Repeat using the 50-100 cards and halving. Ask: *Which ones do not have answers that are whole numbers?* (The odd numbers.)

Differentiation

Less confident learners: Ask these children to make simple similarity statements about the following numbers: 2 and 20; 8 and 16; 50 and 100.

More confident learners: Give these children the following sets of four numbers: 15, 30, 28, 14; 60, 15, 22, 21; 17, 47, 20, 100. Ask them to make statements such as: Think of properties that are true for two of them and false for the other two. Think of some other ways of linking these numbers.

Main teaching activities

Explain to the children that they are to use all their number knowledge to write statements or recognise patterns or similarities in numbers. Write in the middle of the board the numbers 12 and 24. Ask: *What is the same about these numbers? What is different? Can you tell me any relationships between these two numbers?* Write the statements about the numbers. Encourage the children to discuss factors and multiples, doubles, halves, odd or even. Repeat with the numbers 36 and 6.

Independent work: Ask the children to investigate relationships and patterns between the following numbers: 14 and 49; 18 and 36; 50 and 0.5.

Review

Ask the children to talk about, reason and explain their statements and how they decided upon them. Ask: *What do you look for when seeking patterns? What possibilities could there be? Can you suggest more pairs of numbers with more than one similarity?*

Lesson 7 (Teach and practise)

Starter

Refine and rehearse: Write the number 30 on the board and ask the children to find all of the factors. Explain how they found them all in a systematic way. Repeat with 42, this time reminding the children to extend beyond their known times tables (eg 21 × 2).

Main teaching activities

Whole class: Odd or even? Explain to the children that they have a number of strategies, including estimation and knowledge of odd and even numbers, which will assist with accuracy in calculation. For example, with 470 + 380 ask yourself 'Odd or even?'

Previous knowledge should inform children that an even + even = even. Estimation will bring the calculation closer, ie 500 + 400 = 900 (even). So calculating should be easier:

$$400 + 300 = 700$$
$$70 + 80 = 150 \quad \text{(near double)}$$
$$850$$

Repeat with differences. 810 – 380. Odd or even? Even – even = even.

Estimate:	800	–	400	=	400
Calculate:	380	+	(20)	=	400
	400	+	(400)	=	800
	800	+	(10)	=	810

Therefore the difference is 430. *Can anybody suggest an alternative method?* Ask them to explain why they find this more logical. *Does it work with decimal numbers? How efficient are these strategies?*

Repeat the strategies with a decimal number: 81 – 38 or 8.1 – 3.8; 7.4 + 9.8, etc.

Independent work: Explain to the children that they must complete the activity sheet 'Predict and Estimate' to practise these skills. They should use their knowledge of odd and even numbers and estimation to aid calculation of numbers given.

Differentiation

Less confident learners: Use the support version of the sheet, which uses one- and two-digit numbers and multiples of 10.

More confident learners: Use the extension version of the sheet, which uses two- and three-digit odd and even numbers.

Review

Write 3.52 + 3.58 on the board. Ask: *How would you calculate this?* 3.52 + 3.58 = 6.00 + 1.00 + 0.1 = 7.1. *Can you suggest a strategy for helping someone to calculate using decimals? Should it be any different from HTU if you have a good grasp of place value? Explain why.*

Now calculate 0.01 + 0.02 + 0.14. Take alternative suggestions for strategies. Ask the children to explain why it works for them. Discuss with the children the method that is the most efficient, and lead to the least number of possibilities for error. Encourage children to make informal jottings to avoid errors. (For example, do hundredths first = 0.03 + 0.14 = 0.17.)

▶ Generate new calculations by picking random digit cards and discussing ways to solve them.

Lesson 8 (Teach and practise)

Starter
Rehearse: Draw a Venn sorting diagram on the board. Label one ring multiples of 10 and the other numbers greater than 100. Take suggestions for numbers to fit inside each ring and numbers to fit inside the intersection. Ask: *Think of a number that does not fit in this Venn diagram.* Add the number 105 into the intersection. Ask for a volunteer to explain why it is incorrect.

Main teaching activities
Whole class: Explain that today's activity is about using familiar number facts and adjusting them in order to calculate with more difficult numbers. They are going to add and subtract near multiples of 10 or 100. Ask: *Can you round 49 to the nearest 10?* (50.) Explain that as 50 is easier to add than 49, we can add 49 quickly by rounding and adjusting. For example: 49 + 114 is 1 short of 50 + 114 = 164. So the answer is 164 - 1 = 163.

Demonstrate how this can help with subtracting: 204 - 57 is 4 more than 200 - 57 = 143. So the answer is 143 + 4 = 147. Repeat with several examples of addition and subtraction to make sure the children know which way to adjust the answer after rounding up or down. For example: 39 + 46; 156 + 206; 49 - 23; 203 - 189. Remind the children that informal jottings can help us to keep track, especially when rounding and adjusting.
Independent work: Distribute the 'Close to ten' activity sheet. The children can use this to practise addition and subtraction by rounding and adjusting near multiples of 10 or 100.

Differentiation
Less confident learners:
Provide the support version of the sheet, which uses only two-digit numbers.
More confident learners:
Provide the extension version with more challenging addition and subtraction problems, requiring informal jottings.

Review
Write 1003 - 69 on the board. Ask for a volunteer to come and work it out: 1003 - 69 is (3 + 1) less than 1000 - 70 = 930 so the answer is 930 + 4 = 934. Ask: *How can this method help us to calculate money?* (We can round to the nearest £1 or £10). Ask the children: *I have £29.58 and my aunt has sent me £15. How much do I have now?* (£29.58 is 42p short of £30 + £15 = £45, so answer is £45 - £0.42 = £44.58.)

Lesson 9 (Practise)

Starter
Refine and Rehearse: 'Pairs to 1000 Bingo'. Indicate the multiples of 50 on the board and ask each child to jot down any five of the numbers. Now shout out multiples of 50, and if a child has the matching pair that adds to 1000 they must cross it off their list. The first child to cross off all their numbers is the winner and must shout 'BINGO!'

Main teaching activities
Whole class: Write '35 + 37' on the board. Ask the children to suggest ways of calculating this. Hopefully someone will notice that these numbers are near doubles. Explain that we can use this fact to double and adjust: 35 + 35 = 70 so the answer is 70 + 2 = 72.

Encourage the children to use informal jotting to track their use of near doubles. Explain that they can use the same method to find near doubles of decimal numbers, such as 3.5 + 3.7. The digits are the same as double 35, but the decimal place needs to be kept to arrive at the correct place value answer: 3.5 + 3.5 = 7.0 so answer is 7.0 + 0.2 = 7.2.

Repeat with other near doubles generated by throwing two or three dice. Throw one dice to generate the tens number for both parts of the sum, then throw two dice for the units numbers. So if we throw a 5 followed by a 3 and a 4, the sum generated is 53 + 54. Three dice could be used to generate

BLOCK B Securing number facts, understanding shape

pairs of three-digit numbers or decimal numbers.

Paired work: Encourage the children to use dice to generate near doubles to add, including one-place decimals. Ask them to record their findings using informal jottings.

Review

Write some two-digit numbers such as 65, 27, 33, 38, 29, 17, 32, 35 on the board. Ask: *Can all these numbers be doubled easily? Which ones are more difficult? Which ones do you know straight away? Why do some numbers greater than 50 start to cause difficulty when we are doubling? How could doubling help me to solve this problem: 24 × 4?* Ask the children to use repeated doubling to multiply other two-digit numbers by 4.

Differentiation

Less confident learners: The children can use two dice to create two-digit numbers or one-place decimals as appropriate.
More confident learners: The children can use three dice to create three-digit numbers or two-place decimals.

Lesson 10 (Review and teach)

Starter

Rehearse: Write up two 4-digit numbers on the board, for example 2004 and 5782. Ask: *What is the best estimate for adding these two numbers?* Record the suggestions given which may range from 7000 to 7700 to 8000. Discuss which the most helpful estimate is and why it is not necessary to be precise. Rounding is designed to indicate the relative size of the answer. Repeat with two more numbers and subtraction as well as addition.

Main teaching activities

Whole class: Revise column addition (see Block A Unit 1). It is probable that some children will be using the expanded method, adding the most significant digit first, and some will be using the standard compact method and 'carrying' digits. (You will need to refer to your school calculation policy to plan the development of various methods.) The most important thing is that each child should have a reliable and accurate written method of addition that they can use with confidence.

```
  H T U
  2 1 6
+ 1 4 8
```

Ask for volunteers to solve these problems using their chosen method. Each time, also demonstrate the standard written method, emphasising the 'carried' digit. Remind them of the value of rounding and estimating their answer first.

Independent work: Distribute the 'Written methods for addition' activity sheet for the children to work through using their chosen method. You may wish to use this time to focus on a group who are ready to move from the expanded method to a more compact one.

Review

It may be useful to go through some of the problems from the sheet, asking individuals to demonstrate and talk through their method on the board. Ask: *Can a written calculation be used for adding more than two numbers?* (Both methods will work for adding multiple numbers, though the standard compact method can accommodate larger 'carried' digits more easily.) Ask for a confident volunteer to demonstrate how they would add three HTU numbers:

```
  1 2 1
  2 3 4
+ 1 9 7
  5 5 2
  1 1
```

Differentiation

Less confident learners: The children can use the support version of the activity sheet, with simpler three-digit addition problems and using the expanded written method.
More confident learners: The children can use the extension version, with four-digit numbers, including decimals.

Lesson 11 (Teach and practise)

Starter

Reason: Explain that today the children must visualise shapes from a description. Tell them that after each part of the description you will stop and they can guess the shape. Say to the class, *I am thinking of a regular 2D shape. It has 4 sides and four right angles, and the sides are of equal length.* Discuss with the class the minimum amount of information that they need to be sure of the name of the shape. Repeat with other shapes such as a scalene triangle or a rectangle.

Main teaching activities

Whole class: Explain to the children that they are going to carry on adding more than two numbers. The following shopping list should be written on the board.

crisps		64p
sweets		26p
carrots		39p
a banana	+	43p
		172p = £1.72

Demonstrate this calculation, using the compact method. Encourage the children to look for numbers to 'make 10' when adding a large column of figures. Emphasise that the units add up to 22 – that is, 2 in the units and 2 tens (to be added to the tens column).

Repeat this using decimal numbers, as shown here:

apples		£1.54	Keep the place
squash		£1.29	value by
a chicken		£3.99	including 0
biscuits	+	0.65	pounds.
		£7.47	

Highlight the fact that the decimal points must always stay aligned, one under the other, in all the column numbers including the answer.

Independent work: Ask the children to use the activity sheet 'Emma's Emporium' to create some shopping list sums with three or four numbers. Ask them to record the items and the prices. Encourage careful presentation to make sure that place value is handled correctly.

Review

Ask the children to devise a class rule for helping someone add a long list of prices. They should suggest: line up the decimal points; keep the place value correct; 'carry over' any extra digits to the next place value and record them beneath the sum; remember to add any 'extras' to the next column. Record this as a class 'brainstorm' on a large sheet of paper to be displayed in the classroom for future reference.

Differentiation

Less confident learners: The children can use the support version of the price list, with items priced in multiples of 5p to simplify addition. They can use the expanded method of addition.
More confident learners: The children can use extension version, with more difficult numbers. Encourage them to try longer additions.

Lesson 12 (Review and teach)

Starter

Reason: Tell the children that they are going to visualise shapes again, as they did for Lesson 11; however, this time they must follow a set of instructions in their minds. Say: *I have a square piece of paper. I am going to fold it in half diagonally and then in half again. I am going to cut off two of the points with a pair of scissors. When I open the paper out, what shape is it now?* Ask for volunteers to draw the shape they imagined. The results will depend on which corners they imagined that you cut, and how much you cut off. Demonstrate the possibilities using pieces of paper and discuss the information needed for an accurate picture.

Main teaching activities

Whole class: Revise column subtraction, using both the expanded method and the standard compact method with decomposition. Ask for two volunteers to come and calculate the following using their preferred method (one child using each method):

$$
\begin{array}{l}
\text{H T U} \\
2\ 3\ 9 \\
-1\ 4\ 6 \\
\hline
9\ 3
\end{array}
\qquad
\begin{array}{l}
\overset{100}{\cancel{200}}\overset{130}{\cancel{30}} \\
=\ 200\ +\ 30\ +\ 9 \\
=\ 100\ +\ 40\ +\ 6 \\
\hline
0\ +\ 90\ +\ 3
\end{array}
\qquad
\begin{array}{l}
\text{H}\ \text{T}\ \text{U} \\
{}^{2}\cancel{2}\ {}^{1}\cancel{3}\ 9 \\
-1\ 4\ 6 \\
\hline
9\ 3
\end{array}
$$

Independent work: Distribute the 'Written methods for subtraction' activity sheet. Explain that these are all subtraction questions to be solved by using a written method. While the children are working on the sheet, you might choose to focus on a group who are ready to move on to the standard compact method.

Review

Write the following incorrect calculation on the board.

$$
\begin{array}{l}
\text{H T U} \\
5\ 6\ 2\ = \\
-1\ 7\ 3\ = \\
\hline
3\ 3\ 9\ =
\end{array}
\qquad
\begin{array}{l}
\overset{400}{\cancel{500}}\ +\ \overset{100}{\cancel{60}}\ +\ \overset{12}{2} \\
100\ +\ 70\ +\ 3 \\
\hline
300\ +\ 30\ +\ 9
\end{array}
$$

Ask the children to look at the calculation carefully. Can they spot the error? Ask them to decide where the person has made a mistake. (Instead of taking 70 from 150, the person has taken 70 from 100.) Then ask: *Can you correct this calculation? What tips would you give someone to help them with column subtraction?*

Lesson 13 (Teach and practise)

Starter

Recall: Ask the children to draw a 3 by 3 grid, just as they might do to play 'Noughts and Crosses'. In each of the spaces ask them to write a multiple in their times tables, since they are going to play 'Multiplication Bingo'. You might discuss that there are some numbers that will rarely occur, such as a prime numbers or single digits, whereas some multiples have many different factors. Call out multiplication facts, keeping a note yourself of the multiples used. The children cross out the ones that they have on their card until someone wins and shouts 'BINGO!'

Main teaching activities

Whole class: Continue to support children in learning an efficient method of written subtraction. You may choose to work with children experiencing difficulties, or with those ready to move on to the standard method of written subtraction.

With the class, revise the various strategies available for solving subtraction problems: counting on, counting on using a number line or informal jottings, the expanded method of written calculation and the standard compact method. Discuss briefly when each method might be appropriate (for example, counting on for time or small money differences; a written method for large differences).

Independent work: Provide a variety of subtraction problems, including some which do not require a written method. Remind the children that they can choose from a number of subtraction strategies to solve these problems.

Differentiation
Less confident learners:
Provide the support version of the activity sheet, with simplified two-digit and three-digit numbers. The children should use the expanded method.
More confident learners:
Provide the support version, with more demanding problems. Expect the children to use the standard compact method.

Differentiation

Less confident learners: Provide some simplified subtraction problems where the calculations can be managed using counting on methods. Examples: 76 - 23; Find the difference between 102 and 67; 196 - 23; 95 - 12; 76 - 67; 101 - 98.

More confident learners: Provide problems with more demanding calculations and some two-step problems. Examples: £425.74 - £194.48; £2005 - £899; If a man has £3027 in his bank account and spends £103.89 in the supermarket and £55.99 on a new pair of shoes, how much has he got left? 8833 - 1942; Take the double of 86 away from 217; 3852 - 1073.

Examples: Find the difference between 89 and 102; 1937 - 376; 2004 - 1997; 8638 - 749; £309 - £215; £82.40 - £19.38; 375 minus 98.

Review
Write a time problem on the board (such as: 'Westweekers' starts 19.15, ends 20.35). Ask: *Is it appropriate to do a written subtraction calculation with this problem? Which method did you use?* Ask for a volunteer to demonstrate how to find the answer by counting on, using informal jottings to keep track of the hours and minutes. Ask: *Which sort of question definitely needed a written column subtraction? Which are mental calculations?*

Write '156 - 93' on the board. Say: *Think of a word problem that could be solved by using this calculation. What method would you use to solve it?* Take a few suggestions for word problems. Ask for volunteers to solve the problems in their chosen way. Repeat with 1373 - 894.

Lesson 14 (Teach)

Starter
Refine and rehearse: Repeat 'Multiplication Bingo' from Lesson 13; however, this time explain to the children that you are going to use multiples of 10, so instead of calling out 4 × 6 you might say 40 × 6. Therefore their multiples must all be multiples of 10 and end with a zero. Play as before.

Main teaching activities
Whole class: Explain to the children that they are going to explore patterns and relationships of numbers. Draw an intersecting Venn diagram on the board. Label one circle, 'Multiples of 5' and the other 'Even numbers'. Tell the children that they may use any number from 1 to 30 to complete the diagram. Discuss what to do with numbers that fit both criteria (they fit into the intersection), or numbers such as 1 which do not fit into either circle (they are recorded outside the circles). Repeat with another example such as 'Factors of 24' and 'Even numbers'.

Paired work: Provide each pair with ready prepared criteria cards that you want them to use to make decisions about numbers, for example 'Factors of 32', 'Multiples of 3'; 'Odd numbers', 'Even numbers', 'Multiples of 4'. Explain that you want them to discuss the reasons for placing the numbers between themselves.

Review
Draw a Venn diagram onto the board. One circle should be labelled 'Multiples of 10' the other labelled 'Numbers greater than 50'. Fill in some numbers on the diagram with the children's help. Also add some incorrect ones and ask the children to spot your mistakes and to explain why they are incorrect.

Differentiation

Less confident learners: These children might find the sorting exercise easier with two intersecting hoops and number cards 1-30 in order to focus their thinking. Provide them with the simpler criteria to sort, such as 'Multiples of 2', 'Multiples of 5', 'Odd numbers', 'Even numbers'.

More confident learners: These children could have three criteria to sort and use higher numbers where appropriate, for example 'Square numbers', 'Multiples of 7', 'Odd numbers', 'Prime numbers', 'Factors of 48', 'Factors of 72'.

Lesson 15 (Practise and apply)

Starter
Refine and rehearse: Play 'Division Lotto' from Lesson 2 but this time include division facts which are multiples of 10 such as 240 ÷ 60 or 420 ÷ 70.

Main teaching activities
Whole class: Tell the children that they are going to continue to reason about numbers. In order to do this they need to be clear about some mathematical terms. Revise the terminology, factor, multiple, square numbers, common multiple. Ask the class to generate some examples of these, for example square numbers less than 100 or factors of 42. Explain that sometimes they will be asked to think beyond their known multiplication facts. However, they must use the knowledge that they have to work them out. For example, most children in the class should know the factors of 42 are 1, 6, 7 and 42 from their known times tables. However, they need to

remember to include 3 × 14 which they could generate from 6 × 7. Ask: *What is the relationship? How did I work this out?*

Paired work: Explain to the children that they must use the digit cards 3, 5, 1 and 2 to make two-digit numbers that fit the following criteria:

- A square number
- A multiple of 7
- A factor of 24
- A common multiple of 3 and 4
- A prime number
- A multiple of 13
- A factor of 100

For each example, ask the children to record their thinking.

Review

Ask the children to explain some of their answers and how they arrived at them. Write up on the board, 15, 7, 3, 5. Ask: *Three of these numbers are a factor of a two-digit number. What is the number? Which is the odd one out?*

Differentiation

Less confident learners: These children will probably need adult support to help them to reason about number. They may find a calculator helpful to support their working out.

More confident learners: These children should be able to explain their thought processes more clearly. An extension task would be to ask them to select their own four digits and create questions for each other.

⊔SCHOLASTIC

Name _____   Date _____

Drawing quadrilaterals

Use these coordinates to draw quadrilaterals on the grid. Label each shape.

Shape A: (B,3), (B,1), (E,1), (E,3)
Shape B: (B,6), (B,10), (C,10), (C,6)
Shape C: (A,10), (A,5), (G,5), (G,10)
Shape D: (G,5), (E,8), (G,10), (J,7)

Is Shape D a rectangle?

_____

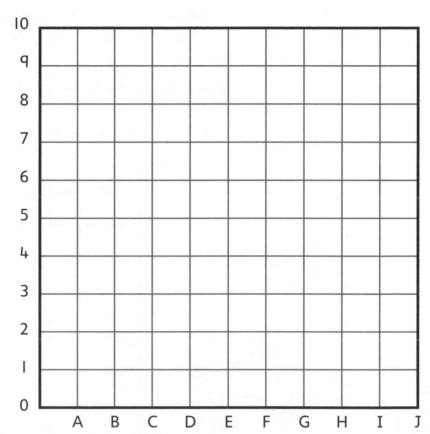

Now write the coordinates of the points in each shape drawn below.
They are all rectangles.

Shape E: _____

Shape F: _____

Shape G: _____

Shape H: _____

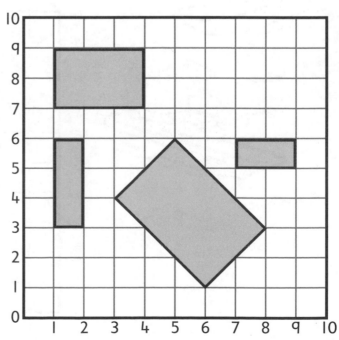

Name _____   Date _____

Quadrilateral battleships

On the first grid, draw five different quadrilaterals. Colour-code them (all different colours) and label the points with their coordinates. Do not let your partner see them.

Take turns with your partner to call out coordinates in an attempt to find one of their points. Do not count landing inside one of the shapes: it must be a direct hit on the point itself. If your opponent scores a hit, you must tell them what colour that shape is. Use the second grid to record where you have made guesses and hits on your partner's territory.

The winner is the player who finds all their opponent's shapes first.

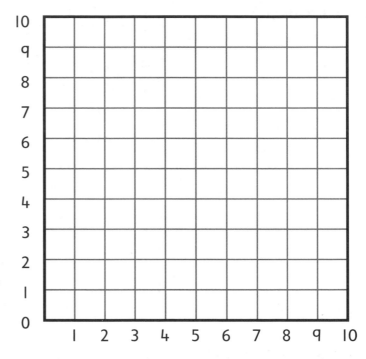

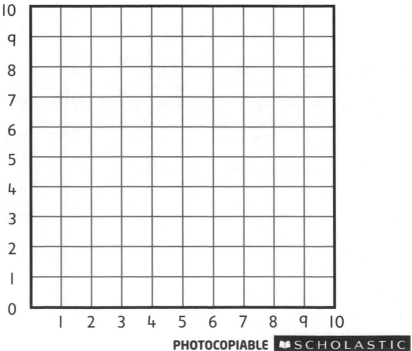

Name _____   Date _____

Predict and estimate

Use your knowledge of odd and even numbers and estimation to help you to calculate the following.

The first one has been done for you.

98 + 64

Odd or even? _E + E = E_____

Estimate: _100 + 60 = 160_____

Calculate: _98 + 64 = 100 + 62 = 162___

---

1. 79 + 92

Odd or even? _____

Estimate: _____

Calculate: _____

2. 104 + 299

Odd or even? _____

Estimate: _____

Calculate: _____

3. 89 – 13

Odd or even? _____

Estimate: _____

Calculate: _____

4. 128 – 92

Odd or even? _____

Estimate: _____

Calculate: _____

5. 244 – 83

Odd or even? _____

Estimate: _____

Calculate: _____

6. 482 – 98

Odd or even? _____

Estimate: _____

Calculate: _____

7. 28.9 – 18.7

Odd or even? _____

Estimate: _____

Calculate: _____

8. 82.5 + 56.1

Odd or even? _____

Estimate: _____

Calculate: _____

BLOCK B Counting, partitioning and calculating

Securing number facts, understanding shape

Lesson	Strands	Starter	Main teaching activities
1. Teach	Use/apply	Recall quickly multiplication facts up to 10 × 10, use to multiply pairs of multiples of 10 and 100 and derive quickly corresponding division facts.	Explore patterns, properties and relationships and propose a general statement involving numbers or shapes; identify examples for which the statement is true or false.
2. Practise	Use/apply	As for Lesson 1	As for Lesson 1
3. Teach and practise	Use/apply	**Use knowledge of place value and addition and subtraction of two-digit numbers to derive sums and differences, doubles and halves of decimals, eg 6.5 ± 2.7, halve 5.6, double 0.34.**	As for Lesson 1
4. Practise	Use/apply	As for Lesson 3	As for Lesson 1
5. Practise and apply	Use/apply Knowledge	Recall quickly multiplication facts up to 10 × 10, use to multiply pairs of multiples of 10 and 100 and derive quickly corresponding division facts.	• Explore patterns, properties and relationships and propose a general statement involving numbers or shapes; identify examples for which the statement is true or false. • Represent a puzzle or problem by identifying and recording the information or calculations needed to solve it; find possible solutions and confirm them in the context of the problem. • Use knowledge of rounding, place value, number facts and inverse operations to estimate and check calculations.
6. Review and teach	Shape	As for Lesson 5	Identify, visualise and describe properties of rectangles, triangles, regular polygons and 3D solids; use knowledge of properties to draw 2D shapes and identify and draw nets of 3D shapes.
7. Practise	Use/apply Shape	As for Lesson 5	• Explore patterns, properties and relationships and propose a general statement involving numbers or shapes; identify examples for which the statement is true or false. • Identify, visualise and describe properties of rectangles, triangles, regular polygons and 3D solids; use knowledge of properties to draw 2D shapes and identify and draw nets of 3D shapes.
8. Practise	Shape	As for Lesson 5	As for Lesson 7
9. Review and teach	Use/apply Shape	As for Lesson 5	• As for Lesson 7 • Complete patterns with two lines of symmetry and draw the position of a shape after a reflection or translation.
10. Practise	Use/apply Shape	As for Lesson 5	As for Lesson 9
11. Teach	Use/apply Shape	Explain what each digit represents in whole numbers and decimals with up to two places, and partition, round and order these numbers. (Revision of Block A, Units 1, 2 and 3)	As for Lesson 9
12. Teach and practise	Use/apply Shape	As for Lesson 11	As for Lesson 9
13. Practise	Use/apply Shape	**Use knowledge of place value and addition and subtraction of two-digit numbers to derive sums and differences, doubles and halves of decimals, eg 6.5 ± 2.7, halve 5.6, double 0.34.**	As for Lesson 9
14. Apply	Use/apply	As for Lesson 13	• Explore patterns, properties and relationships and propose a general statement involving numbers or shapes; identify examples for which the statement is true or false. • Represent a puzzle or problem by identifying and recording the information or calculations needed to solve it; find possible solutions and confirm them in the context of the problem.
15. Apply	Use/apply	Recall quickly multiplication facts up to 10 × 10, use to multiply pairs of multiples of 10 and 100 and derive quickly corresponding division facts.	As for Lesson 14

Unit 2 ▭ 3 weeks

Speaking and listening objectives
- Present a spoken argument, sequencing points logically.

Introduction
Lessons 1 to 5 of this unit give children the opportunity to explore strategies of mental and written calculations and to look for patterns to support their calculating. Lessons 6 to 13 revisit and build on the work covered in Block B, Unit 1 about shape. The language of shape is explored and then children are encouraged to visualise shapes. They are taught about symmetry and creating reflections in a mirror line. The final two lessons give children opportunities to investigate a number pattern. For some this may be a simple repetitive pattern exercise, for others it will provide an opportunity to make generalisations and express a pattern as a formula. All children are encouraged to explain why their way of working was successful and to present their argument to others.

Use and apply mathematics
- Explore patterns, properties and relationships and propose a general statement involving numbers or shapes; identify examples for which the statement is true or false.
- Represent a puzzle or problem by identifying and recording the information or calculations needed to solve it; find possible solutions and confirm them in the context of the problem.

Lessons 1-5

Preparation
Lesson 1: Write on one side of the board random multiples of 6, 7, 8, 9 and 10, and on the other side a colour key such as red = ×6, blue = ×7, black = ×8, green = ×9. Draw a table on the board with the headings: ×2 ×5 ×10 ×100.
Lesson 2: Write on the board random multiples of 50 up to 1000. Make up 'Multiples snap' cards for each group of four.
Lesson 3: Write three or four number patterns for the children to recognise and continue.
Lesson 4: Put 15 two-digit decimals between 0.1 and 9.9 on the board.

You will need
Photocopiable pages
'Multiples snap' (page 76) and 'Multiples bingo' (page 77), for each group.
CD resources
General resource sheets: '0-9 digit cards', 'Number cards 1-100', 'Number fans'.
Equipment
Calculators; squared paper; dice (one for each pair) labelled 6, 7, 8, 9, blank, blank; coloured pencils.

Learning objectives

Starter
- Recall quickly multiplication facts up to 10 × 10, use to multiply pairs of multiples of 10 and 100 and derive quickly corresponding division facts.
- Use knowledge of place value and addition and subtraction of two-digit numbers to derive sums and differences, doubles and halves of decimals, eg 6.5 ± 2.7, halve 5.6, double 0.34.

Main teaching activities
2006
- Explore patterns, properties and relationships and propose a general statement involving numbers or shapes; identify examples for which the statement is true or false.
- Represent a puzzle or problem by identifying and recording the information or calculations needed to solve it; find possible solutions and confirm them in the context of the problem.
- Use knowledge of rounding, place value, number facts and inverse operations to estimate and check calculations.
1999
- Solve mathematical problems or puzzles, recognise and explain patterns and relationships, generalise and predict. Suggest extensions asking 'What if...?'
- Recognise and extend number sequences.
- Make and investigate a general statement about familiar numbers or shapes by finding examples that satisfy it; explain a generalised relationship (formula) in words.
- Choose and use appropriate number operations to solve problems, and appropriate ways of calculating: mental, mental with jottings, written methods, calculator.
- Check results of calculations.

Vocabulary
Multiple, factor, divisible by, decimal, decimal point, decimal place, add, subtract, multiply, divide, sum, total, difference, plus, minus, product, quotient, double, halve, round, estimate, approximate, fraction

Lesson 1 (Teach)

Starter

Revisit: Show the children the jumble of multiples of 6, 7, 8, 9 and 10 and the colour key you have written on the board. Ask them to sort the multiples into the correct times tables by telling you which colour to circle each multiple in. Ask them why some numbers have more than one colour circling them.

Main teaching activities

Whole class: Indicate the table headings you have drawn on the board. Invite the children to recall everything that they know about multiples of 2, 5, 10 and 100 (for example: all multiples of 2 are even numbers; all multiples of 10 end in a zero) and write them in the table.

Now explain that the children are going to investigate multiples of 4. *Are there any patterns in the multiples of 4? Can you write a generalisation or a rule about multiples of 4?* Begin by asking the children to recall the multiples of 4. Record them on the board together: 4, 8, 12... 40, 44, 48.

Paired work: Ask the children to work in pairs to investigate multiples of 4 and make some general statements about them (such as 'All multiples of 4 are even'). They should record their observations and then test them by generating higher multiples of 4 using a calculator, such as 16 × 4 or 42 × 4. Are the observations true for all cases?

Review

Make a record of the children's observations on the board. Most children should be able to tell you that all multiples of 4 are even and that the units digit follows a pattern of 0, 4, 8, 2, 6 which repeats. Ask the children to find a sequence of higher multiples (such as 22 × 4, 23 × 4 and 24 × 4) to test whether the second generalisation is true. From what the children have found out, ask: *Can anyone make a prediction about multiples of 40 or multiples of 8?*

Differentiation

Less confident learners: The children may need adult support in order to make observations and generalisations about multiples of 4.
More confident learners: Expect a higher level of thinking from this group. For example, they may spot or recall the link with the 2-times table (halves of the 4-times table) or the 8-times table (doubles).

Lesson 2 (Practise)

Starter

Rehearse: Point to one of the multiples of 50 on the board. Ask the children to show you, using their number fans, the number that would make 1000 when added to it. They can work in pairs to display the numbers, showing one digit each.

Main teaching activities

Whole class: Refer to the work on multiples of 2, 4, 5 and 10 from Lesson 1. Ask: *What is 30 divisible by?* (6, 5, 15, 2, 1, 30.) *These are the factors of 30. Think of a number that is divisible by 4 and 2.* (Any multiple of 4 is also divisible by 2. Likewise any multiple of 8 is divisible by both 4 and 2.)

Group work: Play 'Multiples snap' in groups of four. Distribute the cards from the activity sheet. Explain that this game will help the children to practise knowledge of divisibility, and also to test the generalisations they made in Lesson 1 for multiples of 2, 4, 5 and 10.

The cards are shuffled and shared out evenly among the group. Each player in turn places a card face upwards on the discard pile. This continues until two numbers from the same times table appear consecutively. The first player to say 'Snap!', and then to say what both numbers are divisible by, wins the whole of the discard pile. The first player to gain all the cards wins. For instance, if 25 and 50 are turned over consecutively, the common factor or divisor is 5 (or 25).

Review

Discuss how we can tell whether a number is divisible by 4. Ask: *Which of your observations about multiples of 4 help us with divisibility? Which ones*

Differentiation

Less confident learners: The children could be asked to look for specific divisors – for example, to look for numbers that are divisible by 2 or 5.
More confident learners: On completion of the game, the children could use blank cards to create their own number cards, including numbers divisible by 9 (or higher numbers outside the 10 × 10 times tables) to add to the game.

don't? What about numbers that are divisible by 9? What observations can you make? (The digits of the 9 times table add up to 9, so they are easy to spot. For example, 18 → 1 + 8 = 9.)

Lesson 3 (Teach and practise)

Starter
Rehearse: Explain to the children that they are going to double two-digit decimal numbers. Ask: *Does the same strategy apply as when doubling two-digit whole numbers?* Encourage them to see that crossing the decimal barrier has the same calculating difficulties as crossing the next ten. Use digit cards to generate two-digit decimals and ask for volunteers to double them.

Main teaching activities
Whole class: Indicate these number patterns, written on the board:

105, 90, 75, 60, ___, ___, ___
2.0, 1.5, 1.0, 0.5, ___, ___, ___
4.7, 4.5, 4.3, 4.1, 3.9, ___, ___, ___

Discuss the patterns and how to continue them. State a rule for each one, such as: 'This pattern is decreasing by 15 each time.'
Paired work: On squared paper, each pair must create a number pattern wordsearch using a run of four numbers in the same number pattern, for example 4, 8, 12, 16. These may run vertically, horizontally or diagonally. On completion, swap with another pair and solve the puzzle.

Review
Check that everyone has found all the number patterns in their paired work activity. Ask: *Do all number patterns have to be made by adding or subtracting? What is the pattern here: 1.0, 0.1, 0.01, 0.001...* or *3, 0.03, 0.0003... Can you state a rule?*
Ask each pair to create a number pattern that uses division or multiplication. In turn, each pair can hold up their pattern for the rest of the children to continue and state a rule.

Differentiation
Less confident learners: With adult support, create simplified patterns of only 2s, 5s and 10s.
More confident learners: Aim to create more complex patterns, for example using negative or decimal numbers.

Lesson 4 (Practise)

Starter
Rehearse: 'Pairs to make 10 Bingo'. Indicate the list of decimals on the board. Ask the children to jot down any five of them. Call out the pair to make 10 of one of the numbers on the board (ie if 6.2 is on the board, say: *3.8*). The children who have the matching pair on their board cross it out. Repeat for the remaining decimals. The winner is the first to cross out all their numbers and shout 'BINGO!'

Main teaching activities
Whole class: Distribute the 'Multiples bingo' activity sheet. Explain that today's activity is an opportunity to practise remembering multiples of 6, 7, 8 and 9. Ask the children to tell you some examples of multiples of each to get them started. Record them on the board as shown in the illustration. Ask: *Are there any observations you can make about multiples of 6, 7, 8 or 9?* (For example, 'Multiples of 8 are all even numbers' or 'The digits of a multiple of 9 add up to 9'.)
Paired work: Give each pair of children a copy of the 'Multiples bingo' game sheet. Explain that the grid contains some multiples of 6, 7, 8 and 9 all jumbled up. The children will need a dice marked with these numbers and two blank faces, and a different coloured pencil each. Go through the rules as described on the sheet. The children take turns to roll the dice and colour a multiple of the number rolled. If they roll a blank, or if there is no appropriate

BLOCK B — Securing number facts, understanding shape

multiple left, they miss a turn. The winner is the player with more squares coloured at the end.

Review

Ask for four volunteers to write the multiples of 6, 7, 8 and 9 (up to 10 × each) in order on the board. Ask: *Did you observe any other patterns or generalisations that might help you to recognise numbers that are divisible by 6, 7, 8 or 9?* Take suggestions. These might include the fact that all multiples of 6 or 8 are even, or that the multiples of 6 or 8 follow a pattern with their unit numbers (for example, 6, 12, 18, 24, 30, 36, 42, 48, 54, 60). With the multiples of 7, you just have to know them!

Lesson 5 (Practise and apply)

Starter

Refine: Ask the children to spot the link between the number fact 35 ÷ 5 = 7 and the question *What is $\frac{1}{5}$ of 35?* They should be able to see that a fraction of a number can be found by using division. Ask some division fraction questions, such as *What is $\frac{1}{2}$ of 18?... $\frac{1}{3}$ of 90... $\frac{1}{4}$ of 36... $\frac{1}{7}$ of 42?* Discuss how fractions are linked to dividing up a number or a shape.

Main teaching activities

Whole class: Ask the children to listen carefully to your description of a mystery number, then raise their hands to offer the answer. Explain that they can use jottings to note important pieces of information. They must be sure of their answer, not just guessing. Say each question twice.

● *I am thinking of a number that is an even number. It is a multiple of 10. Its digits add up to the name of the times table it belongs to. Its factors include 5 and 18.* (90)
● *This is an odd number. It is a multiple of 7. It is a square number. What is it?* (49)
● *I am thinking of an even number that appears in four different times tables in a 10 × 10 grid. Half of this number is an even number. 6 is one of this number's factors.* (24)

Paired work: Ask the children to make up some clues to a mystery number of their own to test on a partner. They can use a multiplication square to help them think of clues. Ask them to make sure that there is only one correct answer to their puzzle.

Review

Work through some of the examples from the lesson and discuss what key information they jotted down and how to check whether the answers are correct. Ask: *What words or numbers did you think were important? What method would you use to check that you have got the right answer?*

Differentiation

Less confident learners: The children could give an answer based on estimation or mental calculation, and then use a calculator to check by dividing.
More confident learners: Pairs can play against the clock. Which pair can complete the grid accurately in the fastest time?

Differentiation

Less confident learners: It may help some children if you suggest the numbers that they might write clues for. Some numbers have more 'properties' than others. Suggest 6, 15, 4, 25 and so on.
More confident learners: The children should be able to think of clues involving square numbers, factors and so on.

■SCHOLASTIC

Lessons 6-13

Preparation

Lesson 6: Prepare some × questions for the starter.
Lessons 9-10: Prepare sets of shapes from the 'Shapes' general resource sheet.
Lesson 10: Prepare some ÷ questions for the starter.
Lessons 11-13: OHTs of 'Blank axes'.
Lesson 13: Write on the board some number sentences with blanks for the starter.

You will need

Photocopiable pages
'Match the nets' (page 78), one for each child, and 'Symmetrical patterns' (page 79), for display.

CD resources
Support and extension versions of 'Match the nets'. General resource sheets: 'Blank axes', for display and individual use, 'Number fan cards 0-9', one set per child, 'Number cards 1-100', 'Shapes', one set for each child/group. 'Reflections' interactive resource.

Equipment
Clixi or Polydron; a selection of 3D shapes; mirrors; large sheet of paper to make a recording chart; strips of paper for children's statements; lots of coloured counters.

Learning objectives

Starter

● Recall quickly multiplication facts up to 10 × 10, use to multiply pairs of multiples of 10 and 100 and derive quickly corresponding division facts.
● Explain what each digit represents in whole numbers and decimals with up to two places, and partition, round and order these numbers. (Revision of Block A, Units 1, 2 and 3)
● Use knowledge of place value and addition and subtraction of two-digit numbers to derive sums and differences, doubles and halves of decimals, eg 6.5 ± 2.7, halve 5.6, double 0.34.

Main teaching activities

2006

● Explore patterns, properties and relationships and propose a general statement involving numbers or shapes; identify examples for which the statement is true or false.
● Identify, visualise and describe properties of rectangles, triangles, regular polygons and 3D solids; use knowledge of properties to draw 2D shapes and identify and draw nets of 3D shapes.
● Complete patterns with two lines of symmetry and draw the position of a shape after a reflection or translation.

1999

● Solve mathematical problems or puzzles, recognise and explain patterns and relationships, generalise and predict. Suggest extensions asking 'What if...?'
● Recognise and extend number sequences.
● Make and investigate a general statement about familiar numbers or shapes by finding examples that satisfy it; explain a generalised relationship (formula) in words.
● Recognise properties of rectangles; classify triangles (isosceles, equilateral, scalene), using criteria such as equal sides, equal angles, lines of symmetry.
● Make shapes with increasing accuracy; visualise 3D shapes from 2D drawings; identify different nets for an open cube.
● Identify different nets for a closed cube (from Year 6).
● Recognise reflective symmetry in regular polygons, eg know that a square has four lines of symmetry and an equilateral triangle has three.
● Complete symmetrical patterns with two lines of symmetry at right angles (using squared paper or pegboard).
● Recognise where a shape will be after reflection in a mirror line parallel to one side (sides not all parallel or perpendicular to the mirror line).

Vocabulary

2D, 3D, two-dimensional, three-dimensional, regular, irregular, polygon, side, parallel, perpendicular, names of shapes, including equilateral triangle, isosceles triangle, scalene triangle, quadrilateral, cube, cuboid, pyramid, prism, face, vertex, vertices, edge, coordinates, reflection, reflective symmetry, line of symmetry, mirror line, rotation, translation, origin, coordinates, x-coordinate, x-axis, y-coordinate, y-axis, net

Lesson 6 (Review and teach)

Starter

Rehearse: Ask the children random multiplication fact questions (up to 10 × 10). They can work in pairs to display the answers with their number fans when you say *Show me*.

Main teaching activities

Whole class: Demonstrate what a cube looks like using Clixi or Polydron. Revise how many faces (6), vertices (8) and edges (12) it has. Open up the net of the cube. Explain that a net is the flat 2D shape made when a 3D shape is opened up. Ask: *Is this the only possible net? Can you visualise what another net of this cube might look like? Can you draw it?* As a volunteer draws his or her visualisation on the board, ask another child to build the net and fold it into a 3D shape to check whether it creates a cube. Discuss possible rotations of this net. Repeat with other nets suggested by children.

Paired work: Ask the children to investigate and draw a variety of different nets to make a closed cube, using Clixi to help. How many different ones can they find? Warn the children that some nets are just rotations of others. Most children should be able to find and draw 8–10 different nets.

Review

Use Clixi or Polydron to create and display the nets of a cuboid, a prism and a square-based pyramid. Ask the children to identify the solid shapes from their nets. Ask: *Are there any other ways of making nets for these shapes? Can you visualise and draw what the other nets might look like?*

Differentiation

Less confident learners: Support the children's drawing and decision making. Discuss how rotated or inverted shapes are still the same shapes. Provide square templates to assist drawing.

More confident learners: Ask the children to record the nets of successful open cubes and 'failed' nets that do not form a closed cube. Ask them to explain, in the latter cases, why the shape would be incomplete.

Lesson 7 (Practise)

Starter

Rehearse: Repeat the starter from Lesson 6. Then reverse the activity by asking the children (in pairs) to show you two factors of a given multiple, using their number fans. For example, if you say 42, the children could hold up 7 and 6 on their number fans

Main teaching activities

Whole class: Display a variety of solid shapes: square-based pyramid, triangular-based pyramid, cuboid, prism and so on. Spend some time identifying and counting faces, vertices and edges. Ask the children whether any of these shapes would have an easily identifiable net. *Why?* (For example, the net for a square-based pyramid would contain a square and four triangles.)

Group work: Ask the children to investigate the shapes and try to draw nets for them without opening up the shapes, passing each shape from group to group. Ask them to complete the 'Match the nets' activity sheet, working individually to make the nets and match the correct nets to the solids.

Review

Say: *Looking at our results, are there any generalisations we can make? For example, do shapes with more sides have a greater number of possible nets?* Share and record on the board the nets discovered by the children. Discuss the reflections and rotations of nets that the children have found. Draw a net of a cuboid and ask: *Can somebody visualise and draw this net rotated through 90°… through 180°?* Draw an incomplete net of a cube and ask: *What needs to be added to this to make it an accurate net of a cube? Can you draw it?*

Differentiation

Less confident learners: Provide the support version of the activity sheet, with cubes and cuboids only.

More confident learners: Provide the extension version, which includes an octahedron (8-sided solid shape) and a decahedron (10-sided solid shape).

Lesson 8 (Practise)

Starter

Rehearse: Play a multiplication challenge game. Arrange the children into a circle. One child starts by calling out another child's name and a multiplication fact question (such as '7 times 6'). That child must reply quickly and correctly or sit down. If they answer correctly, they can call another name and multiplication question. The winners are those still standing after approximately five minutes of playing the game.

▷ **Main teaching activities**

Ask the children to look again at the 'Match the nets' activity page from Lesson 7. Explain that you want them to continue with their visualisations, trying to identify which face would represent the top and the bottom of the cuboids when the net is open. Less confident learners may have to actually build the nets to find the base and the lid, whilst more confident learners may be able to draw other nets of 3D shapes, identifying the top and bottom faces.

Review

Look at the shapes created and discuss ways in which individuals are able to visualise different orientations.

Lesson 9 (Review and teach)

Starter

Refine and rehearse: Play a divisibility game. Split the class into four groups and give each group a number card: 2, 4, 5 or 10. Call out numbers that are divisible by at least one of those numbers. The group that has a correct 'divisibility card' should stand up. Discuss why more than one group stands up for some numbers. Call out 16, 15, 30, 40, 18, 35, 20, 12, 100, 50 and 120. At the end, find out whether anyone remembers which numbers everyone stood up for.

Main teaching activities

Whole class: Establish what is meant by 'reflective symmetry'. Demonstrate by folding card shapes along lines of symmetry. Ask: *How many lines of symmetry has an equilateral triangle or a square? Why does a square have diagonal lines of symmetry when a rectangle does not?*

Using the shapes from the general resource sheet 'Shapes', revise reflective symmetry of regular polygons such as equilateral triangles and squares. Revise symmetry of a rectangle and discuss why it only has two lines of symmetry instead of four, as in a square. (Two longer sides, not a regular shape.) Demonstrate how lines of symmetry can be checked using a mirror or tracing paper. Remind the children that a reflected shape 'flips' over on the opposite side of a mirror line.

Independent work: Ask the children to investigate the lines of reflective symmetry of a variety of polygons. They could draw around the shapes and then find the lines of symmetry using a mirror.

Differentiation

Less confident learners: This group could fold regular card shapes to find the lines of symmetry. These could be stuck down for recording purposes.
More confident learners: This group should investigate patterns in lines of symmetry of regular polygons. Is there a relationship they could spot and predict for other many-sided polygons? They might also investigate non-regular polygons.

Review

Begin a 'results table' on the board or on a large sheet of paper for display purposes.

Regular shape	Number of sides	Lines of symmetry
Equilateral triangle	3	3

Ask: *Can anybody spot a pattern? Can anybody predict how many lines of symmetry a 20-sided regular polygon might have?* Ask: *Is the same true for irregular polygons?*

Lesson 10 (Practise)

Starter

Rehearse: Play 'Division Lotto' as in Block A, Unit 3, Lesson 5. Shuffle a pack of several sets of number cards 2–10 and give six cards to each group of children. Call out a division fact question (such as 24 ÷ 6). Any group holding the answer turns that card face down. The first group to turn all its cards face down and shout 'Lotto' wins.

Main teaching activities

Continuing from Lesson 9, explain to the children that we suspect that there may be a relationship between the number of sides and the number of lines of symmetry but it is unlikely that enough samples were tested in one lesson.

Ask the children to continue the investigation, encouraging them to 'fill the gaps' in the recording table from Lesson 9. Ask questions such as: *Do all triangles or shapes with one right angle have the same number of lines of symmetry?*

Review

Continue the recording chart and ask the children to write a statement about the relationship between the number of sides and the number of lines of symmetry in regular shapes. Ask: *Are there any other patterns we noticed – for example, in triangles, or all shapes with one right angle?*

Distribute strips of paper to the groups of children and ask them to write a statement about their observations. Display these statements with the recording chart.

Differentiation

Less confident learners: Let these children continue to find lines of symmetry by folding but also check by using the mirror – moving towards finding lines of symmetry using the mirror alone.
More confident learners: Encourage these children to look for patterns in other irregular shapes.

Lesson 11 (Teach)

Starter

Refine and rehearse: Play 'Human numbers'. Create some five-digit numbers using digit cards. Ask five children to hold one card each. The rest of the class read the number and re-order it by giving the human digits instructions. For example: *The tens number moves to the thousands.* Create the largest and smallest odd and even numbers. Repeat with other children and digit cards.

Main teaching activities

Whole class: Display the 'Reflections' interactive resource on the interactive whiteboard. Explain that the dark lines represent mirrors and that any shape in any quadrant will need to be reflected vertically and horizontally.

Demonstrate this by clicking on a square. Reflect the shape by counting the squares to the mirror line and then by counting the same number away from the mirror line on the opposite side. Click on the appropriate square and then click 'Show reflection' to see if it is correct. Repeat with the other mirror lines so that the pattern or counter appears in all four quadrants. Repeat as necessary using patterns with two or three squares.

Alternatively complete this activity on the 'Blank axes' resource sheet on an OHP.

Independent work: Distribute the 'Blank axes' general resource sheet. Give the children counters to practise reflecting from square to square into all four quadrants. Then ask them to create a coloured pattern which should be reflected square by square in both mirror lines.

Review

Display the activity sheet 'Symmetrical patterns'. Ask the children what is wrong with the reflection shown. Ask for volunteers to check by counting the squares or corners to the mirror lines.

Then ask for a volunteer to create a pattern using coloured counters or crosses. Ask the children to reflect the pattern in both mirror lines. Ask the children: *What rule would you write to help others know how to reflect shapes in a mirror line?*

Differentiation

Less confident learners: This group may need more adult support to complete the activity.
More confident learners: Encourage this group to use unusual shapes in their pattern such as diagonal lines, where each corner needs to be counted for reflection.

Lesson 12 (Teach and practise)

Starter

Refine and rehearse: Repeat the activity from Lesson 11 but also round the numbers created to the nearest 10, 100, 1000 by adding in zeros.

Main teaching activities

Whole class: Develop the pattern-making ideas from Lesson 11. Introduce the vocabulary 'parallel' and 'perpendicular' as they refer to orientation of lines on a set of axes.

● Parallel: Lines or planes continuously at the same distance from one another.
● Perpendicular: At a right angle to another line or surface.

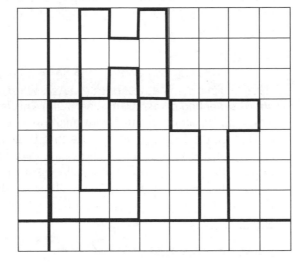

Display on an OHP the 'Blank axes' resource sheet, on which you have drawn a 2D shape such as a 'T' or 'H'. Ask for two volunteers, one to describe the position of the lines and another to attempt to draw them on the OHT. The person describing should give instructions using the words 'perpendicular' and 'parallel'. For example: There is a line, one square in from the mirror line 'y' which is parallel to the mirror line. It is four squares long starting at coordinate (1, 1). There is a second line perpendicular with the first line starting at (1, 5). Finally ask for another volunteer to reflect these lines into all four quadrants.

Paired work: Ask the children to use the 'Blank axes' sheet to plot some lines on the first set of axes and to describe them to a partner, using the vocabulary 'parallel' and 'perpendicular'. The second child should attempt to follow the instructions and draw duplicate lines on their second set of axes. This could take the form of a sort of 'Battleships' game. A line of four squares represents a battleship, three, a submarine, two, a tug, etc. Remind the children that the lines must be along the lines marked on the squares. Roles of describer and scribe are reversed and then both sets of lines are to be reflected into all four quadrants.

Review

Check understanding of the terms 'parallel' and 'perpendicular' by saying: *Hold your hand parallel to the table/floor/door… Now hold it perpendicular to the table, walls, board.*

Now use the OHT and point to lines asking the children to describe them in terms of parallel or perpendicular to the mirror lines.

Differentiation

Less confident learners: This group may be more confident giving the coordinates of the line first before being encouraged by an adult to think of a line parallel or perpendicular.
More confident learners: Ask this group to describe letters on their grids such as H or T or U.

Lesson 13 (Practise)

Starter

Rehearse: Indicate the following number sentence written on the board. ____ + ____ = 1. Ask: *What could the two missing numbers be? They should be two different numbers. What strategies are you using?* Repeat with ____ + ____ = 1.2.

Main teaching activities

Whole class: Display an OHT of 'Blank axes' and draw an equilateral triangle in one quadrant. Label the corners ABC, and reflect it by counting the distance from the mirror line. Repeat for all four quadrants. Label the reflected points A1, B1, C1, A2, B2, C2, etc.

Independent work: Distribute copies of the 'Blank axes'. This time use the two sets of axes to draw a right-angled triangle and a rectangle to reflect in all four quadrants.

Review

Ask: *What do you notice about the pattern created by your four shapes?* (They make a symmetrical pattern.) Ask: *What observations could you make about reflecting a shape?* (It 'flips' over.) This is distinct from a translation which 'slides' along to a different position. Use a 2D shape and a blank set of axes on the OHP to demonstrate this. Draw around the shape and ask for a volunteer to reflect it in one of the mirror lines. Label the reflection R. Next, demonstrate how a shape may be translated by simply sliding it by five squares to the left or seven squares downwards. Label this shape T. Ask the children to tell you the differences they can see.

Differentiation

Less confident learners: May need adult support to ensure accurate reflection of shapes.

More confident learners: Encourage this group to draw a four- or six-pointed star and an irregular polygon of their own creation to reflect. Each reflective point should be relabelled A1, B1, C1; A2, B2, C2, etc.

Lessons 14-15

Preparation

Lesson 14: Write on the board number sentences with blanks for the starter.

You will need

CD resources
General resource sheet: '0-9 digit cards', for teacher's use.

Equipment
Multi-link cubes or counters to support visualisation of triangular numbers.

Learning objectives

Starter

● Use knowledge of place value and addition and subtraction of two-digit numbers to derive sums and differences, doubles and halves of decimals, eg 6.5 ± 2.7, halve 5.6, double 0.34.

● Recall quickly multiplication facts up to 10×10, use to multiply pairs of multiples of 10 and 100 and derive quickly corresponding division facts.

Main teaching activities

2006

● Explore patterns, properties and relationships and propose a general statement involving numbers or shapes; identify examples for which the statement is true or false.

● Represent a puzzle or problem by identifying and recording the information or calculations needed to solve it; find possible solutions and confirm them in the context of the problem.

1999

● Solve mathematical problems or puzzles, recognise and explain patterns and relationships, generalise and predict. Suggest extensions asking 'What if...?'

● Recognise and extend number sequences.

● Make and investigate a general statement about familiar numbers or shapes by finding examples that satisfy it; explain a generalised relationship (formula) in words.

Vocabulary

problem, solution, calculate, calculation, equation, method, explain, reasoning, reason, predict, pattern, relationship, formula, rule, classify, property, criterion/criteria, generalise, general statement, triangular numbers

Lesson 14 (Apply)

Starter
Rehearse: Write up on the board: 7.5 – ____ = 1.9. Ask: *How would you solve this problem? Talk me through your method.* Repeat with 8.2 – 1.7 = ____ and ____ – 2.4 = 5.8.

Main teaching activities
Whole class: Introduce the principle of triangular numbers, demonstrating using cubes, squares or dots on the board. Say: *We start with one, then to add another row that will make a triangle or pyramid we need two more underneath. The next row has three blocks on the bottom...*

The triangular numbers are 1, 3, 6, 10 (although for the purposes of this investigation one can be ignored since it cannot really be considered a 'triangle').

Individual work: Ask: *How does this series continue?* Ask the children to write it down.

Review
Ask: *Has anybody spotted a pattern in the number? Have you been able to find the next numbers in the series without drawing them? Can you explain how? Why is your method so successful? Convince me!*
(Triangular number pattern is 3, 6, 10, 15, 21, 28, 36, 45, 55, ...)

Lesson 15 (Apply)

Starter
Recall: Use the digit cards to create two- or three-digit numbers. Revise and apply knowledge of the tests of divisibility for 2, 4, 5, 10 or 100. Decide as a class whether the number you are holding up is a multiple of 2, 4, 5, 10 or 100. *How do you know?* Check using a calculator: 245 – multiple of 5; 245 ÷ 5 = 49.

Main teaching activities
Continue with the investigation from Lesson 14. As an extension ask: *Which numbers less than 50 cannot be made by combining two or more triangular numbers?* For example, 3 + 6 = 9. However, it is not possible to make 4, 5, 7, 8, 11, 14, 17. Encourage the children to record their findings graphically and numerically.

Review
Ask the children to explain their findings and to make the case for their particular recording method.

Differentiation
Less confident learners: These children will almost certainly want the support of drawing or building the triangular numbers until the numbers involved become too large.
More confident learners: These children should quickly progress from drawing the triangles to recognising a numeric pattern. Some may wish to express the pattern as an algebraic formula.

Name _____ Date _____

Multiples snap

A game for four players.

Cut out these playing cards and use them to play 'Multiples snap'.

25	42	8	12
14	15	28	18
60	52	35	26
13	5	24	38
60	52	35	26

20	36	22
32	10	50
44	30	48
17	6	9
44	21	75
		8
		100

Name _____   Date _____

Multiples bingo

A game for two players.

You need:

- a dice labelled 6, 7, 8 and 9 with two blank faces
- a colouring pencil each.

Throw the dice and colour a multiple of the number thrown. If you throw a blank or there are no multiples of the number you have thrown left, you miss a turn.

The winner is the player with more multiples coloured at the end.

9	49	40	42	18
14	36	6	48	21
7	81	35	90	63
64	24	32	56	45
42	56	72	28	70
80	36	12	27	30
24	63	48	54	16

Name _____   Date _____

Match the nets

Use Clixi or Polydron to make these nets.

Fold each net to make a 3D shape. Tick the diagram if it makes a complete solid shape. Put a cross by it if it doesn't.

Label each correct net with the name of the 3D shape it makes.

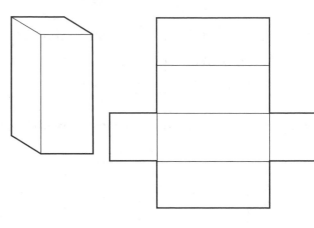
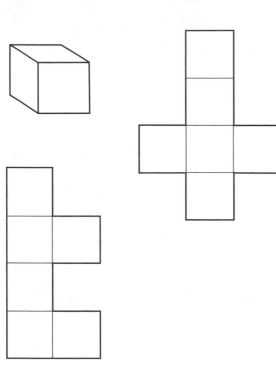
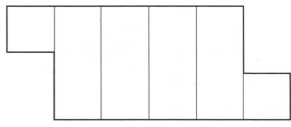

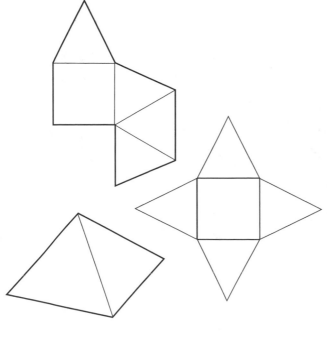
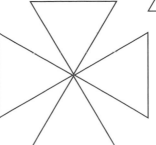

Name _____   Date _____

Symmetrical patterns

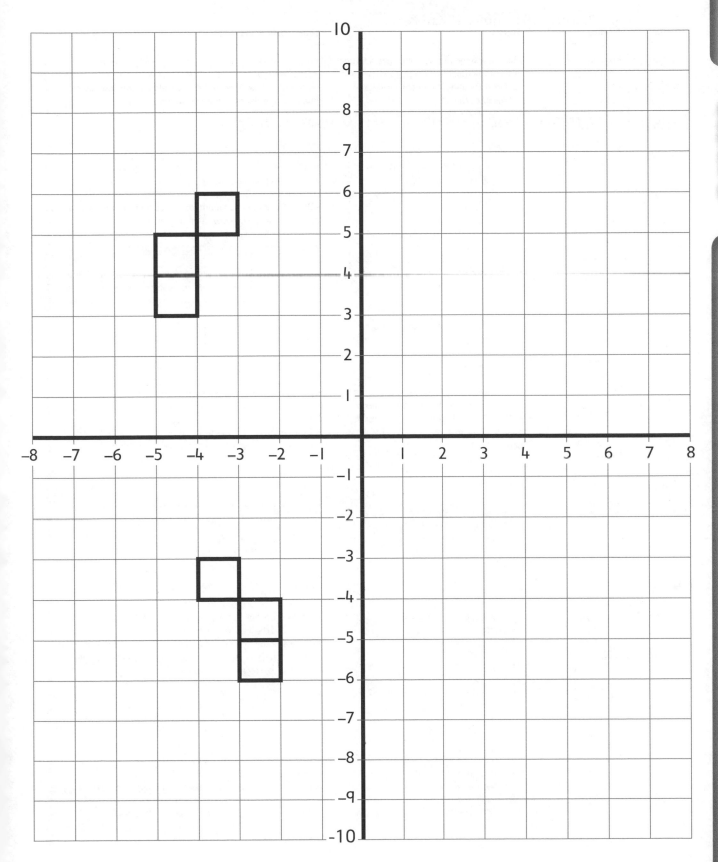

Securing number facts, understanding shape

Lesson	Strands	Starter	Main teaching activities
1. Review	Knowledge Calculate	**Use knowledge of place value and addition and subtraction of two-digit numbers to derive sums and differences, doubles and halves of decimals.**	• Use knowledge of rounding, place value, number facts and inverse operations to estimate and check calculations. • **Use efficient written methods to add and subtract whole numbers and decimals with up to two places.**
2. Teach	Knowledge Calculate	As for Lesson 1	As for Lesson 1
3. Practise	Use/apply Knowledge Calculate	Recall quickly multiplication facts up to 10 × 10, use to multiply pairs of multiples of 10 and 100 and derive quickly corresponding division facts.	• Represent a puzzle or problem by identifying and recording the information or calculations needed to solve it; find possible solutions and confirm them in the context of the problem. • **Use efficient written methods to add and subtract whole numbers and decimals with up to two places.** • Use knowledge of rounding, place value, number facts and inverse operations to estimate and check calculations.
4. Review	Use/apply	As for Lesson 3	Explore patterns, properties and relationships and propose a general statement involving numbers or shapes; identify examples for which the statement is true or false.
5. Teach	Use/apply	Use a calculator to solve problems, including those involving decimals or fractions, eg to find ¾ of 150g; interpret the display correctly in the context of measurement.	As for Lesson 4
6. Review and teach	Use/apply	**Use knowledge of place value and addition and subtraction of two-digit numbers to derive sums and differences, doubles and halves of decimals, eg 6.5 ± 2.7, halve 5.6, double 0.34.**	• Explore patterns, properties and relationships and propose a general statement involving numbers or shapes; identify examples for which the statement is true or false. • Represent a puzzle or problem by identifying and recording the information or calculations needed to solve it; find possible solutions and confirm them in the context of the problem.
7. Teach	Use/apply	As for Lesson 6	As for Lesson 6
8. Practise	Use/apply	Recall quickly multiplication facts up to 10 × 10, use to multiply pairs of multiples of 10 and 100 and derive quickly corresponding division facts.	As for Lesson 6
9. Apply	Use/apply	As for Lesson 8	As for Lesson 6
10. Apply	Use/apply	As for Lesson 8	As for Lesson 6
11. Teach	Knowledge Calculate	Use knowledge of rounding, place value, number facts and inverse operations to estimate and check calculations.	• Use knowledge of rounding, place value and rounding to estimate and check calculations. • Use a calculator to solve problems, including those involving decimals or fractions, eg to find ¾ of 150g; interpret the display correctly in the context of measurement.
12. Practise	Knowledge Calculate	As for Lesson 11	As for Lesson 11
13. Practise	Knowledge Calculate	As for Lesson 11	As for Lesson 11
14. Apply	Use/apply Shape	Identify, visualise and describe properties of rectangles, triangles, regular polygons and 3D solids; use knowledge of properties to draw 2D shapes and identify and draw nets of 3D shapes.	• Explore patterns, properties and relationships and propose a general statement involving numbers or shapes; identify examples for which the statement is true or false. • Identify, visualise and describe properties of rectangles, triangles, regular polygons and 3D solids; use knowledge of properties to draw 2D shapes and identify and draw nets of 3D shapes.
15. Apply	Use/apply Shape	As for Lesson 14	As for Lesson 14

Speaking and listening objectives

- Identify different question types and evaluate impact on audience.

Introduction

The first three lessons of this unit revisit addition and subtraction, further developing written and mental strategies to solve problems. The next set of lessons give opportunities for investigating and becoming familiar with number patterns. Children are encouraged to look for relationships between numbers and make generalisations and predictions. The Speaking and listening strand is covered by a number of opportunities to identify a question to be investigated and also to recognise that there are open-ended and closed questions which require a different response. The final two lessons provide just such an open-ended task to enable children to think creatively and to explore the language and possibilities of shape.

Use and apply mathematics

- Explore patterns, properties and relationships and propose a general statement involving numbers or shapes; identify examples for which the statement is true or false.
- Represent a puzzle or problem by identifying and recording the information or calculations needed to solve it; find possible solutions and confirm them in the context of the problem.

Lessons 1-3

Preparation

Lesson 1: List of 10 decimals on the board.
Lesson 2: Write on the board the question for the group activity.

You will need

Photocopiable pages
'Write to add' (page 93), 'Shopkeeper shuffle' (page 94) and 'A mixed bag of problems' (page 95), one per child.

CD resources
Support and extension versions of 'Write to add', 'Shopkeeper shuffle' and 'A mixed bag of problems'. General resource sheets: Number cards 1-100, for teacher's/LSA's use.

Learning objectives

Starter

- Use knowledge of place value and addition and subtraction of two-digit numbers to derive sums and differences, doubles and halves of decimals.
- Recall quickly multiplication facts up to 10 × 10, use to multiply pairs of multiples of 10 and 100 and derive quickly corresponding division facts.

Main teaching activities

2006

- Represent a puzzle or problem by identifying and recording the information or calculations needed to solve it; find possible solutions and confirm them in the context of the problem.
- Use efficient written methods to add and subtract whole numbers and decimals with up to two places.
- Use knowledge of rounding, place value, number facts and inverse operations to estimate and check calculations.

1999

- Use all four operations to solve simple word problems involving numbers and quantities based on 'real life', money and measures (including time), using one or more steps, including finding simple percentages.
- Choose and use appropriate number operations to solve problems, and appropriate ways of calculating: mental, mental with jottings, written methods, calculator.
- Extend written methods to: addition of more than two integers; addition or subtraction of a pair of decimal fractions (eg £29.78 + £53.34).
- Check results of calculations.

Vocabulary

integer, decimal, decimal point, decimal place, operation, add, subtract, sum, total, difference, plus, minus, round, estimate, approximate

Lesson 1 (Review)

Starter

Refine: Indicate the list of decimals on the board. Ask the children to jot down any five of them. Call out the pair to make 10 of one of the numbers on the board. For example, if 6.2 is on the board, say *3.8*. The children who have the matching pair written down cross it out. Repeat for other decimals. The winner is the first to cross out all their numbers and shout 'BINGO!'

Main teaching activities

Whole class: Write up the sum 349 + 269. Ask children to first round and estimate, and then solve it on their white board using their chosen methods. Some children may use the expanded method:

```
  349
+ 269
  500
  100
   18
  618
```

Some may use compact standard method:

```
  34 9
+ 26 9
  618
  1 1
```

Some children may round and adjust. For example, 350 + 270 – 2 = 350 + 250 + 20 – 2 = 618.

Check progression and use this as an opportunity to assess and decide on groups ready to progress to the standard method. Discuss when a written method is most efficient and accurate. Repeat using 567 – 243 and 422 – 187. Check methods and accuracy as children *'show me'*.

Independent work: Ask the children to solve the range of HTU addition problems from the activity sheet 'Write to add' using their chosen method. Alternatively you may wish to move a group on to a more compact method.

Review

Spend some time checking answers by demonstrating both the expanded and compact method. Write up:

```
  206
+ 347
  543
```

Ask: *What is wrong with this calculation?* Remind the children that using the compact method involves remembering to 'carry' up one into the next place value. This then needs to be included into the calculation: 6 units + 7 units = 13 units. That is one ten 'carried' or put with the tens and three units recorded in the units column. Discuss where this should be put in order not to forget it.

Differentiation

Less confident learners:
Provide the support version of the activity sheet, which asks for a written addition method, but only uses two-digit numbers.
More confident learners:
Provide the extension version, which requires written addition using decimal numbers.

Lesson 2 (Teach)

Starter

Rehearse and reason: Ask the children to write 100 at the top of their board or piece of paper. Explain that they are going to make a subtraction string of numbers (ie keeping a running total and subtracting from that each time). Call out some two-digit numbers to be subtracted. After three or four subtractions, ask the children to compare their final number with a partner. If they are not the same, discuss where the error was made.

Main teaching activities

Whole class: Indicate the question on the board:

▷

● A school makes a profit of £1524 on a sponsored event. It is decided to spend £257 on a visiting theatre group. How much money remains in the school fund? Ask: *How would you calculate this?* Encourage rounding and estimating first and then written responses such as:

Estimate: £1500 - £250 = £1250
    £1524 = £1000 + £500 + £20 + £4
    - £257 = £200 + £50 + £7

readjusted to: Or:
= £1524 = £1000 + £400 + £110 + £14   £ 1 5^4 ^{1}2^1 ^{1}4
  - £257 =   £200 + £50 + £ 7   -   2 5 7
  £1267 = £1000 + £200 + £60 + £ 7   £ 1 2 6 7

Compare both methods and look for similarities, ie 14 - 7 for the units. The readjusted number actually reads the same for both calculations.
   Also revise written addition methods with:

Either:	Or:
£171.28	£171.28
+£138.64	+£138.64
200.00	£309.92
100.00	^{1} ^{1}
9.00	
0.80	
0.12	Again, compare similarities.
£309.92	

Individual work: Give the activity sheet 'Shopkeeper Shuffle', which provides practice at solving money problems of HTU sums with two decimal places.

Review

Ask: *If I have £1072 per month but my house rent costs £350 per month and my supermarket bill is £421 per month, how much do I have left to spend on bills and treats?* Ask: *How would you solve this?* Some may add £350 and £421 together and take it away from £1072. Others may subtract separately. Ask for volunteers to demonstrate their chosen method and discuss the relative merits and margins of error for each. Ask: *How could you estimate first?* Repeat with a similar example.

Lesson 3 (Practise)

Starter

Recall: Hold up a number card such as 7. Ask children to volunteer division facts to match it, for example 42 ÷ 6 = 7. They collect the card for their group if they are correct. The first group to collect five cards wins.

Main teaching activities

Whole class: Remind the children about the checking and estimating techniques practised in previous lessons: even number + even number = even number or odd number + odd number = even number, etc. Also remind them that rounding and estimating gives the relative size of answer.
   Also remind the children that not every calculation needs to be written, as in the case of 140 + 150 = 290. However, care must be taken if numbers become more complicated or bridge 10/100/1000, such as 497 + 836. This would be difficult to calculate accurately using a mental calculation. So written methods become more accurate:

£   500 + 800 = 1300
£ + 0 = 0

Differentiation

Less confident learners:
Provide the support version, which uses three-digit calculations. Some subtractions may still be completed using a number line.
More confident learners:
Provide the extension version, and ask children to use compact methods to solve the calculations.

BLOCK B

Securing number facts, understanding shape

Unit 3 ▢ 3 weeks

```
Either:              Or:          H T U
    H T U                          4 9 7
    4 9 7                        + 8 3 6
  + 8 3 6                         1 2 0 0
   1 3 3 3                         1 2 0
    1 1                              1 3
                                  1 3 3 3
```

One or two children might be able to tell you as a mental calculation 500 + 800 + 36 – 3 but for the majority of the children, this should be a written calculation.

Emphasise the importance of accurate place value.

Independent work: Distribute 'A mixed bag of problems'. Explain that there are a variety of calculations. Some may be solved using mental or informal methods, but many will require a written calculation.

Review

Ask: *If I were to calculate £741.71 – £314.28, would I expect an odd or an even answer?* (Odd. This can be calculated by mentally counting on from 8 to 11, a difference of 3.) Ask: *How would I round and estimate this calculation?* (£750 – £300 → £450.)

Now ask for volunteers to talk through their methods of calculation.

```
  £ 741.71    =    £700 + £40 + £1 + 70p + 1p
 -£ 314.28    =    £300 + £10 + £4 + 20p + 8p
```

Readjusted to:

```
  £ 741.71    =    £700 + £30 + £11 + 60p + 11p
 -£ 314.28    =    £300 + £10 + £ 4 + 20p +  8p
  £ 427.43    =    £400 + £20 + £ 7 + 40p +  3p
```

Emphasise the position of the decimal point and how it remains in the same position.

An alternative calculation would be: £ 7 ³4 ¹1 . ⁶7 ¹1

```
              - 3  1  4 . 2 8
            £ 4  2  7 . 4 3
```

Differentiation

Less confident learners: Provide the support version, which uses simpler numbers.
More confident learners: Provide the extension version, which uses decimal numbers and two-step problems.

Lessons 4–13

Preparation

Lesson 4: Draw a blank ladder grid on the board. Modify a six-sided dice to read 2, 3, 4, 5, 10 (or 11).
Lesson 6: Write on the board the lists of numbers to double and halve.
Lesson 8: Prepare a sheet of 20 single-digit × and ÷ questions.
Lessons 11 and 12: Write up weights and measures as for the Main teaching activities.

You will need

Photocopiable pages
'One, two, buckle my shoe...' (page 96), one per child.
CD resources
Support and extension versions of 'One, two, buckle my shoe...', 'Investigating odd and even numbers', one per child. General resource sheets: 'Blank 100

Learning objectives

Starter

● Recall quickly multiplication facts up to 10 × 10, use to multiply pairs of multiples of 10 and 100 and derive quickly corresponding division facts.
● Use a calculator to solve problems, including those involving decimals or fractions, eg to find ¾ of 150g; interpret the display correctly in the context of measurement.
● Use knowledge of place value and addition and subtraction of two-digit numbers to derive sums and differences, doubles and halves of decimals, eg 6.5 ± 2.7, halve 5.6, double 0.34.
● Use knowledge of rounding, place value, number facts and inverse operations to estimate and check calculations.

Main teaching activities

2006

● Explore patterns, properties and relationships and propose a general statement involving numbers or shapes; identify examples for which the statement is true or false.
● Represent a puzzle or problem by identifying and recording the information or calculations needed to solve it; find possible solutions and

Square', one for each child; 'Multiplication square' and '100 square', 'Number fan cards 0–9'. 'Multiplication square' interactive resource.

Equipment
Six-sided and ten-sided dice (one of each per pair); colouring pencils; stopwatch or similar for timing; OHT/flipchart for recording findings of investigations; OHP or whiteboard calculator; calculators, one per child.

confirm them in the context of the problem.

● Use knowledge of number facts, place value and rounding to estimate and check calculations.

● Use a calculator to solve problems, including those involving decimals or fractions, eg to find ¾ of 150g; interpret the display correctly in the context of measurement.

1999

● Solve mathematical problems or puzzles, recognise and explain patterns and relationships, generalise and predict. Suggest extensions asking 'What if...?'

● Recognise and extend number sequences.

● Make and investigate a general statement about familiar numbers or shapes by finding examples that satisfy it; explain a generalised relationship (formula) in words.

● Use all four operations to solve simple word problems involving numbers and quantities based on 'real life', money and measures (including time), using one or more steps, including finding simple percentages.

● Choose and use appropriate number operations to solve problems, and appropriate ways of calculating: mental, mental with jottings, written methods, calculator.

● Check results of calculations.

● Develop calculator skills and use a calculator effectively.

Vocabulary
Problem, solution, calculate, calculation, equation, method, explain, reasoning, reason, predict, pattern, relationship, formula, rule, classify, property, criterion/criteria, generalise, general statement. Integer, square number, multiple, factor, divisor, divisible by, decimal, decimal point, decimal place

Lesson 4 (Review)

Starter
Recall: Play 'Quick-fire Table Facts'. Using the 'Multiplication square' general resource sheet, shout out a number in the times tables up to 10 × 10 and ask for the corresponding multiples. Ask children to 'show me' using their number fans.

Main teaching activities
Whole class: Explain to the class that in this lesson, they are going to use and investigate number patterns. Point to the ladder grid and explain that one roll of a ten-sided dice will decide how big your steps are. Ask for two volunteers to count up the number pattern. Roll the dice: if it shows a 6, explain that the children must count in constant steps of 6. Roll the dice again to give a starting number, such as 4. The children take turns to add to the number pattern: 4, 10, 16, 22... The first child to cross 100 gets a point for their group or team. Repeat with two more volunteers, using a new starting point and constant step.

Paired work: Working in pairs, the children use a 10-sided dice to create number patterns from random starting points. They should keep a record of the constant step in each pattern, and the numbers they make.

Review
Ask whether anyone can spot the pattern and predict the next three numbers in the following patterns. Say: *2, 5, 8, 11, 14, 17...* (+3) and *5, 11, 23, 47...* (Double and +1). Invite some children to begin a number pattern for the others to identify. Count together up to or over 100 and back to zero, using that sequence.

Differentiation
Less confident learners: The children can use a modified six-sided dice that gives steps of 2, 3, 4, 5 and 10 (or 11).

More confident learners: The children can add the constant step and then multiply by 2. So if the constant step is 3 and the starting point is 2, 2 + 3 = 5 and 5 × 2 = 10. A point goes to the first child to reach 200.

▶

Lesson 5 (Teach)

Starter

Revisit: Ask questions about changing units of measure to larger equivalents, such as: *How many grams in a kilogram?... in 1.5kg?... in 4.5kg?... in 0.25kg? How many millilitres in a litre?... in 3 litres?...in 5.5 litres? How many cm in a metre?... in a kilometre?... in ¼ of a metre?* Ask the children to raise their hands to answer. *How can a calculator help us understand mixed units such as grams and kilograms?*

Main teaching activities

Whole class: Explain that there are many kinds of number sequence: they don't all count on or back in whole-number steps of constant size. Other kinds of regular step are possible as well as adding or subtracting a constant number. Ask: *Can you spot the pattern? 1, 4, 9, 16, 25, 36, 49, 64, 81, 100.* Establish that this is the sequence of square numbers. Remind the children that a number multiplied by itself gives a square number. Ask the children to consider 0.2, 0.4, 0.6, 0.8 1.0, 1.2...(Jumps of 0.2.) *What about 1, 0, -1, -2, -3?* (Counting back in ones, past zero into the negative numbers.)

Explain that a number pattern rule can have more than one step, as long as the pattern follows the rule faithfully. Look at the rule 'Double it and add 1': *start at 1, double it is 2 and add 1 is 3. So the pattern begins 1, 3...* Apply the rule again: *double 3 is 6 and add 1 is 7. So the pattern is 1, 3, 7...* Ask the children to think of the next three numbers in the pattern. Ask whether anyone can invent a new rule for the class to try. Apply it on the board together.

Independent work: Provide the activity sheet 'One, two, buckle my shoe...'. Explain that this is a page of puzzling number sequences. The children must identify the rule for each sequence, then continue it for the next three numbers.

Review

Go through some of the trickier patterns from the sheets. Ask the children to explain the pattern or rule. Ask: *What do you look for when solving a pattern? Do the rules always involve finding a difference?* Explain that a number sequence can follow any mathematical rule that gives a constant pattern.

Differentiation

Less confident learners:
Provide the support version, which uses one-step rules only.
More confident learners:
Provide the extension version, which uses more challenging sequences.

Lesson 6 (Review and teach)

Starter

Recall: Ask the children to jot down both lists of decimal numbers from the board:

Double:	0.3	0.6	1.2	1.5	3.2	4.3	4.8	3.7	2.1	
	2.9	1.8	3.6	4.6	1.6	1.7	2.4	2.5	4.4	
Halve:	6.1	5.3	7.4	3.2	4.2	8.6	9.25	9.6	8.84	1.01
	9.8	8.8	7.2	7.5	4.8	3.6	6.4	2.8	2.2	1.8

Explain that they have one minute to double or halve them. How many can they do in the time? Discuss strategies for getting as many done as possible. Say: *Don't sit trying to work out one of them; go through and do all the ones you know first.*

Main teaching activities

Whole class: Use the 'Multiplication square' whiteboard resource to revise what a factor is (ie numbers multiplied together to give a multiple). Ask the children to find factors of 16, 28 or 35. Show the children how to work out a factor. Explain that a multiplication grid is slightly limiting because it only shows factors up to 10, ie it would not give 2 × 14 for 28. Refer them to Block B, Unit 1 when they used factors outside the 10 × 10 tables. Remind the children that factors of a larger number can be found by partitioning the larger numbers into multiples of known factors. For example 28 = (2 × 10) + (2 × 4) thus 2 and 14 are factors of 28. Revise prime numbers, numbers only divisibly by themselves and 1, such as 17. Ask the children to suggest other prime numbers.

Alternatively, you could use the 'Multiplication square' general resource sheet on an OHP.

Independent work: Distribute a '100 square' to each child. Ask them to work through the numbers and to colour all the prime numbers in one colour. A calculator can be used to check. Next, they must work through the remaining numbers and record all the factors of the first 30 numbers on the bottom or back of the sheet, for example: Factors of 6 are 1, 2, 3, and 6. The activity sheets will be used again in the next lesson.

Review

Ask the children to share their findings of the prime numbers from 1 to 100. Ask: *Would the same pattern be true of the next 100 from 101–200? For example 1, 2, 3, 5, 7 are prime numbers, so would 101, 102, 103, 105, 107 also be prime numbers?* (No, not the even ones such as 102, which is divisible by 2, or 105, which is divisible by 5.)

Remind the children that they can use their knowledge of tests of divisibility and a calculator to work these out. Work through together identifying further prime numbers:

101	103	107	109	113	127	131	137	139
143	149	151	157	163	167	173	179	181
191	193	197	199					

Lesson 7 (Teach)

Starter

Refine and rehearse: Multiplying decimals by 4 by doubling and doubling again. Ask the children questions such as 8.1 × 4; 1.6 × 4; 2.2 × 4; 2.5 × 4; 3.2 × 4.

Ask the children to explain to you their double doubles. Divide the class into two teams and have a quick-fire competition where you call out a question, for example *1.8 × 4* and the first team to put up their hand and say '7.2' gains a point. The first team to 10 are the winners.

Main teaching activities

Whole class: Revise square numbers. (A number multiplied by itself gives a square number.) Ask the class to identify the square numbers they know up to 100 by chanting 1 × 1 = 1, 2 × 2 = 4, 3 × 3 = 9, etc. Display the 'Multiplication square' whiteboard resource and point out the diagonal pattern made by the square numbers. Say, *Can you calculate any square numbers above 100?* For example 20 × 20 = 400 or 13 × 13 = 169.

Explain that, conversely, the square root of a number is the factor that when multiplied by itself gives the square number, ie $8^2 = 64 \rightarrow \sqrt{64} = 8$. Show this on the 'Multiplication square' by highlighting the row 8 and the column 8. Alternatively, you could use the 'Multiplication square' general resource sheet on an OHP.

Independent work: On the '100 square' used in Lesson 6, children must find all the square numbers and colour them a different colour from the prime numbers. *Is there a pattern?* They should then continue to find factors of numbers up to 100.

Review

Ask the children to look at the square numbers they have highlighted. *Is there a pattern?* (Yes, they run diagonally across the page.) *Is the same true for the next 100, 101–200?* (Yes, 11 × 11, 12 × 12, 13 × 13 numbers also run diagonally.)

Ask the children to look at their prime numbers. *Is there a pattern?* (No, not

Differentiation

Less confident learners: This group may be glad of the support of a copy of the 'multiplication square' to begin to find factors and a calculator to check higher factors. They may only find factors of numbers 1–50.
More confident learners: This group should be able to find all the factors of 1–50 mentally. They might take the investigation further, to 100, if there is sufficient time.

Differentiation

Less confident learners: This group will need support in listing all the factors of their numbers, especially to understand that, for example, 28 has factors of 1, 28, 2 and 14 as well as 4 and 7. Point out the relationship: double one factor and halve the other.
More confident learners: This group should extend the prime numbers, square numbers and factor investigation to numbers 101–200 (using the 'Blank 100 square' resource sheet). Fill in the numbers on a blank 100 square and colour and highlight as before. Which numbers follow the same pattern?

▶ really and the arrangement is different for numbers 101–200.)

Finally, ask: *Are there any other generalisations or observations that we can make?* (For example, even numbers have generally more factors than odd numbers.)

Lesson 8 (Practise)

Starter
Recall: Challenge the children to complete a page of 20 single-figure multiplication problems and division problems where the answer is a single number – in less than 3 minutes. As children call out 'Finished!' give them their time – so you will have to keep a close eye on the clock. This will give you an idea of who really knows their tables instantly and those for whom speed compromises accuracy.

Main teaching activities
Whole class: Revise what is already known about odd and even numbers: evens are divisible by 2, even + even = an even answer, etc. Ask the children if, given their knowledge, they can predict: *What happens if you add 3 even numbers together or 4 or 5? What about subtraction? What happens if we subtract 3 even numbers in a row or 3 odd? Or 4 or 5?* Take suggestions and record these on a flipchart/OHT. Explain that the children are going to pose a question, make their own prediction and test the theory to find out the answer.

Independent work: Children must choose one addition or subtraction question to investigate, for example: Do all even numbers give an even answer, irrespective of the number of numbers being added? If I start with an even number and subtract an odd number, what do I get? What happens if I continue to subtract odd numbers until I reach zero? Is there a pattern? They should use the recording sheet 'Investigating odd and even numbers'. Encourage the children to make a prediction: 'I think... because...' and then investigate using a number of examples.

Review
Share findings of addition and subtraction investigations. Ask: *Did any of the results match the predictions that we wrote at the beginning of the lesson? Did anyone not agree with the results of the majority? Why? Are these 'rogue' results which need checking and retesting?* 'Rogue' results are ones that do not fit in with a general pattern, and therefore may be incorrect and need checking.

Ask: *What question should we investigate next?* This may be subtraction for some and multiplication/division for others.

Differentiation
Less confident learners: This group should attempt to investigate a question chosen by the teacher. The level and difficulty will be dependent on the prior knowledge and understanding of odd and even numbers, and will be at the teacher's discretion. A possible question might be to investigate what happens when adding two even numbers together, or two odd numbers, or the outcome of adding one odd and one even.
More confident learners: These children should be able to investigate a question that they have posed independently and then extended to investigate 'What if ...' They should be able to show their mathematical thinking, working in a logical way.

Lesson 9 (Apply)

Starter
Write up on the board the following calculations: 35 × 50; 32 × 40; 48 × 30. Ask the children to simplify these calculations by breaking them down into their constituent factors and re-ordering them for easier multiplying.
For example:
$$35 \times 50 = (7 \times 5) \times (5 \times 10)$$
$$= (5 \times 5) \times 7 \times 10$$
$$= (25 \times 7) \times 10$$
$$= 175 \times 10 = 1750$$

Main teaching activities
Whole class: Ask the children to pose a question that could be investigated as in Lesson 8, but this time looking at the effect of either multiplication or division: *Do all even numbers multiplied together give an even answer? What about using two even numbers? If even numbers are divided by an even number does it always produce an even answer? What if it is divided again?*

Differentiation
Less confident learners: These children should investigate a question set by the teacher. It should be based on the children's current level of understanding and ability to calculate. It might be to investigate repeated subtraction from a given starting number or, more simply, to investigate what happens when an odd number is subtracted from another odd number or from an even number. The children should be encouraged to look for a pattern and make a generalised statement about their findings.
More confident learners: These children should be able to pose a

Unit 3 ☐ 3 weeks

further question to investigate, based on their prior knowledge and understanding of patterns in odd and even numbers. They may already observe that subtracting an odd number from another odd number always results in an even answer. From there they should be able to extend their thinking to: What happens if I repeatedly subtract odd numbers? Is there a pattern? Alternatively they might investigate the behaviour of odd and even numbers when multiplying. These children should be able to predict and then investigate, explaining their results with clear reasons.

Again, use a range of predictions on the flipchart/OHT for later reference in the review session.

Independent work: As for Lesson 8, pose questions for children to investigate. The children should use a further recording sheet 'Investigating odd and even numbers' to note down questions, predict and investigate.

Review

Share findings of investigations by asking individuals to present their evidence to the rest of the class, giving reasons for their original prediction and what they found out.

Compare these with the original predictions. Listen out for clear mathematical reasoning. Ask: *If two even numbers multiplied together give an even answer, is this true for all even numbers of even factors? What about two even factors? Why?*

Lesson 10 (Apply)

Starter

Rehearse: Ask the children to calculate mentally a sum such as 18 × 6; 19 × 4; 21 × 6; 23 × 5, etc, using partitioning, and use their number fans to display their answer when you say *Show me.*

Main teaching activities

Whole class: Explain that in this session the children are going to draw together everything they have learned about calculating using odd and even numbers. Explain that to avoid constantly writing odd and even, it is easier to use letters, ie E = even, O = Odd. In this way we can write a number sentence or formula which shows our findings.

Display a flipchart/OHT to summarise findings about odd and even numbers. Starting with addition, demonstrate how they might record:

E + E = E	Or: O + O = E
E + E + E = E	O + O + O = O
E + E + E + E = E etc	O + O + O + O = E etc.

Independent work: Children must create their own information page giving generalisations about odd and even numbers, with sections for 'Addition', 'Subtraction', 'Multiplication' and 'Division'. They should record their own results as a formula in the appropriate section. As the children work, ask individuals to put up one or two of their results on the class recording sheet for others to use and test for themselves.

Ask the children to try an example of any of the formulae copied from the class record to ensure that they understand and agree:

E × E = E	O × O = O
2 × 6 = 12	7 × 3 = 21
E × E × E = E	O × O × O = O
2 × 6 × 4 = 48	7 × 3 × 3 = 63

Review

Ask: *Are there any odd and even combinations that do not produce a consistent result?* (No, there should be reliable patterns.) *How can this knowledge assist with the accuracy of our own calculations?* (It's not a complete answer, but another checking strategy.) Discuss how consistent application of a rule should produce reliable results in this instance.

Turn the children's findings into a game. Explain that you are going to call out a formula or code calculation such as O + O. The children consult their investigations and put their hands on their head if they think the answer will be odd or stand up if they think the answer might be even.

Differentiation

Less confident learners: Adult support may be needed to ensure that this group understand and can apply the formulae. You may decide that they should use addition and subtraction only.
More confident learners: This group should be able to rigorously test some of the formulae and detect possible anomalies.

Lesson 11 (Teach)

Starter

Recall: Say to the children: *I have a problem to solve. It contains quite large numbers and I don't think the answer is correct so I need to use what I know about number facts to try to solve it. 22,419 + 12,583 = 34,993.* Take their ideas, referring them to adding odd numbers together, rounding the thousands to obtain an estimate, looking for a crossing of the hundreds barrier. Ask for someone to check the findings using a calculator.

Main teaching activities

Whole class: Explain to the children that they are going to use calculators to solve problems. Indicate the weights of parcels that you have written on the board. A = 3.7kg; B = 600g; C = 2½kg; D = 4.300kg; E = ¾kg; F = 75g. Ask them to identify something that might be tricky when calculating using these numbers (they are mixed units). Indicate one of the weights, for example 2½kg. Ask the children: *What would you enter into your calculator to represent this number?* Discuss and revise equivalent weights and measures to ensure that everyone understands how to enter these weights into their calculator. Ask: *What is the combined weight of parcel A and E?* Explain that a calculation is easier to read if it is converted to the same unit of measure, either grams or kilograms. Explain that this calculation could be entered as 3.700 + 0.750 (kg) or 3700 + 750 (g). Ask the children to enter an example into their calculator and to read and explain the answer. Repeat with a second example.

Independent work: Ask the children to answer some more of these weight problems and use their calculator to answer them. They should record the presses they enter into their calculator and ensure that they use the correct unit of measure when reading and recording the answer. Provide questions such as: *Half of C; What is the difference between D and F?; What is the combined weight of B, C and D?*

Review

Share and compare the answers obtained. Ask, *What might an answer of 5.6 mean or 0.7? How do you know? What fact could you use to check your conversions?* (Multiply decimal answers by 1000 in order to convert kilograms to grams.) *How could I convert an answer of 13,500g into kilograms?* (Divide by 1000.)

Differentiation

Less confident learners: These children might be advised to use only grams to begin with and then convert these to kilogram answers with adult help.
More confident learners: These children should be able to make up more questions of this type, including a weight using three decimal places, for example 2.495kg.

Lesson 12 (Practise)

Starter

Recall: Tell the children that you have a similar problem to the starter in Lesson 11, but it is a subtraction problem with a decimal. 8927.77 – 2498.01 = 6429.76. Ask them to use their knowledge of estimating, rounding and odd and even numbers to check this answer and then use a calculator to be certain.

Main teaching activities

Whole class: Explain to the class that this lesson follows on from Lesson 11 but this time the children will need to be able to convert both centimetres and millimetres into metres. Discuss how a calculator could be used to do this. (100cm = 1m and 1000mm = 1 m.) Ask the children to key 1.4m into their calculator and ask them to convert it to centimetres and then millimetres.

Paired work: Provide the children with the following heights and ask them to make up some varied questions, using the information, for each other to solve, using the words taller, smaller, difference, and so on.

● Jane is 1.35m tall
● Aziz is 152cm tall
● Karen is 40mm taller than Jane

Differentiation

Less confident learners: These children will need adult help to discuss the types of questions that might be asked and the appropriate operations needed to solve them. The four operation symbols should be displayed to remind the children and a

SCHOLASTIC

calculator could be used to find the answers.
More confident learners: These children should aim to produce two-step problems, needing more challenging calculations. They may be allowed to add in extra information and to use mm.

- Ali is 1¼m
- Sue is 173cm tall

Review

Share some of the questions that the children have made up and discuss the way that they entered the heights into their calculator. Ask: *How did you find out how tall Karen was? What did you enter into your calculator? Was the answer in metres, centimetres or millimetres?*

Lesson 13 (Practise)

Starter

Refine and rehearse: Write these numbers up on the board:

2018	3864	4503	2845
3699	2330	4440	5500
7193	5883	2911	

Ask the children to challenge each other with questions such as: *I can see two numbers that total approximately 6500. Can anybody see which they are? Can anybody find a pair of numbers with a difference of approximately 1100?* Remind the children about rounding to the nearest 100 or the nearest 1000.

Main teaching activities

Ask the children to think about the weights and measures conversions work they have been doing and to apply what they have learned to solve today's activity. Ask: *If the answer displayed on your calculator is 4.6, what could this possibly mean?* (For example, 4.6m, 4.6km, 4.6kg, 4600g, 460cm £4.60.) Ask them to identify as many possible answers as they can and then write five very different questions that might generate this answer, all linked to weights and measures. Encourage them to be inventive with their questions and the operations that they use.

Differentiation

Less confident learners: Provide adult support for these children.
More confident learners: Encourage these children to generate more questions of their own.

Review

Hear some examples of questions and ask the children to solve some of them to check accuracy. Write up a sample of good questions and ask: *What is the difference between these two types of question: What is the sum of 2.4kg and 2200g? Tell me two decimal numbers that total 4.6 litres.*

Lessons 14-15

Preparation

Lesson 14: Prepare the shape from the 'Shape investigation' resource sheet. Copy the 'Shape investigation' onto A3 or OHT for display purposes.

You will need
CD resources
'Shape investigation', one shape per child. General resource sheet: 'Shapes'.
Equipment
1cm squared paper; card; scissors; adhesive.

Learning objectives

Starter

- Identify, visualise and describe properties of rectangles, triangles, regular polygons and 3D solids; use knowledge of properties to draw 2D shapes and identify and draw nets of 3D shapes.

Main teaching activities
2006
- Explore patterns, properties and relationships and propose a general statement involving numbers or shapes; identify examples for which the statement is true or false.
- Identify, visualise and describe properties of rectangles, triangles, regular polygons and 3D solids; use knowledge of properties to draw 2D shapes and identify and draw nets of 3D shapes.
1999
- Make and investigate a general statement about familiar numbers or shapes by finding examples that satisfy it; explain a generalised relationship (formula) in words.

● Recognise properties of rectangles; classify triangles (isosceles, equilateral, scalene), using criteria such as equal sides, equal angles, lines of symmetry.

Vocabulary
2D, two-dimensional, regular, irregular, polygon, side, parallel, perpendicular, angle, degrees, acute, obtuse, protractor, names of shapes, including equilateral triangle, isosceles triangle, scalene triangle, quadrilateral

Lesson 14 (Apply)

Starter
Rehearse and reason: Remind the children when they played 'I am thinking of a shape' in Block B, Unit 1. Ask them to think of a 2D or 3D shape and describe it to the others, one clue at a time until someone guesses it. If possible, provide some shapes from the 'Shapes' resource sheet for them to select from.

Main teaching activities
Whole class: Display the shape from the 'Shape investigation' sheet. Explain to the children that they are going to use these two 'jigsaw pieces' to make as many different shapes as they can and record them by drawing them onto squared paper. Demonstrate this by creating and drawing some shapes. Ask the children to describe the shapes that you have made using the language of shape that they have learned, for example: this shape has two right angles, this one has two sets of parallel lines.
Individual work: Distribute the prepared shapes from the 'Shape investigation' sheet. Ask the children to cut carefully along the dotted diagonal line. They should then draw the shapes they make onto squared paper, using a ruler.

Review
Share the shapes drawn. Ask: *Are there any regular shapes? Can we name any of them? Which shapes have parallel lines or more than one right angle? Could we start to sort and classify them? By which criteria?*

Differentiation
Less confident learners: These children will probably need adult support to draw the shapes accurately.
More confident learners: Children would be expected to create a variety of interesting shapes.

Lesson 15 (Apply)

Starter
Rehearse and reason: Display a selection of shapes from the 'Shapes' resource sheet. Ask one child to choose one of the shapes, without touching it. In order to ascertain which shape has been chosen, the other children must ask related shape questions, to which the answer is yes or no. Disallow questions relating to colour or material. Ask the children to focus on the language of shape.

Main teaching activities
Continue to sort and classify the shapes drawn in Lesson 14. They could use the following sets: shapes with no right angles; shapes with one right angle; shapes with two or more right angles. Invite them to stick them onto card for display purposes.

Review
Share the sorting criteria and display the work. Ask: *Can we name any of these shapes? Do they all have the same number of sides?*

Differentiation
Less confident learners: Provide adult support for these children.
More confident learners: Ask these children to think of other sorting criteria.

Name _____ Date _____

Write to add

To + Congratulations

Use a written method of addition to solve these questions.

1. 641 + 186 _____	**2.** 1853 + 208 _____
3. £32.50 + £327.10 _____	**4.** 284 + 892 _____
5. £884.10 + £73.00 + £194.01 _____	**6.** 728 + 593 _____
7. 37m + 29.5m + 94m _____	**8.** 471g + 349g _____
9. 288ml + 845ml _____	**10.** £204.50 + £733.20 _____

Name _____ Date _____

Shopkeeper shuffle

Help the shopkeeper to work out these bills, using the methods you have been learning.

1. Mrs Jones had £10.50 in her purse. She bought a bag of apples for £1.89. How much does she have left? _____	**2.** £35.27 – £17.05 _____
3. £128.89 – £84.94 _____	**4.** £394.10 – £178.22 _____
5. Mr Ellis has saved £254.78 towards his holiday. He wants to know how much more he needs to pay the full £870.00. _____	**6.** £701.46 – £263.38 _____
7. £968.19 – £385.77 	**8.** Lucia has been saving for a party and has £305.56. The disco costs £85.77 and the food costs £124.86. How much has she left for decorations and a new outfit? _____

Name _____   Date _____

A mixed bag of problems

Copy and complete:

1.

```
    £ 4 2 0 . 1 0
  + £ 3 6 1 . 4 0
  _____

  _____
```

2.

```
    £ 3 7 2 . 8 1
  + £ 7 2 1 . 3 4
  _____

  _____
```

3.

```
    £ 8 1 4 . 4 2
  − £ 1 1 3 . 1 2
  _____

  _____
```

4.

```
    £ 4 1 7 . 1 4
  − £ 2 8 8 . 3 7
  _____

  _____
```

5. Ellie had saved £48.57 from her birthday money and then received £78.50 for Christmas.

How much money had she saved?

_____

6. 165 boy scouts joined 145 cubs for a camping trip.

How many children attended?

_____

7. I have 6m 52cm of pink ribbon and 4m 47cm of green ribbon.

How much ribbon have I in total?

_____

8. My garden measures 15m in total. The path stretches as far as 7m 28cm.

How much more path do I need before I reach the bottom of the garden?

_____

Name _____ Date _____

One, two, buckle my shoe...

Number patterns to identify and continue

1. 2, 5, 11, 23, _____ , _____ , _____

The pattern is _____

2. 101, 99, 97, 95, _____ , _____ , _____

The pattern is _____

3. 12, 16, 20, 24, _____ , _____ , _____

The pattern is _____

4. 1, 2, 5, 10, 17, _____ , _____ , _____

The pattern is _____

5. 2, 3, 5, 9, 17, _____ , _____ , _____

The pattern is _____

Now make up some number patterns of your own to test a friend.

Handling data and measures

Key aspects of learning
- Enquiry
- Information processing
- Evaluation
- Communication
- C reative thinking
- Empathy

Expected prior learning
Check that children can already:
- construct frequency tables, pictograms, bar charts and line graphs to represent the frequencies of events and changes over time
- collect, select and organise data to answer questions; draw conclusions and identify further questions to ask
- use ICT to collect, analyse, present and interpret information
- find and interpret the mode of a set of data
- describe the occurrence of familiar events using the language of chance or likelihood.

Objectives overview
The text in this diagram identifies the focus of mathematics learning within the block.

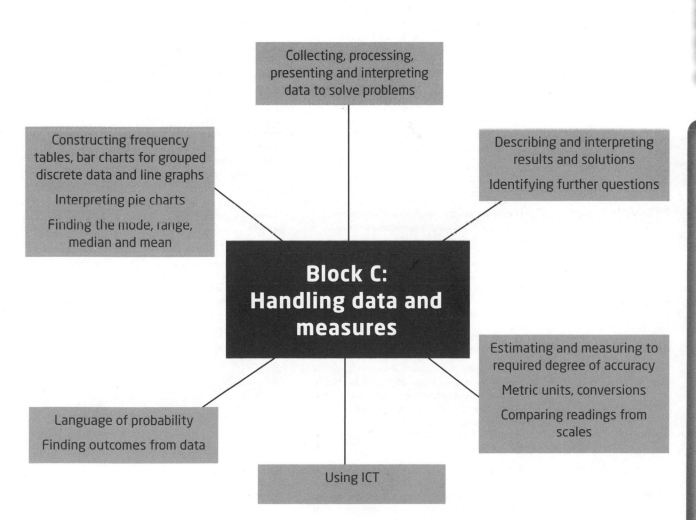

Collecting, processing, presenting and interpreting data to solve problems

Constructing frequency tables, bar charts for grouped discrete data and line graphs

Interpreting pie charts

Finding the mode, range, median and mean

Describing and interpreting results and solutions

Identifying further questions

Block C: Handling data and measures

Estimating and measuring to required degree of accuracy

Metric units, conversions

Comparing readings from scales

Language of probability

Finding outcomes from data

Using ICT

Handling data and measures

Speaking and listening objectives

- Plan and manage a group task over time by using different levels of planning.

Introduction

The first part of this unit gives the children experience in constructing simple graphs and the opportunity to recognise that graphs are used as visual representations of data. As well as being a quick visual reference, children are taught that the 'picture' can be manipulated by changing scales. Lessons 5 to 10 deal with different kinds of measures and measuring equipment. Children are encouraged to notice that there are different sizes of scale and to measure and read scales effectively. They are sometimes required to work in groups, and to plan and work collaboratively. This includes developing clear ideas about time management.

Use and apply mathematics

- Plan and pursue an enquiry; present evidence by collecting, organising and interpreting information; suggest extensions to the enquiry.
- Explain reasoning using diagrams; graphs and text; refine ways of recording using images and symbols.

Lesson	Strands	Starter	Main teaching activities
1. Review	Data	Extend mental methods for whole-number calculations, eg to multiply a two-digit by one-digit number (eg 12 × 9), to multiply by 25 (eg 16 × 25), to subtract one near multiple of 1000 from another (eg 6070 – 4097). (Revision of Block A, Units 1 and 2)	• Answer a set of related questions by collecting, selecting and organising relevant data; draw conclusions, using ICT to present features, and identify further questions to ask. • **Construct frequency tables, pictograms and bar and line graphs to represent the frequencies of events and changes over time.**
2. Teach	Data	Read, choose, use and record standard metric units to estimate and measure length, weight and capacity to a suitable degree of accuracy, eg the nearest centimetre; convert larger to smaller units using decimals to one place, eg change 2.6kg to 2600g.	• Answer a set of related questions by collecting, selecting and organising relevant data; draw conclusions, using ICT to present features, and identify further questions to ask. • **Construct frequency tables, pictograms and bar and line graphs to represent the frequencies of events and changes over time.** • Find and interpret the mode of a set of data.
3. Teach	Data	As for Lesson 2	As for Lesson 2
4. Practise	Data	• Explain reasoning using diagrams, graphs and text; refine ways of recording using images and symbols. • Construct frequency tables, pictograms and bar and line graphs to represent the frequencies of events and changes over time.	As for Lesson 2
5. Review and teach	Measure	As for Lesson 4	Read, choose, use and record standard metric units to estimate and measure length, weight and capacity to a suitable degree of accuracy, eg the nearest centimetre; convert larger to smaller units using decimals to one place, eg change 2.6kg to 2600g.
6. Teach	Measure	As for Lesson 4	As for Lesson 5
7. Practise and apply	Measure	• Read, choose, use and record standard metric units to estimate and measure length, weight and capacity to a suitable degree of accuracy, eg the nearest centimetre; convert larger to smaller units using decimals to one place, eg change 2.6kg to 2600g. • Interpret a reading that lies between two unnumbered divisions on a scale.	As for Lesson 5
8. Teach	Measure	As for Lesson 7	As for Lesson 5
9. Practise	Measure	• Read, choose, use and record standard metric units to estimate and measure length, weight and capacity to a suitable degree of accuracy, eg the nearest centimetre; convert larger to smaller units using decimals to one place, eg change 2.6kg to 2600g.	As for Lesson 5
10. Practise	Measure	Plan and pursue an enquiry; present evidence by collecting, organising and interpreting information; suggest extensions to the enquiry.	As for Lesson 5

■SCHOLASTIC

Lessons 1-4

Preparation
Lesson 1: Draw a blank tally chart on the board or use the 'Doubles in a minute' activity sheet on an OHP.
Lesson 3: Write randomly on the board some pairs of equivalent measurements for matching, such as: 2 litres, 500g, 1.5km, 2000ml, 0.5kg, 1500m, 100cm, 1m, 3.5kg, 4000ml, 4 litres, 3500g.

You will need
Photocopiable pages
'Doubles in a minute' (page 107) and 'Lazy Larry's ice creams' (page 108), one per child.
CD resources
Support version of 'Doubles in a minute'; support and extension versions of 'Lazy Larry's ice creams'; 'Bar chart' interactive resource; 'Pictogram' interactive resource.
Equipment
Interactive whiteboard; a spreadsheet program such as *Microsoft Excel* or *Numberbox 2* (Black Cat Software); calculators.

Learning objectives

Starter
● Explain reasoning using diagrams, graphs and text; refine ways of recording using images and symbols.
● Construct frequency tables, pictograms and bar and line graphs to represent the frequencies of events and changes over time.
● Read, choose, use and record standard metric units to estimate and measure length, weight and capacity to a suitable degree of accuracy, eg the nearest centimetre; convert larger to smaller units using decimals to one place, eg change 2.6kg to 2600g.
● Extend mental methods for whole-number calculations, eg to multiply a two-digit by one-digit number (eg 12 × 9), to multiply by 25 (eg 16 × 25), to subtract one near multiple of 1000 from another (eg 6070 – 4097). (Revision of Block A, Units 1 and 2)

Main teaching activities
2006
● Answer a set of related questions by collecting, selecting and organising relevant data; draw conclusions, using ICT to present features, and identify further questions to ask.
● Construct frequency tables, pictograms and bar and line graphs to represent the frequencies of events and changes over time.
● Find and interpret the mode of a set of data.
1999
● Solve a problem by representing and interpreting data in tables, charts, graphs and diagrams, including those generated by a computer, eg bar line charts, vertical axis labelled in 2s, 5s, 10s, 20s, or 100s, first where intermediate points have no meaning (eg scores on a dice rolled 50 times), then where they may have meaning (eg room temperature over time).

Vocabulary
data, graph, chart, table, horizontal axis, vertical axis, axes, label, title, scale, pictogram, bar chart, bar line chart, line graph, mode, calculate, calculation, explain, represent, interpret

Lesson 1 (Review)

Starter
Revisit: Distribute the 'Doubles in a minute' activity sheet. Look at the set of numbers in Part A. Ask the children to double as many of these as they can in one minute. Say that if one number is more difficult than others, they should miss it out. Afterwards, go through some of the answers, asking the children to explain their strategies. (Recall, partitioning, and so on.) Ask: *Which numbers were more difficult?* (Numbers that bridge a 10.) *Why?*

Main teaching activities
Whole class: Explain that you want to know how many numbers most of the children can double in one minute. To find this out, the children are going to represent their results as a bar chart. Emphasise that drawing a chart helps other people to interpret your data.

Revise tally charts. On the blank chart on the board, fill in the possible scores from zero to the highest number of correct doubles. By a show of hands, fill in the tally chart. For example, part of the chart might show:

Score	0	1	2	3	4	5
Tally	0	I	II	I	IIII	III

BLOCK C Handling data and measures

Say that a tally chart is quite helpful for examining data, but a graph gives a clearer visual impression of the data.

Display the 'Bar chart' interactive resource from the CD-ROM on an interactive whiteboard. Say that the class is now going to represent the information from the tally chart on a bar chart. Emphasise that a graph without labels has no meaning. Give the graph a title, such as: 'A graph to show the scores of Year 5's Doubles in a minute competition'. Agree on what the axes represent and label them. (The *x*-axis, the horizontal axis, is 'Number of correct doubles', the *y*-axis, the vertical axis, is 'Number of children'.) Set the *y*-axis so that one square represents one person from 0 to the highest score.

Ask for a volunteer to draw the first column by clicking on the bar above the number 0 on the *x*-axis once for each person who scored 0. Repeat for the first few bars until pupils understand how to complete the graph. Decide whether all your class are capable of coping with a bar line chart (each value shown by a vertical line ending with a cross), or whether some of them would be more comfortable using solid bars.

Independent work: Show the children the blank axes on Part B of the 'Doubles in a minute' sheet. Ask the children to complete the graph using the tally chart data but using a different *y*-axis scale, this time in twos. Ask: *What happens when we want to record three people?* (The level on the *y*-axis will be halfway between 2 and 4.) Note: you may have to alter the *y*-scale if there is an even distribution of children for each score. Alternatively they could use a spreadsheet program such as *Microsoft Excel* or *Numberbox 2* to draw the graph.

Review

Look at and compare the children's graphs. Are they consistent? Complete the graph on the whiteboard and use it to extract information by asking, for example: *Which score did the most people get? Did a greater number of people score more or less than 7? How many people scored above 10? What can we say about Year 5's doubling ability? Is there a trend? Did more people score above 10 than scored below 10?* Now ask: *Why are graphs used to represent and compare data? Where might you see graphs? Are they all the same kind as ours?*

Lesson 2 (Teach)

Starter
Revisit: Revise the relationships between grams and kilograms, millilitres and litres and millimetres, centimetres, metres and kilometres. Ask questions such as: *How many metres make 4 kilometres? How many millilitres in 3 litres? How many millimetres in 8 centimetres? How many millimetres in 1 metre? How many grams in 5.5 kilograms?*

Main teaching activities
Whole class: Build on the review session from Lesson 1. Explain that a graph or chart provides information visually and so makes it easy to extract information. Introduce the concept of the mode or most popular result: the tallest bar or bar line. Encourage the children to investigate questions such as: *Did more people score higher than the mode or lower?* They can use the calculator to check, adding all of the bars above the mode score and all of those below. They can also calculate the range: the difference between the highest and lowest scores.

Independent work: Ask the children to write six questions to elicit information from the chart, then swap questions with a partner and answer them.

Review
Ask some children to read out one of their questions; the other children can try to answer them by interpreting their graph. Discuss the importance of

---

Differentiation

Less confident learners: The children can use the support version of 'Doubles in a minute', which has easier numbers to double. They can draw a bar chart with support (especially to check that they are representing odd-numbered values correctly as coming halfway up a square on the *y*-axis).

More confident learners: When the children have completed their chart, ask them what the graph would have looked like if they had used five squares per person. *Why is getting the scale right important? Would we have used two people per square if we had collected this data from the whole school? Why? What would have been a better scale?* (Too much space for each unit means the chart will not fit on the page, too little space means the difference in the bar lines is too difficult to see.)

Differentiation

Less confident learners: The children can concentrate on reading off straightforward facts such as 'eight people scored five doubles'.

More confident learners: The

---

children should be able to make comparisons and create questions that require a calculation, such as: How many more people scored more than the mode? How many people scored more than 6 but less than 15?

carefully drawn, accurate graphs. Emphasise the importance of adding labels and a title. Ask questions to assess the children's level of understanding: *What is the x-axis showing? What about the y-axis? Why would this graph be unhelpful if it did not have titles and labels? Pretend that the titles and labels are missing – what could this graph be about?* (For example, shoe sizes, age, pets.) *What is the range? What is the mode?*

Lesson 3 (Teach)

Starter
Rehearse: Show the children the random measurements written on the board. Explain that each one has a matching equivalent. Ask for volunteers to come and link matching pairs using a coloured pen line (for example, linking 2 litres to 2000ml).

Main teaching activities
Whole class: Explain that the scale used on the *y*-axis of a graph is very important. Firstly, it has to fit on the page. Secondly, because graphs and charts present information visually, changing the scale can produce graphs that look very different, and this can be misleading.

Distribute the 'Lazy Larry's ice creams' activity sheet. Explain that the chart of figures shows the number of ice creams a van driver has sold over an eight-month period. He is hoping for a bonus, so he wants the graph that he presents to his boss to look as impressive as possible. On the first graph, the *y*-axis (representing the number of ice creams sold) is marked in 2s; on the second, it is marked in 20s. Ask the children to put the data onto both graphs in the form of a bar chart or bar line graph.

Independent work: The children complete both graphs from the information given in the chart, then answer the questions. Alternatively they could use a spreadsheet program such as *Microsoft Excel* or *Numberbox 2* to draw the graphs.

Differentiation
Less confident learners:
Provide the support version of the activity sheet on which the second graph is already drawn; the children can draw the first graph and concentrate on answering the question.
More confident learners:
Provide the extension version, which asks the children more challenging questions about the two graphs.

Review
Discuss the visual impact of each graph, emphasising that both versions display the same data. Ask the children which graph makes the salesman look more hardworking and successful. (Graph 1, because the upward trend of the graph is steeper.) Ask: *How many more ice creams did Larry sell in June than in January? Is this what you would expect? Why? Do you think he may have taken some secret days off during the summer? What excuses might he have for not increasing his sales more during the summer? Do you think his boss will be very impressed? How can you explain the difference between the two graphs?*

Lesson 4 (Practise)

Starter
Revisit: Use the 'Pictogram' interactive resource to create a pictogram as a class, using one symbol to represent two items. Add labels and a key and then use the pictogram to extract information and make statements. Ask: *What is indicated by half a symbol?*

Main teaching activities
Whole class: Explain that the children are going to investigate the probability or likelihood of making one total more often than any other when throwing two dice. Discuss which is likely to produce more accurate results: throwing the dice twice, ten times or 100 times. The dice throwing can be simulated using a program such as *NumberBox 2* (Black Cat Software). Explain that throwing the dice more times will increase the accuracy of the conclusions.

Explain that the children will then use a spreadsheet program (*Microsoft Excel* or *Numberbox 2*) to draw a bar chart to display their results. Discuss

BLOCK C

Handling data and measures

what scale might be suitable for the *y*-axis (this will depend on how many throws each pair decide to do). Remind the children to give their graph a title and label the axes.

Paired work: Instruct the children to throw the dice a minimum of 250 times and record the results. They must then use a spreadsheet program to represent the data in a bar chart, choosing a suitable *y*-axis scale, labels and a title.

Differentiation

Less confident learners: The children will need help with drawing the chart axes and choosing a scale. You might like to ask an adult helper to do this for them.
More confident learners: The children should be able to decide independently what scale to use.

Review
Ask the children: *What is the mode of your results?* (It should be 6 or 7.) *Why is this?* (There are more combinations of two dice scores that add up to 6 or 7 than add up to any other number.) *Why is there no bar for 1?* (Impossible with two dice.) *How could we make this investigation more reliable and accurate? Why would a sample of 500 throws give a more accurate result? What about 5000? Was your investigation fair? How could you standardise your method of throwing the dice* (unless the children used a computer)? *Is this like the way you work in a science investigation?*

Lessons 5-10

Preparation
Lesson 5: Find a pictogram (from the internet or a text) to display, enlarged as necessary. Each symbol should represent 5 items.
Lesson 6: A pictogram with the key and labels covered.
Lesson 7: Write on the board the list of measures for the starter.
Lesson 8: Write or print a set of cards or labels (one for each item of measuring equipment) saying 'Divisions of ____ '.

You will need
Photocopiable pages
'Problems with measures' (page 109), 'Reading scales' (page 110) and 'Rise and fall' (page 111), one per child.
CD resources
Support and extension versions of 'Problems with measures', 'Reading scales' and 'Rise and fall'; 'Measuring jug' interactive resource; 'Thermometer' ITP and 'Measuring scales' ITP.
Equipment
A collection of instruments that measure using scales: a top pan balance, a set of bathroom scales, a spring balance, a measuring jug, a measuring cylinder, a stopwatch, a thermometer, a tape measure, a metre stick, a ruler and so on; items (or pictures of items) for children to match to measuring equipment (see Lesson 5); interactive whiteboard; calculators.

Learning objectives

Starter
● Plan and pursue an enquiry; present evidence by collecting, organising and interpreting information; suggest extensions to the enquiry.
● Explain reasoning using diagrams, graphs and text; refine ways of recording using images and symbols.
● Construct frequency tables, pictograms and bar and line graphs to represent the frequencies of events and changes over time.
● Read, choose, use and record standard metric units to estimate and measure length, weight and capacity to a suitable degree of accuracy, eg the nearest centimetre; convert larger to smaller units using decimals to one place, eg change 2.6kg to 2600g.
● Interpret a reading that lies between two unnumbered divisions on a scale.

Main teaching activities
2006
● Read, choose, use and record standard metric units to estimate and measure length, weight and capacity to a suitable degree of accuracy, eg the nearest centimetre; convert larger to smaller units using decimals to one place, eg change 2.6kg to 2600g.
1999
● Use, read and write standard metric units (km, m, cm, mm, kg, g, l, ml), including their abbreviations, and relationships between them. Convert larger to smaller units (eg km to m, m to cm or mm, kg to g, l to ml).
● Suggest suitable units and measuring equipment to estimate or measure length, mass or capacity.

Vocabulary
Units of measurement and their abbreviations (m, cm, mm and so on).

Lesson 5 (Review and teach)

Starter
Revisit: Repeat the starter from Lesson 4. However, this time the symbol on the pictogram should represent 5 units. Discuss the difficulties that this might bring.

Main teaching activities
Whole class: Show the children the collection of measuring equipment. Ask

them to tell you what could be measured with each one, and in what units. Discuss the need for a range of units of measure. Explain that different types of measuring equipment use different units, and that particular units are more suitable for some things than for others. For example, the spring balance scales would be useful for weighing flour, pencils or raspberries within the range of a few grams to 3 or 4 kilograms. However, standing scales are more appropriate for weighing people in kilograms or stones and pounds, as weighing a person in grams would result in a large and awkward number.

At this point, it is a good idea to address the fact that Britain still has 'imperial' units in common usage, such as pints (for milk and beer), gallons (for the fuel consumption of a car, though petrol has to be sold in litres) and stones and pounds (for people's weight and sometimes foodstuffs - though again, by law, food (whether packaged or loose) must be sold in kilograms. Explain that it is useful to be aware of these imperial units because they are still widely used, but in school we calculate using litres, grams and centimetres.

Independent work: Provide a variety of items (or pictures of items) for children to match to appropriate measuring equipment.

Review

Discuss the activity; hear the children's ideas and correct any misconceptions. A common error is to think that we measure the distance from Edinburgh to London in metres. Ask: *What would you use to measure petrol for a car?* (Litres.) *So why do people talk about fuel consumption in miles per gallon?* (By law we must sell petrol in litres, but the gallon is a more familiar unit, and so is still used for comparison.) Ask the children to help you sort all the measuring equipment that you have gathered together into 'length', 'capacity' and 'weight'.

Differentiation

Less confident learners: The children may find it helpful to have examples of measuring apparatus in front of them, so that they can check the sizes of the units.

More confident learners: Ask these children to choose appropriate equipment with no units of measure provided, so they have to think of these units without help, and estimate their mass.

Lesson 6 (Teach)

Starter

Reason: Indicate the pictogram that you have displayed that has the labels and key blanked out. Take suggestions from the children as to what the graph might be about. Ask them to consider what value each symbol might represent. Discuss likely sizes. For example, if it is a graph about cars in a car park, the symbol might represent 20 or 50 cars, whereas if it is about toys in a toy box, the symbol may only represent 2 or 5. Discuss how graphs have little meaning without titles and labels, and, in the case of pictograms, a key.

Main teaching activities

Whole class: Explain that while it is important to choose the correct unit of measure, sometimes it is more convenient to use mixed units than just to use one unit. For example, if we want 1.5 kilograms of dried fruit for a cake, it is easier to measure 1kg and 500g than to measure using only grams or kilograms.

In order to measure accurately, it is useful to know the equivalent amounts for each unit. Ask the children to look at the ruler and tell you how many millimetres are equal to 1 centimetre (10); then look at the metre stick and tell you how many centimetres are in 1 metre (100); and so on (1000 grams = 1 kilogram; 1000 metres = 1 kilometre; 1000 millilitres = 1 litre). It may help them to remember that 'kilo' means 1000 and 'milli' means 1/1000.

Independent work: Ask the children to create a table of these equivalents and then use it to convert some given measures, for example 1400g = 1kg 400g.

Review

Ask the children: *How many millilitres in 1 litre?... half a litre?...3.5 litres? How many metres in 1 kilometre?... 2.5km?... 0.25km? Which is the most likely distance to the end of our playground: 8.5cm, 88cm, 8m, 18m, 8km?*

Differentiation

Less confident learners: The children can use a calculator to multiply by the appropriate amount. They may need help with putting $2\frac{1}{2}$ (2.5) into the calculator, for example 1500g ▶ 1.5kg, or 2.5km ▶ 2.5 × 1000 = 2500m.

More confident learners: Ask children to find equivalents of, for example, 7412g ▶ 7kg 412g.

What is the most likely height of a boy in Year 5: 15cm, 1.5m, 15m, 1.5km? How much tea would an average-sized mug hold: 50ml, 500ml, 5 litres? Which is bigger: 5000g or 6kg? ...1500ml or 2 litres? ...2750m or 2.5km?

Lesson 7 (Practise and apply)

Starter
Revisit and reason: Ask the children to consider likely weights of items. *Do you know your own weight in kilograms?* They could use this knowledge for a comparison. Indicate the weights you have written on the board: 20kg; 70kg; 30kg; 60g; 140g. Ask the children to suggest something that might weigh these amounts. Ask them to decide which weight matches the following: a man (70kg); a suitcase to take on holiday (20kg); a child (30kg – dependent on age); an apple (140g); an egg (60g).

Main teaching activities
Whole class: Explain to the children that they are going to use their knowledge of equivalent units of measurement to help them solve problems. We sometimes need to convert measurements to the same units in order to work out a problem. For example: *Sally wants to put three shelves up in her kitchen. Each shelf is 80cm long. In the DIY store, shelving wood is sold in 2m lengths. How many lengths will she have to buy? How much wood will be wasted?* Work through this problem together on the board:
1. These are mixed units. What needs to be converted to make calculating easier? (2m to 200cm)
2. To turn the problem into a calculation, identify the operation needed to solve it: 200cm – 80cm = 120cm and 120cm – 80cm = 40cm. Sally can get two shelves from one piece of wood.
3. To make three shelves, Sally needs to buy two lengths of wood.
4. She will waste 40cm + 120cm = 160cm.
   Explain that some of the questions on the activity sheet will need formal calculations and some will need informal jottings; but they will all need the word 'converting'. Assess the methods and thought processes the children have used.
Independent work: Ask the children to work through the word problems on the 'Problems with measures' activity sheet.

Differentiation
Less confident learners: Provide the support version of the activity sheet, which has only one-step problems.
More confident learners: Provide the extension version, which has a final challenge for the children to try.

Review
Ask for volunteers to talk you through the methods they used to solve some of the problems. Talk about information in word problems that is redundant or irrelevant, as in the question about the race track: you don't need to know how long the track is to work out its width. Provide pairs of children with individual whiteboards or paper and pencils; ask them to write a measures question, including some redundant information, for the others to solve.

Lesson 8 (Teach)

Starter
Reason: Use this starter to encourage children to calculate with weights and measures, and to round and estimate. Ask: *If an apple weighs 140g how many apples would I get in 1kg? If an egg weighs 60g, how heavy is a box of six eggs? Will it be exact? There are 14 satsumas in a 1kg net. Approximately how much does one weigh?* Discuss the calculations needed and variation in size since not all fruits are uniform weight and shape, which means that a certain amount of rounding up or down may be necessary.

Main teaching activities
Whole class: Show the children the collection of measuring equipment. Explain that they have to decide what units of measure are being used for each item, and how big the divisions are. For example, a top pan balance may measure in divisions of 25g. Ask a child to complete the label, for example

ⓜSCHOLASTIC

'Divisions of 25g', and place it on the balance. Do this with other items of measuring equipment. Some may have two labels; for example, a stopwatch may measure seconds and tenths of seconds. Explain that the children will need to look for clues on the equipment; for instance, weighing scales often have the weight divisions written on the dial. Noticing the divisions is important for accurate measuring and reading from a scale. It also means that some pieces of apparatus are more appropriate for certain jobs than others; for example, you wouldn't need a scale with 1ml gradations to measure fuel for a car.

Paired work: The children work in pairs to examine the equipment and complete a table to record the unit that each piece of apparatus uses for measurement. For example:

Apparatus	Division of measure
Top pan balance	25g

Review
Hold up an item of measuring apparatus, such as a measuring cylinder. Ask: *What division of measure does this scale go up by? What would it be useful to measure?* Repeat this with several more items of equipment. Hold up two different containers that measure in ml, such as a 2 litre jug and a 50ml measuring flask. Ask: *How many of these small flasks would it take to fill this large one?* Repeat using other items, such as a metre stick and a tape measure or a metre stick and a ruler.

Lesson 9 (Practise)

Starter
Reason and rehearse: If possible have available different types of weighing scales, including a balance, electric scales, top pan dial scales, bathroom scales and a spring balance. Ask the children: *Which weighing implement would you choose to weigh: a kitten, one counter, a ball, one portion of grapes, a person, a suitcase?* Ask them to explain their reasoning. Estimate their likely mass.

Main teaching activities
Whole class: Explain to the children that they are going to read some scales accurately using what they know about measuring equipment and units of measurement. Display the 'Measuring jug' interactive resource. Fill the jug to an amount (eg 100ml) and ask children to read off the number on the scale. Repeat with other amounts, including some where the value is in between the numbered divisions. Repeat with the ITPs 'Thermometer' and 'Measuring scales' if time allows.

Independent work: Ask the children to work through the 'Reading scales' activity sheet. For each picture, they should read the scale and record the correct value and unit of measure.

Review
Talk through the activity sheet, noting some children's answers. Discuss any errors and misconceptions that arise. Ask the children to give their answers both in whole units (eg 2.5kg) and in whole units and smaller ones (2kg 500g). Avoid using terms such as '2½ hours', which do not refer to any actual scale. Sometimes children may become confused by mixed-number measures and say, for example, '2kg and ½kg'. Encourage the children to count on from whole kilograms or litres in metric steps: for example, 2kg, 2kg 250g, 2kg 500g... or 1 litre, 1 litre 100ml, 1 litre 200ml...

Differentiation
Less confident learners: Give this group four pieces of equipment with appropriate labels already filled out. Ask them to match each label to the correct item of equipment, then draw and label the items.
More confident learners: Challenge this group to add an extra column to their table, suggesting items that could suitably be measured using each kind of apparatus.

Differentiation
Less confident learners: Provide the support version of the activity sheet, in which the values to be read on the scale are whole numbers.
More confident learners: Provide the extension version of the activity sheet, which contains a second sheet with an extra activity.

BLOCK C

Handling data and measures

Lesson 10 (Practise)

Starter
Rehearse and reason: Tell the children that in groups of three and four, they should imagine that they have one hour to find out which is the favourite chocolate bar of all the children in the class. They must write a time plan to show how they would find out and present the information. They must have a clear idea of how much time they would allocate to each part of the process. Explain that each group must then present their plan to the class for discussion.

Main teaching activities
Whole class: Display the 'Thermometer' ITP from the CD-ROM set at -10 to 10, with intervals of 1. Use the pointer to pose questions such as:
- *The temperature was -2°C at 7am, but had risen by 4 degrees by 11 o'clock. What was the new temperature?*
- *The temperature fell from 7°C to -1°C. By how many degrees did it fall?*
- *The temperature rose from -4°C by 10 degrees. What was the new temperature?*

Teach the children to count from the start temperature through zero to the new temperature. Some children will add 10 degrees to -4°C and say the result is 14°C. Discuss why this is wrong. (It does not take account of the negative number.) Demonstrate how to enter a negative number into a calculator, and use it to check the temperature calculations. Emphasise that a negative number is less than zero.

Independent work: Distribute the 'Rise and fall' activity sheet. Ask the children to calculate the temperature differences and check them with a calculator.

Review
Share feedback of the children's work to assess their confidence in calculating with negative numbers. Then ask: *If it is -8°C in Helsinki and 2°C in London, what is the temperature difference?* (10°C) *Cairo is 33°C hotter than Oslo. In Oslo it is -3°C. What is the temperature in Cairo?* (30°C) *Can anyone suggest a rule for calculating temperature differences across 0°C?* (Count down to zero and on from there.)

Differentiation
Less confident learners: The children may need additional support and encouragement to count using the thermometer as a number line. Help them to understand the distance to zero and then count on.
More confident learners: Provide the extension version, with a scale from 20°C to -20°C.

Name _____ Date _____

Doubles in a minute

PART A
How many of these numbers can you double in one minute?

15	24	12	34	17	22	27
45	50	29	39	46	13	18
26	38	16	25	19	10	37

Tally chart of scores

Score	0	1	2	3	4	5	6	7	8	9	10	11	12	13	14	15	16	17	18	19	20	21
Tally																						

PART B
Using this information, draw a bar line graph to show the scores.

Use one square for every two children on the vertical axis (the 'y-axis').

Don't forget to label the axes and give the graph a title.

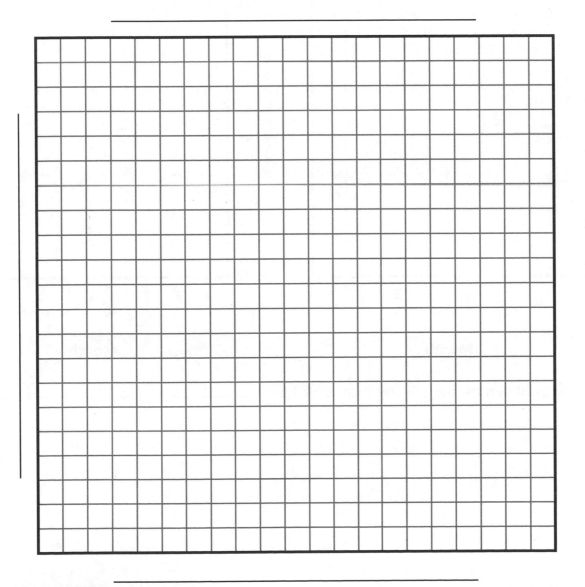

BLOCK C

Handling data and measures

Name _____   Date _____

Lazy Larry's ice creams

**Larry the ice cream salesman needs to create a graph that
will make his sales figures for January to August look good.**

Transfer the data from his sales chart onto the two graphs provided
below. They have different scales.

Month	Jan	Feb	March	April	May	June	July	Aug
Ice creams sold	162	166	164	170	170	176	174	178

Sales Graph 1

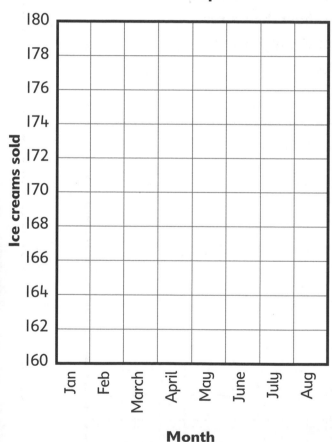

Sales Graph 2

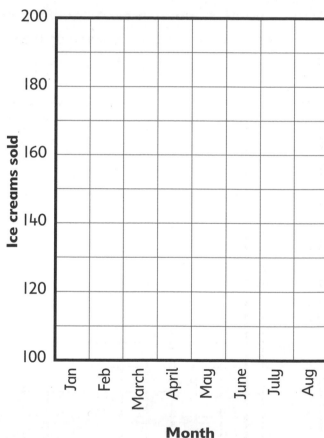

Which graph shows the sales figures in the best light? _____

BLOCK C   Handling data and measures

Unit C1 ▢ **Lesson 7**

Name _____   Date _____

Problems with measures

Solve these word problems. Show how you calculated the answers.

A recipe for scones uses 500g of flour to make 16 scones. How many scones could be made with a 3kg bag of flour?	
Wood can be bought in 2m lengths. Ahmed is making a picture frame that is 45cm by 60cm. How many lengths of wood does he need to buy, and how much will be left over?	
Jon walks 850m to school. His friend Sam walks 1.5km to school. What is the difference between the distances the two boys walk?	
My little sister is 89cm tall. I am 1m 27cm tall. What is the difference between our heights?	
A paper clip uses 3.5cm of wire. How many paper clips could I make from 2m of wire?	
A house is 7m 40cm tall. A ladder is 395cm tall. How much longer would the ladder have to be to reach the top of the house?	
A race track is 100m long. Each lane is 75cm wide. There are six lanes. How wide is the race track?	

BLOCK C

Handling data and measures

Name _____   Date _____

Reading scales

**Look carefully at the dials and scales below.
Can you see what each mark on the scale represents?**

Beneath each picture, write the amount being measured.

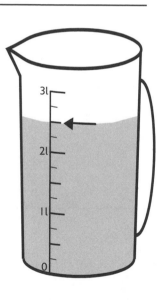 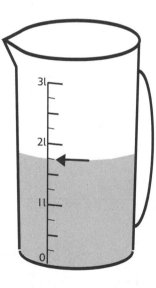 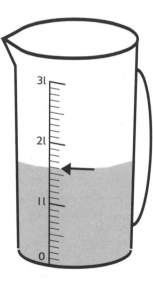 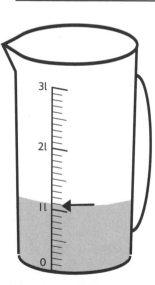

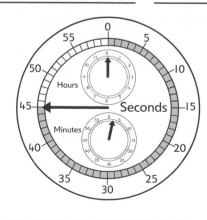 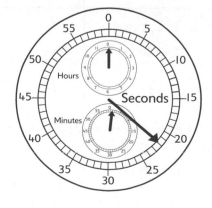 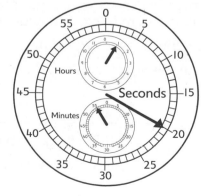

Name _____   Date _____

Rise and fall

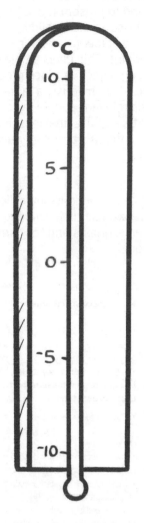

```
10 ┤
 9 ┤
 8 ┤
 7 ┤
 6 ┤
 5 ┤
 4 ┤
 3 ┤
 2 ┤
 1 ┤
 0 ┤
−1 ┤
−2 ┤
−3 ┤
−4 ┤
−5 ┤
−6 ┤
−7 ┤
−8 ┤
−9 ┤
−10 ┤
```

Use the number line above to help you calculate the following:

1. At 6am the temperature was −2°C. By midday, it had risen by 10 degrees. What was the temperature at midday? _____

2. The temperature has fallen from 10°C to −3°C. How far has it fallen? _____

3. There is a difference in temperature of 12 degrees between the classroom and the playground. The classroom is warmer. It is at 9°C. How cold is the playground? _____

4. The daytime temperature is 6°C, but by evening it has fallen by 9 degrees. What is the temperature in the evening? _____

5. The temperature rises by 6 degrees from −6°C. What is the new temperature?

_____

Handling data and measures

Speaking and listening objectives
- Understand and use the processes and language of decision making.

Introduction
This unit allows children to make enquiries for themselves in a real-life context, to research some data and to present it in a graphical form for the use by others. The first five lessons allow children to research some information which may be useful to someone in their school and then to produce evidence for their findings. This gives ample opportunity for covering the speaking and listening objective, since groups must make a number of independent decisions. It is obviously a more meaningful activity if the results are presented to the relevant people in school. Lessons 6 and 7 are an introduction to probability, and the final lessons deal with reading from a scale, especially when the intervals between numbers need to be worked out.

Use and apply mathematics
- Plan and pursue an enquiry; present evidence by collecting, organising and interpreting information; suggest extensions to the enquiry.
- Explain reasoning using diagrams, graphs and text; refine ways of recording using images and symbols.

Lesson	Strands	Starter	Main teaching activities
1. Review and teach	Data	Read, choose, use and record standard metric units to estimate and measure length, weight and capacity to a suitable degree of accuracy, eg the nearest centimetre. convert larger to smaller units using decimals to one place, eg change 2.6kg to 2600g.	• Answer a set of related questions by collecting, selecting and organising relevant data; draw conclusions, using ICT to present features, and identify further questions to ask. • **Construct frequency tables, pictograms and bar and line graphs to represent the frequencies of events and changes over time.**
2. Practise and apply	Use/apply Data	As for Lesson 1	• Plan and pursue an enquiry; present evidence by collecting, organising and interpreting information; suggest extensions to the enquiry. • Explain reasoning using diagrams, graphs and text; refine ways of recording using images and symbols. • Answer a set of related questions by collecting, selecting and organising relevant data; draw conclusions, using ICT to present features, and identify further questions to ask. • **Construct frequency tables, pictograms and bar and line graphs to represent the frequencies of events and changes over time.**
3. Practise and apply	Use/apply Data	As for Lesson 1	As for Lesson 2
4. Practise and apply	Use/apply Data	As for Lesson 1	As for Lesson 2
5. Practise and apply	Use/apply Data	Explain reasoning using diagrams, graphs and text; refine ways of recording using images and symbols.	As for Lesson 2
6. Teach	Data	As for Lesson 1	Describe the occurrence of familiar events using the language of chance or likelihood.
7. Practise	Data	• Read, choose, use and record standard metric units to estimate and measure length, weight and capacity to a suitable degree of accuracy, eg the nearest centimetre. • Interpret a reading that lies between two unnumbered divisions on a scale.	As for Lesson 6
8. Teach and practise	Measure	As for Lesson 7	• Read, choose, use and record standard metric units to estimate and measure length, weight and capacity to a suitable degree of accuracy, eg the nearest centimetre. • Interpret a reading that lies between two unnumbered divisions on a scale.
9. Practise	Measure	Describe the occurrence of familiar events using the language of chance or likelihood.	As for Lesson 8
10. Apply	Measure	As for Lesson 9	As for Lesson 8

Unit 2 ▢ 2 weeks

Preparation
Lesson 1: Find a line graph for display purposes.
Lesson 5: Find some examples of graphs for the starter.
Lesson 6: Write some probability statements onto the board and prepare a sheet with other examples, one per child.

You will need
Photocopiable pages
'Every picture tells a story' (page 120), one per child.
CD resources
Support version of 'Every picture tells a story'; 'Thermometer' ITP.
Equipment
Squared or graph paper; large sheets of paper or card; scissors; adhesive; interactive whiteboard.

Learning objectives

Starter
● Read, choose, use and record standard metric units to estimate and measure length, weight and capacity to a suitable degree of accuracy, eg the nearest centimetre; convert larger to smaller units using decimals to one place, eg change 2.6kg to 2600g.
● Explain reasoning using diagrams, graphs and text; refine ways of recording using images and symbols.
● Interpret a reading that lies between two unnumbered divisions on a scale.

Main teaching activities
2006
● Plan and pursue an enquiry; present evidence by collecting, organising and interpreting information; suggest extensions to the enquiry.
● Explain reasoning using diagrams, graphs and text; refine ways of recording using images and symbols.
● Answer a set of related questions by collecting, selecting and organising relevant data; draw conclusions, using ICT to present features, and identify further questions to ask.
● Construct frequency tables, pictograms and bar and line graphs to represent the frequencies of events and changes over time.
● Describe the occurrence of familiar events using the language of chance or likelihood.
1999
● Explain methods and reasoning, orally and in writing.
● Solve a problem by representing and interpreting data in tables, charts, graphs and diagrams, including those generated by a computer, eg bar line charts, vertical axis labelled in 2s, 5s, 10s, 20s or 100s, first where intermediate points have no meaning (eg scores on a dice rolled 50 times), then where they may have meaning (eg room temperature over time).
● Discuss the chance or likelihood of particular events.

Vocabulary
data, information, survey, questionnaire, graph, chart, table, horizontal axis, vertical axis, axes, label, title, scale, bar chart, bar line chart, line graph, mode, maximum/minimum value, problem, solution, calculate, calculation, method, explain, reason, reasoning, predict, pattern, relationship, classify, represent, analyse, interpret, probability, probability scale, fair, unfair, risk, doubt, unlikely, likelihood, certain, uncertain, probable, possible, impossible, chance, good chance, poor chance, no chance, outcome

Lesson 1 (Review and teach)

Starter
Rehearse: Ask various questions about equivalent measures of length, such as: *How far in metres is 1.75km?... 3.7km? How far in kilometres is 3295m... 500m? How many centimetres are there in a metre? How many millimetres are equivalent to 250cm?... 385cm?... 1514cm? What unit of measurement would you use to measure the distance from here to France... the length of your pencil?*

Main teaching activities
Whole class: Explain that this set of activities is all about graphs and how they represent information in a visual form from which others can easily extract information. Revise with the children the types of graph most

BLOCK C — Handling data and measures

appropriate for different kinds of data. Ask: *If I wanted to compare the number of visitors to a shopping centre on different days of the week, what sort of graph would be most appropriate? Can you suggest other kinds of information that might be shown on a bar chart or a bar line graph? How would my graph look different if I wanted to compare the numbers of boys and girls who visited the centre on each day?*

Remind the children that sometimes bar charts can be used to compare two sets of data. In this example, we could draw two bars in different colours for each day, comparing the numbers of male and female visitors. This is called a comparative bar chart, and it extends the number of different factors that can be presented.

Now display a line graph and ask: *What do we call this type of graph? What kind of information is displayed on a line graph? Why is it not a suitable way of displaying a comparison - for example, of shoe sizes?*

Display a graph of any type, without a title or any labels. Discuss how graphs need titles and labels to tell the reader what was being measured or compared. Ask the children to guess what your unlabelled graph might be showing. Can they suggest a title and suitable labels for the axes?

Independent work: Distribute the 'Every picture tells a story' activity sheet. Explain that this page shows some graphs, but somebody forgot to write the titles and label the axes. Remind the children that all graphs 'tell a story'. Ask them to think about what each graph might represent, and to label and title it accordingly.

Review

Ask what the graphs on the activity sheet might represent. Suggestions might include: visitors to a library, noise in a dining hall, rainfall in two different places. Ask: *Who might use this graph? Why do people represent information on a graph instead of writing it?* Explain to the children that graphs tell people things, and often more useful information can be presented in a single graph than could be explained in several pages of writing. However, graphs give no information at all if they do not have appropriate titles and labels.

Lesson 2 (Practise and apply)

Starter

Rehearse: Explore capacity equivalents by asking questions such as: *How many millilitres in a litre? How many millilitres make 3.5 litres... 6.8 litres... 5.2 litres... 4.9 litres? Convert these amounts into litres: 4500ml... 1300ml... 550ml... 250ml.* The children volunteer answers by raising their hands.

Main teaching activities

Whole class: Explain that the next few activities are going to involve collecting information, creating a database and presenting the data graphically. Each group will collect data to find the answer to a question. If possible, it should be a question of practical use and of interest to people in, or connected with, the school. Discuss what questions the groups might wish to ask, and what information they will need to collect. Suggestions might include:

● What are the most/least popular dishes served for school lunch?
● What PE equipment is used in the school? (This could be divided into indoor and outdoor equipment to make the data collection more manageable.)
● Which computer program do we spend the most time working with? (This could be applied to the computer suite or the classroom computers. A log could be kept next to the computer, and times and programs entered for a day or a week.)

There are many possible surveys related to the school. Emphasise that they must be manageable in terms of data collection and the time available. Discuss how the children intend to collect the data - they can't stand in

BLOCK C

Handling data and measures

Differentiation
Less confident learners: Provide the support version of the activity sheet; the labels and titles are provided in a jumbled-up order for the children to relate to the appropriate graphs.
More confident learners: Ask the children to generate an 'unlabelled graph' of their own for a friend to label. They should decide what the labels should be before they draw the graph.

Differentiation
Less confident learners: Guide the children towards a simple comparison of data, such as the numbers of different balls used

for PE, netball, tennis and so on.
More confident learners: Guide the children towards making a comparative line graph. For example, they could carry out a time audit to compare the amount of computer use in the computer suite, in a classroom and in the office each hour over a day.

one place all day logging data. Encourage them to produce a tally chart for efficient data collection.

Paired/group work: Ask each pair or group to plan an investigation posing a question which can be solved by collecting and displaying data.

Review

Check the groups' progress, and discuss the manageability of their projects with them. Ask each group to report to the class what data they are going to collect, how they intend to represent the information and who they think will find it useful.

Lesson 3 (Practise and apply)

Starter

Rehearse: Explore equivalent measures by asking such questions as: *Which is heavier, 3.2kg or 2300g?... 3.5kg or 3400g?... 6kg or 600g?* Remind the children how many grams are in a kilogram. Ask: *How many grams are in ½ or ¼ or ¾ of a kilogram? Convert these masses to kilograms: 2350g, 4170g, 2381g.*

Main teaching activities

Let the groups or pairs carry out the data collection they planned in Lesson 2. This may be ongoing if collection is to take place over a day. Decide which groups or pairs need more support, or can be guided towards a more challenging investigation.

Review

Use the Review to check the children's progress and iron out any difficulties. Ask: *How are you going to turn the data into a graph? What type of graph will it be?*

Lesson 4 (Practise and apply)

Starter

Rehearse: Ask questions about changing units of measure to larger equivalents, such as: *How many grams in a kilogram?... in 1.5kg?... in 4.5kg?... in 0.25kg? How many millilitres in a litre?... in 3 litres?...in 5.5 litres? How many centimetres in a metre?... in a kilometre?... in ¼ of a metre?* Ask the children to raise their hands to answer

Main teaching activities

Whole class: Before the children go on to create their graphs, either by hand or with a computer program such as *Number Box* or *Microsoft Excel*, they need to establish a viable and manageable scale for the *x*- and *y*-axes. For children counting items of PE equipment, a *y*-axis scale in ones might be used. For children investigating the use of a computer, a time scale on the *x*-axis of 09:00–15:00 in steps of 15 or 30 minutes might be used. The necessary scale will depend on the data collected and the size of the sample. Remind the children that the graph must fit on one page, and that changing the scale can make the data look very different.

Paired/group work: The children should create a graph to represent their data.

Review

Establish that all the children are well on the way to creating a graph. Display some of the graphs that have been manipulated to 'look different' by using different scales. Discuss the effect. *Why would anyone want to do this?*

Differentiation

Less confident learners: It may help the children to have the scale of the graph provided for them.
More confident learners: The children should be able to create a comparative line graph on a computer, if one is available. They might like to experiment with changing the scales on the *y*-axis to manipulate the 'look' of their graph. This can be linked to the Year 5 QCA unit for ICT 'Introduction to databases'.

Lesson 5 (Practise and apply)

Starter

Revisit and reason: Ask the children to consider the types of graphs that they know and have used. Ask for a volunteer to describe the appearance and function of a bar chart, a bar line chart, a line graph and a pictogram. Show the children an example of each. Stick the examples up on the board and ask the children which graph they would choose to represent the following:

- Goals scored by a team throughout the season
- Visitors to an ice rink each month
- Number of books read by four members of the class
- Noise levels in a playground.

Main teaching activities

Whole class: Explain that the children now have a visual image of their data, and they can use this to inform or persuade other people. Model an example based on one of the graphs used in the starter: *This graph clearly shows…* or *From this graph we can draw the conclusion…*

Revise the idea of the mode: the 'most popular' option or highest bar in a bar chart. Teach the idea of the median: the middle number in a range when the numbers are written in order of increasing size. For example, scores of 3, 6, 4, 2, 1, 8, 9 can be written in size order: 1, 2, 3, 4, 6, 8, 9. The median is the middle number or bar - in this case, 4. Explain that if the number of numbers or bars is even, the median is calculated by adding the two middle values and dividing by 2.

Paired/group work: Ask each group to create a presentation based on their findings. This should include a statement beginning 'Our graph shows…' and an outline of the process, including the planning, a tally chart, details of any problems, the graph and a conclusion. Their presentations will also be used in a display, and perhaps used to inform the relevant person in the school - for example, the kitchen staff might like to know which dishes are most popular, or the PE staff might find an equipment audit helpful.

Encourage the children to think of any suggestions that might follow from their findings. For example: Our graph shows that we need to buy more tennis balls before next summer. Or: Perhaps we could persuade the kitchen staff not to cook cabbage, because our graph shows that nobody likes it.

Review

Use this time to reflect on the process of this sort of investigation and for the groups to present and persuade using their graphs. Ask questions such as: *How would your data be different if you had monitored the use of the computer over a longer period of time? How would your graph be different if you had asked the whole school about their food choices? How would you have changed the scale of the graph?*

Differentiation

Less confident learners: The children should make simple statements based on their graph, such as 'The most popular food is…'

More confident learners: The children should be able to look at further implications of their findings. For example: 'We found out that there are three fully inflated basketballs. We need to inflate the others or buy new ones, since this is not enough for a class lesson.'

Lesson 6 (Teach)

Starter

Recall: Ask the children questions about suitable methods and units of measure. Ask: *What could I be measuring if I used a 1 litre jug? … a metre stick? … a ruler? … an electronic weighing scale? … a spring balance? … a 10ml measuring cylinder? … a 5ml spoon?* Discuss appropriate units of measure.

Main teaching activities

Whole class: Introduce the children to the language of probability. Indicate the questions written on the board such as: *What is the likelihood that it will snow tomorrow? … that we will have a power cut tonight? What are the chances of a cat wandering into our classroom?*

Explain that it is necessary to standardise the language and that this is usually: impossible; unlikely; possible; probable; certain. Explain that there are shades of meaning in between these statements. Ask them to sort the probability of the statements that you have written onto the board into these categories.

Independent work: Distribute your prepared list of statements, which may include:

What is the probability that:

- Manchester United will win a major title next season?
- I will find fairies at the bottom of my garden?
- We will do maths today?
- An alien spaceship will land in the playground?
- There will be salad for lunch?

Ask the children to write the probability headings into their books and sort the statements under the correct headings.

Review

Ask the children to tell you an event that is certain or impossible. Ask them how they know. Ask: *At the beginning of a hockey match, what is the probability that one of the sides will win? Or that one of the sides may score a goal?* Discuss how some events may have an even chance of occurring.

Differentiation

Less confident learners: These children may cut and stick the statements for speed, discussing them with an adult.
More confident learners: These children should be able to make up and add more examples to their lists.

Lesson 7 (Practise)

Starter

Rehearse: Using the 'Thermometer' ITP from the CD-ROM, indicate temperatures on the scale and ask children to read them. Include negative numbers.

Main teaching activities

Continue to add statements to a probability scale ranging from 'Impossible' to 'Certain'. Ask the children to think of at least three examples for each point on the probability scale. They could present it as a table with the headings 'Impossible', 'Unlikely' and so on.

Review

Discuss how difficult it is to find things that are certain or events that have an even chance of occurring. Pose the question: *Do you think the language of probability is the same in all countries? Do you think some languages have words with different shades of meaning?*

Lessons 8-10

Preparation
Lesson 9: Draw a probability scale on the board.

You will need
Photocopiable pages
'A scaly problem' (page 121), one per child.
CD resources
Support and extension versions of "A scaly problem. 'Thermometer' ITP, 'Measuring scales' ITP; 'Measuring jug' interactive resource.
Equipment
Interactive whiteboard; counting sticks (unnumbered) or/and strips of paper 1 metre in length; a ream of A4 paper; ruler; spring balance scales; counters.

Learning objectives

Starter
- Read, choose, use and record standard metric units to estimate and measure length, weight and capacity to a suitable degree of accuracy, eg the nearest centimetre.
- Interpret a reading that lies between two unnumbered divisions on a scale.
- Describe the occurrence of familiar events using the language of chance or likelihood.

Main teaching activities
2006
- Read, choose, use and record standard metric units to estimate and measure length, weight and capacity to a suitable degree of accuracy, eg the nearest centimetre.
- Interpret a reading that lies between two unnumbered divisions on a scale.

BLOCK C

Handling data and measures

▷

1999
● Record estimates and readings from scales to a suitable degree of accuracy.

Vocabulary
Units of measurement and their abbreviations (m, cm, mm and so on).

Lesson 8 (Teach and practise)

Starter
Rehearse: Use the 'Thermometer' ITP to count differences between temperatures. Demonstrate, using the scale, how to count through the 0 when calculating differences between positive and negative temperatures.

Main teaching activities
Whole class: Explain to the children that they are going to be reading from different scales. Use the 'Measuring scales' ITP from the CD-ROM to ask them to read amounts from the scale, first with all the numbers in place and then with the scale numbers hidden. Discuss with the children how they work out the small divisions between main numbers. For example, display the 'Measuring jug' interactive resource from the CD-ROM. Set the scale to 0–100ml and fill it to somewhere between 40ml and 50ml. Explain that there are four lines in between these two main divisions, which indicates five spaces or jumps. The difference between 50ml and 40ml is 10ml and this is divided by five, making each small line worth 2ml. They should then be able to read the amount. Repeat with other examples and scales.
Individual work: Distribute the activity sheet 'A scaly problem' and explain to the children that the lines on the sheet have the main divisions marked on but that they will have to work out what the smaller divisions in between represent in order to work out where each letter is pointing.

Differentiation
Less confident learners: Provide the support version of the sheet, with scales that begin at 0 and have divisions of 2, 5 and 10.
More confident learners: Provide the extension version of the sheet, which includes decimal divisions.

Review
Say: *Tell me a rule for working out the smaller divisions on a scale. What information must I have to be able to do this?* Use a number of examples.

Lesson 9 (Practise)

Starter
Rehearse: Indicate the probability scale you have drawn on the board. Pose a variety of statements and ask individuals to come and indicate where on the line they would place the probability of each event. For each statement they must discuss their reasons.

Main teaching activities
Whole class: Remind the children what they learned about reading smaller divisions on a scale from Lesson 8. Explain that for today's lesson they are going to use unmarked measuring equipment to measure given amounts. For example, you will ask them to use the unmarked measuring stick, or metre length of paper to measure 46cm. Ask them how they will do this with a measuring stick only marked in 10cm divisions or a plain length of paper. They may be able to suggest that they need to fold the paper up into equal divisions of 10cm in order to estimate the divisions in between.
Paired work: Children should find items that are as close as possible to the measures that you suggest to them – some might be over 1 metre, for example 85cm, 24cm, 46cm, 18cm, 66cm, 1m 20cm. They can be encouraged to mark smaller divisions to show how they have used their paper metre stick. Remind them that they will be estimating first.

Differentiation
Less confident learners: These children may need some extra adult help and to use a counting stick or piece of paper that already has some divisions marked on it to support measuring.
More confident learners: These children should be able to estimate and measure to a greater degree of accuracy.

Review
Ask the children for their results and ask a volunteer to measure the item accurately, using a marked metre stick. Discuss degrees of accuracy. Ask:

■■SCHOLASTIC

What intervals did you need to work out on your home made metre stick? What calculations did you have to do?

Lesson 10 (Apply)

Starter
Rehearse: Repeat the starter activity from Lesson 9, also asking: *Tell me an impossible event. Why? Tell me a certain event. How could I make it certain that I should throw a 6 using a dice? What would I have to do? What is the probability of my throwing a number bigger than 3?*

Main teaching activities
Whole class: Tell the children that they are going to use what they have learned about reading in between scales at different intervals to solve a problem. They have explored larger scales without numbers, and now they have to devise a way of working out the measurement of something very small.

Group work: Ask: *How would I find out the thickness of one piece of A4 paper?* Ensure that everyone understands that you mean the thickness not the width. Say: *There is a ream of paper here and you may use any measuring implement you wish and you may use a calculator. You must be able to explain how you arrived at your answer to the rest of the class.*

Review
Hear suggestions for solving this problem. Ask groups to describe their way of working. Discuss margins of error and how it is very difficult to be accurate with such a very small measurement.

Differentiation
Less confident learners: These children will probably need a lot of adult support to decide on a method to solve this problem. (Measure 50 or 100 sheets and divide by 50 or 100 to find the thickness of one sheet.)
More confident learners: This group should be able to devise a way of working and explain it. An extension for them might be to find the mass of one counter, using only spring balance scales, not digital ones.

BLOCK C

Handling data and measures

Name _____   Date _____

Every picture tells a story

Using your imagination and your knowledge of graphs, think about what each of these graphs might be showing. Label the axes of each graph and give the graph a title.

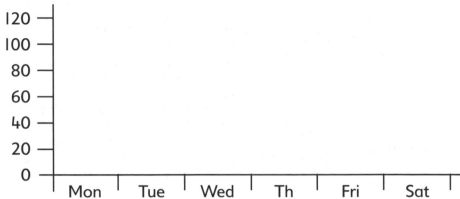

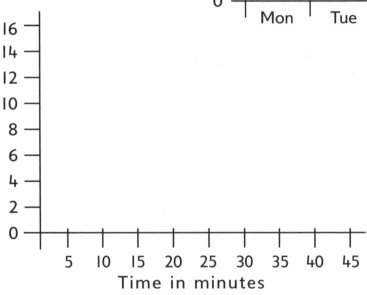

A graph to show contrasting temperatures in _____ and _____

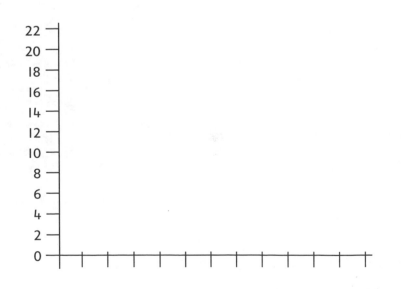

Name _____ Date _____

A scaly problem

Work out where each letter is pointing.

1.

20   A   B   C   D   E   120

A = _____   B = _____   C = _____   D = _____   E = _____

I noticed that this scale goes up in steps of _____

2.

60
J
I
H
G
F
0

F = _____   G = _____   H = _____

I = _____   J = _____

I noticed that this scale goes up in steps of _____

3.

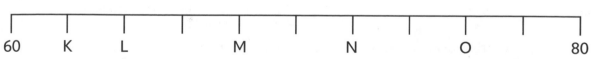

60   K   L   M   N   O   80

K = _____   L = _____   M = _____   N = _____   O = _____

I noticed that this scale goes up in steps of _____

Handling data and measures

Speaking and listening objectives

- Understand different ways to take the lead and support others in a group.

Introduction

During this unit children have the opportunity to explore different sorts of graphs and charts to record information for three different but related data handling activities evaluating the school visits undertaken by one school in a year. They have to plan their activities and work as a group or in pairs to record their findings and present their results. Through this they are fulfilling the speaking and listening objective of taking different roles within a group and supporting each other. The final three lessons develop the probability theme introduced in Unit 2 and revisited as a starter in this unit. This time children are taught to express probability as a fraction or a decimal fraction.

Use and apply mathematics

- Plan and pursue an enquiry; present evidence by collecting, organising and interpreting information; suggest extensions to the enquiry.
- Explain reasoning using diagrams, graphs and text; refine ways of recording using images and symbols.

Lesson	Strands	Starter	Main teaching activities
1. Review and teach	Use/apply Data	Read, choose, use and record standard metric units to estimate and measure length, weight and capacity to a suitable degree of accuracy, eg the nearest centimetre; convert larger to smaller units using decimals to one place, eg change 2.6kg to 2600g.	• Plan and pursue an enquiry; present evidence by collecting, organising and interpreting information; suggest extensions to the enquiry. • Explain reasoning using diagrams, graphs and text; refine ways of recording using images and symbols. • Answer a set of related questions by collecting, selecting and organising relevant data; draw conclusions, using ICT to present features, and identify further questions to ask. **• Construct frequency tables, pictograms and bar and line graphs to represent the frequencies of events and changes over time.** • Find and interpret the mode of a set of data.
2. Practise	Use/apply Data	As for Lesson 1	As for Lesson 1
3. Practise	Use/apply Data	As for Lesson 1	As for Lesson 1
4. Practise	Use/apply Data	As for Lesson 1	As for Lesson 1
5. Practise	Use/apply Data	Describe the occurrence of familiar events using the language of chance or likelihood.	As for Lesson 1
6. Practise	Use/apply Data	As for Lesson 5	As for Lesson 1
7. Apply	Use/apply Data	Find and interpret the mode of a set of data.	As for Lesson 1
8. Review and teach	Data	As for Lesson 7	Describe the occurrence of familiar events using the language of chance or likelihood.
9. Teach	Data	• Read, choose, use and record standard metric units to estimate and measure length, weight and capacity to a suitable degree of accuracy, eg the nearest centimetre. • Interpret a reading that lies between two unnumbered divisions on a scale.	As for Lesson 8
10. Practise	Data	As for Lesson 9	As for Lesson 8

Lessons 1-7

Preparation

Lesson 2: Prepare some equivalent measures cards and stick them randomly on the board.
Lessons 3-4: Write on the board some mixed measures for children to sort and order.
Lesson 5: For the Starter, draw on the board a probability scale from impossible to certain. Write on the board the three lists of numbers for the Review activity.
Lesson 6: Draw on the board probability scale from no chance to definite.
Lesson 7: Enlarge or copy and project some of the graphs for presentation to the class.

You will need

Photocopiable pages
'The Archimedes Science and Technology Centre' (page 131), 'Thrills and spills' (page 132), 'Fair's fair?' (page 133), one per child.
CD resources
Support and extension versions of 'The Archimedes Science and Technology Centre', 'Thrills and spills' and 'Fair's fair?'.
Equipment
Graph paper; Blu-Tack.

Learning objectives

Starter

● Read, choose, use and record standard metric units to estimate and measure length, weight and capacity to a suitable degree of accuracy, eg the nearest centimetre; convert larger to smaller units using decimals to one place, eg change 2.6kg to 2600g.
● Describe the occurrence of familiar events using the language of chance or likelihood.
● Find and interpret the mode of a set of data.

Main teaching activities

2006
● Plan and pursue an enquiry; present evidence by collecting, organising and interpreting information; suggest extensions to the enquiry.
● Explain reasoning using diagrams, graphs and text; refine ways of recording using images and symbols.
● Answer a set of related questions by collecting, selecting and organising relevant data; draw conclusions, using ICT to present features, and identify further questions to ask.
● Construct frequency tables, pictograms and bar and line graphs to represent the frequencies of events and changes over time
● Find and interpret the mode of a set of data.

1999
● Explain methods and reasoning, orally and in writing.
● Solve a problem by representing and interpreting data in tables, charts, graphs and diagrams, including those generated by a computer, eg bar line charts, vertical axis labelled in 2s, 5s, 10s, 20s or 100s, first where intermediate points have no meaning (eg scores on a dice rolled 50 times), then where they may have meaning (eg room temperature over time).
● Find the mode of a set of data.

Vocabulary

data, information, survey, questionnaire, graph, chart, table, horizontal axis, vertical axis, axes, label, title, scale, pictogram, bar chart, bar line chart, line graph, mode, maximum/minimum value, problem, solution, calculate, calculation, method, explain, reason, reasoning, predict, pattern, relationship, classify, represent, analyse, interpret

Lesson 1 (Review and teach)

Starter

Revisit: Revise converting units of measure by asking: *How many millilitres in a litre?... metres in a kilometre?...grams in a kilogram?...centimetres in a metre?* Ask questions such as: *How many grams are there in 1.5kg? 2000m is equal to how many kilometres? How many metres are equivalent to 300cm?*

Main teaching activities

Whole class: Explain to the children that in this unit of work, they will carry out three different (but related) data handling activities. These activities are all about investigating and evaluating the school visits undertaken by one school in a year. Revise the way in which different graphs are used for different types of data: bar charts or bar line graphs for comparisons of discrete (separate) data, line graphs for continuous data.

Explain that there are three types of value we can use when talking about a set of numbers:

▷ **1. Mode:** the value that occurs most often. Write this list of numbers on the board: 3, 4, 7, 7, 8, 1, 2, 3, 3, 8, 1, 1, 2, 3, 3. Ask for a volunteer to come and re-order these in ascending order. Now ask the class to decide which value occurs most often. In this case the mode is 3.

2. Median: the middle value of a sequence of numbers arranged in ascending order, or the average (add together and divide by 2) of the two middle values if there is an even number of values in the sequence. Ask the children to look at the re-ordered data again and find the median value. In this case it is also 3.

3. Mean: this is what we would call the 'average' in everyday life. It is normally calculated by adding all the values together and dividing their sum by the number of values. Write the following on the board: 3, 17, 13. Ask the children to add these values together and divide by the number of values: 33 ÷ 3 = 11, so the mean of these values is 11. Repeat with other sets of values such as 5, 3, 4, 3, 5 (mean = 4) and 9, 2, 3, 10 (mean = 6).

Independent work: Set groups of children to work as individuals on the activity sheets. Talk through each activity with the group beforehand. Most children will complete all three of the following activities in six days; others may need an extension activity such as writing (and answering) their own questions to append to the graphs. You may wish to set up a 'carousel' of simultaneous activities and work with different groups each day.

Activity 1: The Archimedes Science and Technology Centre

Use the table of data on the activity sheet 'The Archimedes Science and Technology Centre' to create a bar line graph showing the monthly number of visitors to the Centre in a year. Label the vertical axis with two squares for every 10,000 people. Use your graph to answer the questions.

Notes: The children's answers should reflect some reasoning about the changing seasons – for example, 'Fewer people go to outdoor places like parks when the weather is bad.' The higher numbers of visitors between May and August is probably a consequence of children being on school holidays and therefore being able to visit the Centre with their families. Encourage the children to see that the information extracted from a graph can be used to make hypotheses and even to predict. They need to think of the data in a 'real life' context in order to draw conclusions from it.

Activity 2: Thrills and spills

A Year 5 class visits the Speed and Sound science fair each year. Their favourite features are the rides demonstrating speed. Look at the 'Thrills and spills' activity sheet, which has a line graph showing the speed of the Rocking Roller Coaster during its 3-minute ride. Draw a similar line graph for the Hill and Dale Dipper using the data in the table. Use the two graphs to answer the questions.

Notes: 1. A comparison of speeds between two fairground rides. **2.** To find the mean speed of each ride, add up all the readings shown on the graph (including 0 readings at the beginning and the end). Mean speed for the Rocking Roller Coaster = 192 ÷ 10 = 19.2mph. Mean speed for the Hill and Dale Dipper = 25mph. **3.** To find the speed at a particular time, read it off the *y*-axis of the graph. For the Rocking Roller Coaster, speed at 70 seconds is 25mph and speed at 30 seconds is 11mph. For the Hill and Dale Dipper, speed at 70 seconds is 32–33mph and speed at 30 seconds is 10mph.

Activity 3: Fair's fair?

Look at the 'Fair's Fair' activity sheet. Use the data from the tables showing the average waiting time and the duration of the ride for each of five rides at the Speed and Sound fair to draw one comparative bar chart showing all the information. Use all the data to compare the rides. List them in order of value for money and write a report commenting on the waiting times, the ride times and the value for money of each ride.

Notes: Look for the use of two different colours to represent the two sets ▷ of times on the graph. The children's decisions about value for money should

▪SCHOLASTIC

use all of the available data, not just one or two parameters. The Wall of Fear is the best value for money at 27p per minute with only 10 minutes' waiting time and a 10-minute ride. Squashed costs 60p per minute and is a 5-minute ride, but has a very long waiting time. The Hill and Dale Dipper costs 77p per minute and has a very short waiting time, so may be considered better value than Squashed. The Rocking Roller Coaster costs 83p per minute, with 15 minutes' waiting time, so comes fourth. The poorest value for money is the Hole of Horror, which costs 90p per minute with 18 minutes' waiting time, and is the shortest ride.

NB: Answers are for the core version. For the support and extension versions see the CD-ROM.

Review
Each day, check the progress of each group and correct any misconceptions. Ask questions such as:
● *Why does this activity use a bar line chart when this activity uses a line graph?*
● *Look at these numbers: 8, 4, 7, 8, 9, 2, 8. Find the mode and the median. Find the mean of the numbers. What advice would you give to someone calculating a mean?*
● *When would you use a calculator? Have any of you needed a calculator to answer the questions?*

Differentiation (Lessons 1-7)
Less confident learners: The children can use the support versions of the activity sheets, with simpler numbers and graph frames with axes and divisions provided.
More confident learners: Expect the children to work with greater independence. They can use extension versions of the activity sheets, with more difficult numbers and more challenging questions.

Lesson 2 (Practise)

Starter
Refine and rehearse: Indicate the randomly displayed weights and measures cards on the board. Ask individual children to find matching pairs such as 1.5l = 1500ml.

Main teaching activities
Ask the children to continue with the carousel of activities (see Lesson 1). Revise when a bar or bar line graph is appropriate and when to use a line graph. (The latter measures something over a period of time, eg temperature of a person in 24 hours.)

Review
Ask the children to consider when finding the mean of a set of data might be useful. (It gives an overall 'snapshot' or measure of data, for example average rainfall in July or 'mean' number of visitors to a zoo each day.)
   Invite a group who have been working on 'The Archimedes Science and Technology Centre' to share their work so far. Ask questions such as: *What was difficult about drawing this graph? Why would it have been inappropriate to draw a line graph for this? Why do you think there were more visitors in some months than in others? How might a graph like this help the Centre to organise its publicity and 'special events'? Who might be interested in this data?*

Lesson 3 (Practise)

Starter
Refine and rehearse: Write up a list of mixed measurements on the board. Ask the children to sort these into sets of measurements and then order them, smallest first: 1.2 litres; 250g; 4000g; 1.5kg; 1.8km; 350m; 650cm; 2000ml; 3500ml; 2.5 litres; 700m; 40g.

Main teaching activities
Ask the children to continue with the carousel of activities (see Lesson 1). Revise 'mode' or most represented or popular result of data. *When might this have practical use?* (For example, to find the most popular chocolate bar sold in a shop or the most representative shoe size or height.)

▷ ### Review

Ask a group who have been working on 'Thrills and spills' to report back about their work to the rest of the class. Then ask: *What sort of graph did you draw? Why? Which of the questions would you have been unable to answer if you had drawn a bar chart?* (The ones that involve reading intermediate points.) *Who might find this information of value?*

Lesson 4 (Practise)

Starter

Refine: Ask the children to convert the mixed measures used in Lesson 3 to smaller units: 1250ml = ? l, 1½kg = ? g; 440cm = ? m; 50mm = ? cm. Revise 1000g = 1kg; 1000ml = 1 litre; 100cm = 1m, and so on.

Main teaching activities

Ask the children to continue with the carousel of activities (see Lesson 1).

Review

Ask a group who have been working on 'Fair's fair?' to report their findings and views. Some other groups who have looked at this activity may have different views, and can be invited to discuss these. Ask: *What facts do we need to look at when deciding which is the 'best' ride? Does it depend on your own preferences? Do some people value the thrill of a longer ride more than not having to wait a long time? How can you calculate the price per minute of a ride?*

Lesson 5 (Practise)

Starter

Revisit: Indicate the probability scale ranging from impossible to certain:

| impossible | unlikely | uncertain | possible | probable | certain |

Pose some scenarios and ask the children to decide where along the scale that they should be placed. For example: *It will rain tomorrow. I will learn to drive a car by the time I am 30. I can score 0 when I throw a die.*

Main teaching activities

Ask the children to continue with the carousel of activities (see Lesson 1). Explain that the children's data handling work will be displayed, and that they need to be able to present their findings to the class as if they were telling the owners of the Science Centre or the Speed and Sound Fair. They will thus need to have clear results and explanations, and be ready to answer questions. They should prepare a statement to go with each activity sheet. A statement might be a comparison of length of ride or value for money or popularity. Ask the children to consider how data can be presented to show the same results in different lights, for example by increasing the vertical scale on a bar chart, differences can be made to look visually bigger. Demonstrate using differences of waiting time on a vertical scale of 1 square = 1 minute and compare this to a vertical scale of 1 square = 5 minutes.

Review

Ask the children to calculate the mean of each set of numbers that you write on the board. Write:
13, 11, 12
4, 5, 3, 2, 4, 2, 1
7, 8, 4, 6, 10, 1
2, 3, 1, 4, 3, 2, 2, 1, 1, 1

The children in each group should work together. At the end of all the calculations, they should try to spot what the mean numbers all have in common. (They are all factors of 12.)

Lesson 6 (Practise)

Starter
Refine: Indicate the probability scale ranging from no chance to definite:

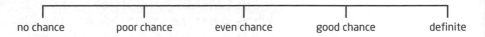

| no chance | poor chance | even chance | good chance | definite |

Make up more statements and ask the children to decide where on the scale they should go. Discuss what an even chance might mean and suggest examples for it. (For example, There is an even chance that Team A might beat Team B.)

Main teaching activities
Ask the children to continue with the carousel of activities (see Lesson 1). With any children who have finished the carousel already, revise or teach other types of diagrams that represent and sort information – for example, Carroll diagrams.

Tell the children: *A group of children were asked what rides they preferred at the fairground. Each child was asked whether they had chosen fast rides or slow rides, with queues of more or less than 15 minutes.* Copy this diagram onto the board:

	Slow fairground rides	Fast fairground rides
Rides with queues of more than 15 minutes	5	35
Rides with queues of less than 15 minutes	40	10

Ask questions such as: *How many children were prepared to queue for longer than 15 minutes for any ride? How many children were questioned altogether?*

Ask the children who have completed the main teaching activities to consider some types of information that a Carroll diagram could sort, such as the contents of lunchboxes on a school trip: egg sandwiches and other sandwiches; brown bread and white bread. Can they draw Carroll diagrams to sort this information?

Review
Invite the children who have been working on Carroll diagrams to display their charts. Ask the class: *What kind of information does this chart give us? Would it be suitable for displaying the number of visitors to a museum each month? Would it be suitable for sorting the number of people visiting the Archimedes Centre or the Speed and Sound Fair? How could we do this?* Demonstrate on the board, using a simple survey:

	Have visited the Archimedes Centre	Have not visited the Archimedes Centre
Have visited the Museum of Speed, Light and Sound	190	120
Have not visited the Museum of Speed, Light and Sound	214	400

BLOCK C

Handling data and measures

Lesson 7 (Apply)

Starter
Reason: Write up the following statement on the board: *I threw a dice ten times. The mode was 4.* Ask the children to explain what this means and to put it into a context. They might wish to demonstrate their meaning using diagrams or charts.

Main teaching activities
Whole class: This lesson should be the culmination of the children's work on handling data. Before the lesson, if possible, select a variety of the children's graphs to copy onto OHT sheets. Use these to allow the children to share their results and findings. Compare the appearance of some graphs that are showing the same information, but look different due to a larger or smaller scale being used on the *y*-axis.
Group/independent work: Ask various groups to present their findings as if they were either the science centre or science fair owners or visitors waiting in a queue. Invite the class to ask each group questions.

Review
Use this session to gather and reinforce all the children's learning about data handling in this unit of work. Ask:
● *Why are graphs and charts useful? When are they most often used? Who might find these graphs and charts useful?*
● *What action might the owner of the science centre want to take after seeing this data? Should visitors be given this kind of data as part of their guide book? Would it encourage or discourage visitors?*
● *Can you think of any other information about the science centre that would be useful?* (For example, a line graph showing price increases over the last five years.) *Who might be interested in this?*
● *Can the 'picture' conveyed by a graph sometimes be deceptive? How? Why might someone want to manipulate the data?*
  Give the children strips of paper to write down what they have learned from this work, or what they know now about data handling that they didn't know before. Display these, or store them as a record.

Differentiation (Lessons 1-7)
Less confident learners: The children can use the support versions of the activity sheets, with simpler numbers and graph frames with axes and divisions provided.
More confident learners: Expect the children to work with greater independence. They can use extension versions of the activity sheets, with more difficult numbers and more challenging questions.

Lessons 8-10

Preparation
Lesson 8: Draw on the board a probability scale showing both words and the decimal fractions.

You will need
Photocopiable pages
'How likely?' (page 134), one per child.
CD resources
'Measuring scales' ITP; 'Measuring jug' interactive resource.
Equipment
Interactive whiteboard; playing cards, coins, coloured counters, dice and so on, for probability.

Learning objectives

Starter
● Find and interpret the mode of a set of data.
● Read, choose, use and record standard metric units to estimate and measure length, weight and capacity to a suitable degree of accuracy, eg the nearest centimetre.
● Interpret a reading that lies between two unnumbered divisions on a scale.

Main teaching activities
2006
● Describe the occurrence of familiar events using the language of chance or likelihood.
1999
● Discuss the chance or likelihood of particular events.

Vocabulary
fair, unfair, risk, doubt, unlikely, likelihood, certain, uncertain, probable, possible, impossible, chance, good chance, poor chance, no chance, outcome

Lesson 8 (Review and teach)

Starter

Reason and recall: Ask the children to work together to find the mode of the ages on their table. Ask them to explain to you how they did it. Write up seven empty squares on the board. Ask for a volunteer to fill the boxes with digits so that the mode of the numbers is 7. Ask: *What advice can you give our volunteer to do this?*

Main teaching activities

Whole class: Remind the children of how they have been expressing probability as a likelihood, using language such as certain or impossible. Practise some examples. Then explain that in different countries, different languages have a variety of words to express likelihood. Probability can however be expressed numerically, as a division of 1.

Indicate the probability scale on the board, showing both the words and decimal fraction version of probability.

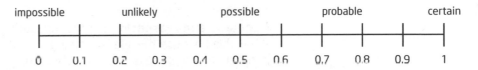

| impossible | unlikely | possible | probable | certain |

0   0.1   0.2   0.3   0.4   0.5   0.6   0.7   0.8   0.9   1

Ask the children to think of some statements and to express the probabilities as decimal fractions, using the number line to help them.

Independent/paired work: Ask the children to draw their own decimal number line from 0 to 1 and to write a list of events for which they can estimate a probability. They should give each event a letter and place it onto their probability number line. For example, if A = 'It will snow tomorrow', the letter A should be placed at 0.2. When they have completed their statements the children should discuss them with a friend to see if they agree with the letter placing.

Review

Review: Ask questions such as: *Tell me an event that would score 1 or 0. How can you decide on an event which will score 0.5? Explain how you decided this.*

Differentiation

This will largely be by outcome and level of adult support. Less confident learners will probably need the support of the written likelihoods whereas more confident learners will be able to just use the numeric scale.

Lesson 9 (Teach)

Starter

Rehearse and reason: Display the 'Measuring scales' ITP from the CD-ROM. Hide the numbers on the scale and ask the children to work out what each of the divisions might represent. Change the maximum weight on the scales and repeat the exercise. Ask: *What difference do you have to calculate?* (For example, the difference between each main division.) *What other information do you need to know?* (The maximum weight or some of the main divisions.) Add some weights to the pan and ask the children to tell you the mass shown.

Main teaching activities

Whole class: Explain that today's lesson continues with probability but this time the children will be predicting expected probability. This is where simple events such as scoring using a spinner or tossing a coin is measurable and is expressed as a fraction. For example, the probability of throwing heads when tossing an ordinary 10p coin is 1 chance out of a possible 2. That is ½. All expected probability events can be expressed in this way since:

expected probability = the number of ways an event can happen
the number of possible outcomes

BLOCK C Handling data and measures

Demonstrate this again by throwing an ordinary, 'fair' dice. The probability of throwing a 2 is $^1/_6$.

Paired work: Indicate to the children the items that you have provided for finding a probability. Ask them to write probability statements about these items, for example: There is a $^4/_{52}$ (or $^1/_{13}$) chance of picking a king from a pack of playing cards.

Review
Share the statements made by the children and demonstrate how these can be proved. Ask: *How would you label a blank dice so that the probability of obtaining an odd number is $^5/_6$? How do you know?* Show the children a plastic wallet or bag containing three blue counters, two red counters and one green counter. Invite the children to make statements about the probability of picking each colour and ask them to explain how they worked them out.

Lesson 10 (Practise)

Starter
Rehearse and reason: Repeat the measuring scale activity from Lesson 9 but this time use the 'Measuring jug' interactive resource. Again hide the numbers on the scale and ask the children, given the maximum capacity of the measuring cylinder, to work out how much the smaller divisions are worth. Change the scale several times. Then partially fill the cylinder and ask them to read the amount either in millilitres or litres.

Main teaching activities
Whole class: Remind the children about the probability work undertaken so far. Ask some revision questions such as: *What is the probability of this class having PE today? If I spin a 1-8 spinner, what is the probability of landing on an even number?* Explain that they are going to answer some questions to show that they can express a probability as both a decimal fraction and a fraction.

Independent work: Distribute the activity sheet 'How likely?' and ask the children to work through the problems.

Review
Share some of the more difficult answers from the sheet and discuss how they were solved. Ask: *If I threw two coins together what is the probability of throwing two heads?* Explain how you worked it out.

Differentiation
Less confident learners: These children will need to actually use the items provided to test the probability - for example, they will need to actually flip the coin to understand the chances of throwing a head.
More confident learners: These children should be able to predict more adventurous probabilities such as the chances of picking a red king or a black card or a picture card.

Differentiation
Less confident learners: These children may need some apparatus in front of them, such as coloured counters, and additional adult support.
More confident learners: These children may be able to go on to solve the extension activity on the sheet.

■ SCHOLASTIC

Name _____   Date _____

The Archimedes Science and Technology Centre

Use the information in the table to draw a bar line graph on a sheet of squared paper, showing the number of visitors to the Archimedes Science and Technology Centre in each month of a year. Label the vertical axis with two blocks for every 10,000 people.

Month	No. of visitors	Month	No. of visitors
January	25,000	July	40,000
February	20,000	August	45,000
March	18,000	September	30,000
April	25,000	October	25,000
May	40,000	November	17,000
June	38,000	December	15,000

Use your graph to answer the questions below.

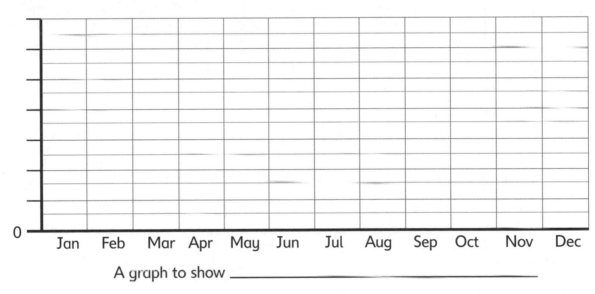

A graph to show _____

1. Which was the most popular month for visiting the centre? Why do you think that?

_____

2. Which was the least popular month? Why?

_____

3. How many more people visited the centre in the most popular three months than in the least popular three months?

_____

4. What is the range of this data?

_____

5. Why would it not be appropriate to represent this data as a line graph?

_____

Name _____   Date _____

Thrills and spills

Look at this graph for the Rocking Roller Coaster.

On the same set of axes, plot a line graph to show the speeds reached by the Hill and Dale Dipper, which also lasts for three minutes. The data you need is in the table below.

A graph to show _____

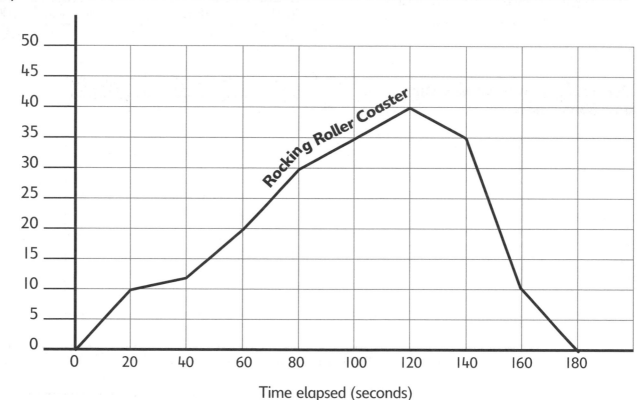

Hill and Dale Dipper

Time (secs)	Speed (mph)
0	0
20	5
40	15
60	28
80	38
100	42
120	42
140	50
160	30
180	0

Use the information on the graph to answer these questions.

1. Give the graph a title.

2. Use a calculator to find the mean speed for each ride. Show how you did it.

3. What was the approximate speed of each ride at 70 seconds?

4. What was the approximate speed of each ride at 30 seconds?

Name _____ Date _____

Fair's fair?

Look at the table of data below.

Draw one comparative bar chart to show the average queuing time and the ride length for five rides at the Science Fair. Use one big square of graph paper for every five minutes.

Ride	Queuing time (minutes)	Length of ride (minutes)	Cost
Rocking Roller Coaster	15	3	£2.50
Hole of Horror	18	2	£1.80
Squashed	25	5	£3.00
Wall of Fear	10	10	£2.70
Hill and Dale Dipper	5	3	£2.30

Now consider the cost of each ride. Use all your data to write a short report, comparing the rides in terms of value for money. List the five rides in order of preference, stating your reasons.

Child's report

BLOCK C

Handling data and measures

Name _____ Date _____

How likely?

1. Kit picked one card at random from a pack of 52. Write down the probability that he will pick:

   a) a ten _____ **b)** a red card _____

   c) a heart _____ **d)** the ace of diamonds _____

2. A bag contains two white counters, five red counters, three blue counters and one green counter. Write down the probability of picking out:

   a) a green counter _____ **b)** a red counter _____

   c) a white counter _____ **d)** a black counter _____

3. Jill says that there is a probability of 0.2 that the weather will be sunny and warm tomorrow. Tom disagrees and says that the probability is more likely to be 1. Who, if either of them, is correct? _____

   _____

4. There are three toffees and one mint left in a bag of sweets. Alfie says that the probability of picking the mint is $\frac{1}{3}$ because there are three toffees and only one mint.

   Is he correct? _____

5. There are two spinners, one showing numbers one to six and the other displaying numbers one to seven. Erin says that she is more likely to throw an odd number with the one to seven spinner. Do you agree? Explain what you think. Is she more likely to throw an even number with either spinner?

   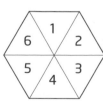

   _____

   _____

   _____

   _____

   Extension task

   Three coins, a 10p, a 20p and a 2p, are tossed together. Write down all the possible combinations that can be thrown. Is there a stronger probability of throwing any one combination? Explain your answers.

   _____

   _____

Calculating, measuring and understanding shape

Key aspects of learning
- Information processing
- Social skills
- Problem solving
- Evaluation
- Communication
- Creative thinking

Expected prior learning
Check that children can already:
- talk about their methods and solutions to one- and two-step problems
- partition, round and order four-digit whole numbers and decimals to two places, and use decimal notation to record measurements, eg 1.3m or 0.6kg
- multiply and divide numbers to 1000 by 10 and 100 (whole-number answers)
- use written methods to add and subtract two- and three-digit whole numbers and £.p, and to multiply and divide two-digit numbers by a one-digit number, including division with remainders, eg 15 × 9, 98 ÷ 6
- know that addition is the inverse of subtraction and that multiplication is the inverse of division, and vice versa
- use a calculator to carry out one- and two-step calculations involving all four operations
- know that angles are measured in degrees and that one whole turn is 360°
- read scales to the nearest tenth of a unit
- measure and calculate perimeters of rectangles and find the area of shapes drawn on a square grid by counting squares
- read time to the nearest minute; use am, pm and 12-hour clock notation, and calculate time intervals from clocks and timetables.

Objectives overview
The text in this diagram identifies the focus of mathematics learning within the block.

Solving multi-step problems, using a calculator where appropriate

Estimating and checking results

Estimating and measuring, weight, length, capacity

Readings from scales

Time: 24-hour clock, timetables, calendar

Estimating, measuring and drawing angles

Angles in a straight line

Drawing shapes with parallel and perpendicular lines

Block D: Calculating, measuring and understanding shape

Multiplication and division by 10, 100, 1000

Addition/subtraction of whole numbers and decimals

HTU × U, TU × U, U.t × U and HTU/U

Area and perimeter of regular/irregular polygons

Formula for area of rectangle

Coordinates

Two lines of symmetry

Reflection, translation

Unit 1 ▇ 2 weeks

Calculating, measuring and understanding shape

Speaking and listening objectives

- Plan and manage a group task over time by using different levels of planning.

Introduction

The first three lessons of this unit deal with measurement in the form of time and introduce children to calculating time using the 24-hour clock. The following two lessons are on shape, and using coordinates to draw shapes. There are opportunities for children to use their knowledge of common and regular shape to reason about positioning and to work out unknown coordinates. There may be a difference of opinion from one child to another about how to approach this task and there are opportunities for speaking and listening as children describe their thinking.

The final set of lessons in this unit deals with finding areas of squares and rectangles and those of composite shapes. Again, children may have to plan their way of working and explain how they solved a problem.

Lesson	Strands	Starter	Main teaching activities
1. Teach	Measure	Solve one- and two-step problems involving whole numbers and decimals and all four operations, choosing and using appropriate calculation strategies, including calculator use.	Read timetables and time using 24-hour clock notation; use a calendar to calculate time intervals.
2. Practise	Measure	Use understanding of place value to multiply and divide whole numbers and decimals by 10, 100 or 1000.	As for Lesson 1
3. Apply	Measure	Solve one- and two-step problems involving whole numbers and decimals and all four operations, choosing and using appropriate calculation strategies, including calculator use.	As for Lesson 1
4. Review and teach	Shape	As for Lesson 3	**Read and plot coordinates in the first quadrant; recognise parallel and perpendicular lines in grids and shapes; use a set-square and ruler to draw shapes with perpendicular or parallel sides.**
5. Practise	Shape	As for Lesson 3	As for Lesson 4
6. Teach	Measure	Interpret a reading that lies between two unnumbered divisions on a scale.	**Draw and measure lines to the nearest millimetre; measure and calculate the perimeter of regular and irregular polygons; use the formula for the area of a rectangle to calculate the rectangle's area.**
7. Teach and practise	Measure	Use a calculator to solve problems, including those involving decimals or fractions, eg to find ¾ of 150g; interpret the display correctly in the context of measurement.	As for Lesson 6
8. Practise	Measure	**Read and plot coordinates in the first quadrant; recognise parallel and perpendicular lines in grids and shapes; use a set-square and ruler to draw shapes with perpendicular or parallel sides.**	As for Lesson 6
9. Practise	Measure	As for Lesson 8	As for Lesson 6
10. Apply	Measure	Read, choose, use and record standard metric units to estimate and measure length, weight and capacity to a suitable degree of accuracy, eg the nearest centimetre; convert larger to smaller units using decimals to one place, eg change 2.6kg to 2600g.	As for Lesson 6

■SCHOLASTIC

Use and apply mathematics

● Solve one- and two-step problems involving whole numbers and decimals and all four operations, choosing and using appropriate calculation strategies, including calculator use.

Lessons 1-3

Preparation
Obtain some train and bus timetables. Photocopy these to provide one copy of each type of table for each pair of children. Obtain permission from the station manager before taking the timetables, and contact the travel company to obtain permission before photocopying them.
Lesson 1: Write on the board the word problems for the starter.
Lesson 2: Write on the board the word problem for the main activity.

You will need
Photocopiable pages
'A day in the life' (page 145), 'Time and tide' (page 146) and 'Steam train times' (page 147), one per child.
CD resources
Support and extension versions of 'A day in the life', 'Time and tide' and 'Steam train times'. General resource sheets: '24-hour clock', for support; 'Number fan cards 0–9', one per child; 'Number cards 1–100', cards 10–90; and 0–9 digit cards, for teacher use.
Equipment
Clock faces; train or bus timetables.

Learning objectives

Starter
● Solve one- and two-step problems involving whole numbers and decimals and all four operations, choosing and using appropriate calculation strategies, including calculator use.
● Use understanding of place value to multiply and divide whole numbers and decimals by 10, 100 or 1000.

Main teaching activities
2006
● Read timetables and time using 24-hour clock notation; use a calendar to calculate time intervals.
1999
● Read the time on a 24-hour digital clock and use 24-hour clock notation, such as 19:53. Use timetables.
● Solve word problems involving time.
● Use a calendar (Year 4).

Vocabulary
operation, calculation, calculate, multiply, divide, days of the week, months of the year, second (s), minute (min), hour (h), day, month, calendar, timetable, 12-hour clock, 24-hour clock, am and pm

Lesson 1 (Teach)

Starter
Recall: Indicate the word problems shown below, written on the board. Ask the children to solve them and use their number fans to show the answer. Discuss the operations and methods the children have used.

Work out these numbers:

1. Angie has an apple tree in her garden. She picks 96 apples. She stores one-third of them and gives half of what is left to her friend. The remainder she puts in her fruit bowl.
2. On my sweet stall at the school fair, I started with 206 bags of sweets. I have only 39 left. How many bags did I sell?
3. Frankie read four books, each of which had 89 pages. How many pages did he read altogether?

Main teaching activities
Whole class: Explain to the children that they are going to use the 24-hour clock to tell the time. There are 24 hours in each day and night, from midnight of one day to midnight of the following day. Instead of using two lots of 12 hours to tell the time, dividing them into 'am' and 'pm' (as we commonly do), the 24-hour clock uses a continuous increase in the number of hours up to 24. So 1:00pm is 13:00 hours, 2:00pm is 14:00 hours and so on. Time in 'am' and 'pm' is modelled on the analogue clock (with hands), which measures only 12 hours. The 24-hour digital clock does not need to have 'am' or 'pm' added.

Ask the children to work out some o'clock times in the 24-hour system: *What is 8pm?... 8am?... 4pm?... 10pm?... 9pm?... 5am?...* Check that they understand that to work out the 24-hour equivalent of a 12-hour time, we keep the first 12 hours of the day (from midnight to midday) at exactly the same number, but calculate the second 12 hours by adding 12 to the hour. For example, 4pm is 12 + 4 = 16:00 hours. Discuss the notation: hours come first, then minutes, so '16:00 hours' means 16 hours and no minutes.

Independent work: Distribute copies of the 'A day in the life' activity sheet to the children. Explain to them that the diagram on the sheet represents a whole day divided into 24 hours. Ask them to fill in the space for each hour by drawing what they might be doing at that time in a typical school day: eating lunch at 12:00, playing with a friend at 17:00, watching television at 19:00 and so on.

Review

Ask the children:
- *What might you be doing at 16:00 hours?... 21:00?... 7:00? What about 10:30?... 18:15?*
- *How many hours are there in a day and a night?*
- *Tell me these times using the 24-hour clock: 6.30am; 5.30pm; 9.45pm; 11.50pm; 4.35am; 7.15pm.*
- *Tell me these times using 12-hour am or pm time: 13:00; 02:45; 16:20; 17:35; 23:15; 19:30; 06:30.* Turn this into a 'Stand up, sit down' game: you say a time and the children stand up if it is in 12-hour time and sit down if it is in 24-hour time. For example, they would sit when you said 06:00 and stand when you said 6.45pm.

Lesson 2 (Practise)

Starter

Refine: Invite three volunteers to stand at the board: one to multiply by 10, one by 100 and one by 1000. Pick a one place decimal number using the digit cards and ask the three children to record their answers. Ask the class: *Can you tell me a quick rule that they might use to multiply?* (Move the digits up in place value by the number of zeros in the multiple, using zeros to hold the place value.) Repeat multiplying then dividing by 10, 100 and 1000: 98 × 100 = 9800; 9800 ÷ 10 = 980.

Main teaching activities

Whole class: Indicate the following word problem on the board or OHP: *I start watching a programme at 19:30 and it ends at 20:45. How long is the programme?*

Ask the children how they would work out an answer. Take suggestions. Explain that standard written subtraction is not suitable for this problem – it may be tempting when the numbers are written vertically, but it won't give the right answer. Ask: *Can you suggest reasons why it doesn't work?* (Hours are calculated as multiples of 60 minutes rather than in base 10.) Encourage the children to count on in minutes to the next whole hour from the earlier time, and then count on in hours. Suggest that informal jottings are a good way to keep track. For example: 19:30 + 30 minutes = 20:00 and then 45 minutes = 20:45. So time elapsed is 30 + 45 minutes = 1 hour and 15 minutes.' Repeat this with a second example:

Programme begins: 21:30
Programme ends: 22:15

Independent work: Provide the activity sheet 'Time and Tide', which presents questions on time involving the 24-hour clock. The final challenge for the children is to write a time question for a partner to answer.

Review

Ask the children: *If a train left Waterloo station at 12:35 and arrived at Cambridge 1 hour and 25 minutes later, at what time did it arrive?* Discuss whether in this instance it is easier to add on the hours or the minutes first. Give each pair of children one copy of a timetable. Ask them to calculate the time taken for each stage of a journey, using the counting on method. Go

Differentiation

Less confident learners: Give the group a copy of '24-hour clock' to help them convert 12-hour to 24-hour times.
More confident learners: Encourage the children to subdivide the hours into halves and perhaps quarters, so they can indicate times such as 14:30 and 17:45.

Differentiation

Less confident learners: Provide the support version, which involves calculating in whole and half hours only.
More confident learners: Provide the extension version, which uses calculations with more difficult numbers of minutes.

through a timetable as a class, asking individuals to count on aloud.

Lesson 3 (Apply)

Starter
Rehearse: Play 'Pairs to 100'. Distribute the number cards 10–90 randomly among the children. Ask for one child to hold up a number card and call out its value. The child holding the number that adds to the first number to make 100 calls it out, then offers another number from his or her cards. This continues until all the pairs have been found. Once all a child's cards have been used, they must continue to follow the game, checking the accuracy of the pairs making 100.

Main teaching activities
Whole class: Distribute the copies of the timetables you have collected. Discuss with the children how each timetable is arranged, with places and times cross-referenced. You could also discuss how timetables become more complicated when there are weekend and holiday variations. Explain that timetables always use the 24-hour clock to avoid confusion between morning and evening times (for example, 6pm and 6:00 hours). Build the children's confidence in using timetables by asking some simple questions, such as: *What time does the bus leave Warwick? At what time should it arrive at Coventry? How long does the journey take?* Ask the children to make up some questions to challenge the class.
Independent work: Distribute the 'Steam train times' activity sheet. Explain that this sheet presents a timetable; the children have to plan a route and answer some questions, using the 24-hour clock.

Review
Ask for volunteers to describe their planned journey and challenge the rest of the class to calculate how long it will take. Look for consistency in the length of time allocated for a given distance, and sensible judgements about the length of time spent at each place. Check the accuracy of the time calculations (problems often occur with bridging through an hour).

Differentiation
Less confident learners: Provide the support version, on which the journeys take only whole hours and half hours.
More confident learners: Provide the extension version, with times that have more awkward numbers of minutes.

Lessons 4-5

Preparation
Lesson 4: List ten multiples of 50 on the board. Copy the 'Blank axes' resource sheet onto OHT.
Lesson 5: List ten different multiples of 50 on the board. Draw on the board a set of unlabelled axes. Enlarge the 'What's the point?' activity sheet to A3 for support.

You will need
CD resources
Extension version of 'What's the point?'. General resource sheet: 'Blank axes'.

Learning objectives

Starter
● Solve one- and two-step problems involving whole numbers and decimals and all four operations, choosing and using appropriate calculation strategies, including calculator use.

Main teaching activities
2006
● Read and plot coordinates in the first quadrant; recognise parallel and perpendicular lines in grids and shapes; use a set-square and ruler to draw shapes with perpendicular or parallel sides.
1999
● Read and plot coordinates in the first quadrant.
● Recognise perpendicular and parallel lines.

Vocabulary
coordinates, *x*-axis, *y*-axis, *x*-coordinate, *y*-coordinate

Lesson 4 (Review and teach)

Starter
Rehearse: Indicate the list of ten multiples of 50 on the board. Ask the children to write down, against the clock, the numbers that add to them to make 1000 (for example: 200 + 800, 350 + 650, 550 + 450). Ask for answers around the room.

Main teaching activities
Whole class: On an OHT of 'Blank axes' resource sheet, show the children the way coordinates are labelled and written with the x-axis first and then the y-axis with a coordinate written in brackets. Demonstrate some points (in the first quadrant) and ask the children to name the coordinates. Demonstrate how a shape can be drawn if the coordinates are marked and joined up in the order they are written. Draw a square and note down the coordinates as you go. Join up the coordinate points using a ruler.
Individual work: Distribute copies of the 'Blank axes' sheet. Ask the children to mark the points of the coordinates for several shapes (in the first quadrant) and note them down as a list at the bottom of the page. They should join up the points on their own drawing to show the shapes and also label the coordinates.

Review
Ask the children to swap work and check the coordinate lists for each other. Ask: *What do you notice about the coordinates that are perpendicular to the x-axis? If I draw a square which has the coordinates (3, 7) for the bottom left hand corner, what does that tell you about the x-coordinate of the top left hand corner? Can you tell me part of another of the coordinates? Which one? How do you know?*

Differentiation
Less confident learners: These children may find it helpful if you provide coordinates of shapes for them to mark on their grid.
More confident learners: These children should be more adventurous with the shapes they are able to produce and may be able to use all four quadrants.

Lesson 5 (Practise)

Starter
Rehearse: Repeat the starter from Lesson 4, using a new list of ten multiples of 50. Can the children improve their score against the clock?

Main teaching activities
Whole class: Explain that today's lesson carries on from Lesson 4. The children are going to have to work out the missing coordinates of regular shapes from ones that are given. Draw a pair of axes on the board. Do not label them with numbers but draw a rectangle on the diagram. Label the bottom left hand corner as (2, 1) and the top right hand corner as (4, 5). Ask the children to work out how they can label the missing coordinates. Guide them by reminding them that coordinates along a line perpendicular with an axis will all be the same. They may also need reminding that the x-coordinate always comes first.
Individual work: Distribute the 'What's the point?' worksheet and ask the children to fill in the missing coordinates.

Review
Share difficulties or successes. Ask: *Could we write a rule or a set of instructions to help us remember how to do this?* (For example, coordinates along the perpendicular to the axis line will always be the same.)

Differentiation
Less confident learners: These children will need to work together as a group on an enlarged version of the activity sheet with adult guidance.
More confident learners: These children can work on the extension version of the activity sheet, which includes questions without the support of a diagram.

Lessons 6-10

Preparation

Photocopy squared paper onto OHT.
Lesson 6: Make an OHT of a rectangle and a polygon divided into square centimetres.
Lesson 7: Write on the board the calculation for the starter.
Lesson 8: Photocopy the 'Blank axes' resource sheet onto OHT.
Lesson 9: Draw on the board or OHT a set of unlabelled axes.
Lesson 10: Write on the board the word problem for the main activity.

You will need

CD resources
Core and extension versions of 'Count the area'; support and extension versions of 'Calculate the area'.
Equipment
Variety of length measuring equipment: ruler, tape measure, metre stick, and so on; calculators; squared paper.

Learning objectives

Starter

● Interpret a reading that lies between two unnumbered divisions on a scale.
● Use a calculator to solve problems, including those involving decimals or fractions, eg to find ¾ of 150g; interpret the display correctly in the context of measurement.
● Read and plot coordinates in the first quadrant; recognise parallel and perpendicular lines in grids and shapes; use a set-square and ruler to draw shapes with perpendicular or parallel sides.
● Read, choose, use and record standard metric units to estimate and measure length, weight and capacity to a suitable degree of accuracy, eg the nearest centimetre; convert larger to smaller units using decimals to one place, eg change 2.6kg to 2600g.

Main teaching activities

2006
● Draw and measure lines to the nearest millimetre; measure and calculate the perimeter of regular and irregular polygons; use the formula for the area of a rectangle to calculate its area.
1999
● Measure and draw lines to the nearest millimetre.
● Measure and calculate perimeters of rectangles and regular polygons.
● Understand area measured in square centimetres (cm²); use the formula for the area of a rectangle.

Vocabulary

measure, measurement, measuring scale, scales, balance, metre stick, tape measure, ruler, measuring cylinder, metric unit, standard unit, length, distance, perimeter, area, surface area, mass, weight, capacity, units of measurement and their abbreviations

Lesson 6 (Teach)

Starter

Rehearse: Provide a variety of length measuring equipment. Ask: *How tall am I?* Invite all of the children to estimate first and then ask for two volunteers to come and measure. Discuss with the class when there is an issue of a split scale or reading an unmarked scale. Repeat using: *How long is this pen? What is the width of the room? What is the girth or circumference of the bin?*

Main teaching activities

Whole class: Show the children your OHT of a rectangle divided up into square centimetres. Explain that the squares cover the 2D space on the page enclosed by the rectangle. This is known as the area of the rectangle. By counting the squares, we can calculate how much area the rectangle covers. Count the squares all together and record as A = ____cm². Explain that area is measured in square centimetres or cm² because the rectangle can be measured in two ways: length and breadth (width). A line in one direction is measured in cm, but an area is covered by square centimetres. One square centimetre is a square 1cm long and 1cm wide.
    Repeat this, using the other polygon on your OHT.
Independent work: Distribute the 'Count the area' activity sheet. Explain that these are 2D shapes divided into square centimetres. Ask the children to find the area that each shape covers by counting the squares.

Differentiation

Less confident learners: Provide additional support. It may help the children to keep count of the squares if they tick off or colour each square.
More confident learners: Provide also the extension version of 'Count the area', with composite shapes, and with half-squares to count.

Differentiation

Less confident learners: If the children find the calculation difficult, they can find the area by counting the squares. They may also need assistance to draw the shapes accurately.
More confident learners: The children could be encouraged to draw composite shapes made up of two or more different squares or rectangles joined together, find the area of each section and then add them to find the total area.

Review

Using squared paper, shade a rectangle 6cm by 7cm. Ask:
● *What unit do we use to measure area? Can you explain why area is measured in square centimetres?*
● *What is the area of this shape? How do you know? By counting the squares? Can anybody suggest a quicker way to find the number of squares?* (Multiplying the number of squares across by the number down. So 6cm × 7cm = 42cm².)

Draw several more squares and rectangles on squared paper. For each one, ask the children to supply a number sentence that gives the area.

Lesson 7 (Teach and practise)

Starter

Refine and reason: Write up the following calculation on the board:
$150 - \underline{\quad} \rightarrow 78 \div \underline{\quad} \rightarrow 26 \div \underline{\quad} \rightarrow 2.6$

Ask the children to use a calculator to work out the missing numbers and to record on whiteboards or rough paper. Ask them to explain their strategies and the presses that they made.

Repeat with:
$19 - \underline{\quad} \rightarrow 7.9 \times \underline{\quad} \rightarrow 790 \div \underline{\quad} \rightarrow 158$

Main teaching activities

Whole class: Remind the children of how they found areas by counting square centimetres in Lesson 6. Explain that for squares and rectangles, the area can be calculated as length × breadth. Draw a rectangle and label the sides 2cm and 6cm. Apply the formula: area = 2cm × 6cm = 12cm². Check your answer by asking the children to count the squares. Repeat using a number of different squares and rectangles.
Independent work: Ask the children to draw some squares and rectangles on 1cm squared paper (using the printed lines), then measure the sides and apply the length × breadth formula to find the area. They should record the area, then check it by counting the squares.

Review

Check the understanding of how to calculate area by drawing and labelling several rectangles and asking the children to find the area of each. Draw a composite shape such as an 'L' shape, and ask: *How can we find the area if the shape is not a rectangle?* (If it has straight sides, we may be able to divide it into squares and rectangles.) Demonstrate that the 'L' shape is made up of two rectangles. Find the area of each rectangle, then add them together. Repeat with another composite shape.

Lesson 8 (Practise)

Starter

Revisit: On an OHT of the 'Blank axes' resource sheet, ask the children to tell you the way coordinates are labelled and written. Demonstrate some points on the grid and ask the children to name the coordinates. Then say that you are going to give the coordinates of a shape and ask the children to guess what the shape is. Ask for a volunteer to mark the coordinate points as you say them. (2, 1), (3, 3), (4, 1) gives the outline of an equilateral triangle. (5, 2), (4, 4), (2, 4), (3, 2) gives the shape of a parallelogram.

Main teaching activities

Whole class: Draw a rectangle on the board and explain that this represents a field. Label the sides as 4m and 3m. Ask the children to find the area (12m²). Now label the sides 4m and 320cm. Ask the children whether they can see a difficulty with finding this area (there are mixed units). Explain that combining two different units means that the calculation will be incorrect, so we need to make sure that both sides are measured in the same unit: either

4m × 3.2m or 400cm × 320cm. Remind the children that they can partition to help them multiply decimals or multiples of 100. In this case, 4 × 3 = 12 and 4 × 0.2 = 0.8, so area = 12.8m². Alternatively, 400 × 300 = 120,000 and 400 × 20 = 8000, so area =128,000cm². (This value would have to be divided by 10,000 to convert it back to m².)

Repeat this, using other mixed units such as cm and mm or km and m.
Independent work: Distribute the 'Calculate the area' activity sheet. Ask the children to look very carefully at the units of measurement, and to convert each pair of lengths to the same unit before finding the area of each shape.

Review

Draw a rectangle with the sides labelled 2.3m and 300cm. Write in the middle: 'Area = 6.9cm²'. Ask: *Is this area correct? Why not? How can we put it right? What tips would you give to someone who wanted to find the area of this shape?*

Draw a rectangle and label its area as 12m². Ask: *What lengths might the sides be? Is there more than one possible answer? Why?* List all the possible answers. Repeat with another rectangle with the area 18cm² and a square with the area 16cm².

Differentiation
Less confident learners: Provide the support version of the activity sheet, on which the units do not need to be standardised.
More confident learners: Provide the extension version, which involves finding the areas of composite shapes as well as converting units.

Lesson 9 (Practise)

Starter

Refine: On an unnumbered set of axes draw a square with two of the four coordinates labelled. Ask the children to work out what the missing coordinates are from the position on the grid and from the given coordinates. For example, draw a 3 × 3 square and mark on the coordinates (1, 1), (1, 4). The remaining coordinates are (4, 4) and (4, 1). Discuss how the children could work this out, either by using the knowledge of the length of one side and adding 3 onto each of the given coordinates, or by noting the *x*-coordinate for one point and applying the same to the next point, in line with it on the *y*-axis and the same for the other point.

Main teaching activities

Whole class: Ask the children to think about the area of the classroom floor, their living room and bathroom floors, and the playground. Ask: *What units would it be measured in? How would you measure it?* Ask the children to estimate each area.

Now ask: *If the answer is 24cm², what could the question be?* Take suggestions (such as 'What is the area of a rectangle with the sides measuring 2cm and 12cm?') and record some on the board. Repeat with: *If the answer is 1.5l, what could the question be?* Write the answer in the centre of a spidergram and record a variety of questions. As a class, generate more questions and answers on a measures theme.

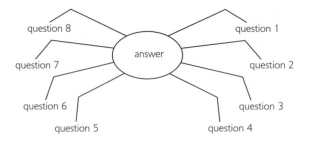

Paired work: The children can work in pairs to generate another three answers each, then swap and write eight possible questions to match each answer.

Differentiation

Less confident learners: Provide answers (such as 25cm, 12cm², 3 litres, 32m², 1500g, 1000ml) for this group to match with questions.
More confident learners: Ask this group to suggest two-step questions. For example, if the answer is 4.2m², the question could be: 'If one of the sides of a rectangle is 0.7m and the other is 600cm, convert them to a common unit and find the area.'

Review

Write on the board: 64.2cm × 5. Ask the children to imagine that they work in a DIY store, and this is a problem they need to solve. Ask them to note down a possible scenario that requires this calculation. Share some ideas and record them for a display. Ask: *Is there another way this answer could have been reached? Could you change your question to make a two-step problem?* For example: 'I am making five bookshelves for my bedroom. Each shelf has to be 64.2cm long to fit into an alcove. How much wood will I need to buy? If wood costs £5 a metre, how much will I need to spend?'

Repeat using (£20 + £17) × 5. Ask the children to write a two-step problem and explain how they would solve it.

Lesson 10 (Apply)

Starter

Recall and rehearse: Ask the children to record on whiteboards or scrap paper something that could be sensibly measured in cm, mm, m or km. Ask: *Why do we use different units of measure for different things? Could we measure the distance to Spain in centimetres?* (Yes, but it would be a very big number.) *What about the length of my pencil point measured in km?* (Again yes, but it would be a very small decimal number.) Ask: *What unit of measure would you choose to measure the perimeter of the playground? … a track for an athletics event? … The length of a minibeast?* Also ask: *If a millipede is 28mm long, what would that be in centimetres or metres?* (2.8cm; 0.028m.)

Main teaching activities

Whole class: Repeat the initial whole-class activity from Lesson 9, but focus on smaller areas in the classroom such as the cover of an exercise book, the cover of an atlas and a lunchbox lid.

Write the following problem on the board:
- A farmer has a field 6m long and 9m wide. What is its total area?
- He then buys a smaller square field adjoining the first one, with a side length of 4m. What is the total area of the farmer's land?

Ask a child to visualise and draw the two adjoining fields (with a shared boundary line), and to label the sides of each field. The drawings should be to scale with the scale marked clearly as a key (for example, 1cm = 1m). Remind the children that the l × b formula only works for squares and rectangles, so the areas of the two fields need to be calculated separately and then added together.

Group and individual work: Ask the children, working in pairs, to measure the dimensions and calculate the areas of the classroom objects discussed in the whole-class session. They should draw the shapes to scale, being very careful to draw as accurately as they can and to mark on the scale. Ask: *How did you work out the area? Was it close to your original estimate? What units does the area have?* Ask them to write the calculation as an l × b sum.

Differentiation

Less confident learners: Provide shapes which have whole cm measurements. Children can find the areas of them, using the straightforward l × b formula.
More confident learners: Ask children to estimate and measure composite shapes such as the area of carpet in the classroom.

Review

Recap on the children's understanding of area. Ask: *How can I find the area of a rectangle? What is the formula or rule that we use?* Now draw a shape consisting of a joined square and rectangle. Ask: *How can we find the area of this shape? Why can it not be solved using one calculation?*

6m × 9m = 54m²
4m × 4m = <u>16m²</u>
total area = 70m²

Name _____   Date _____

A day in the life

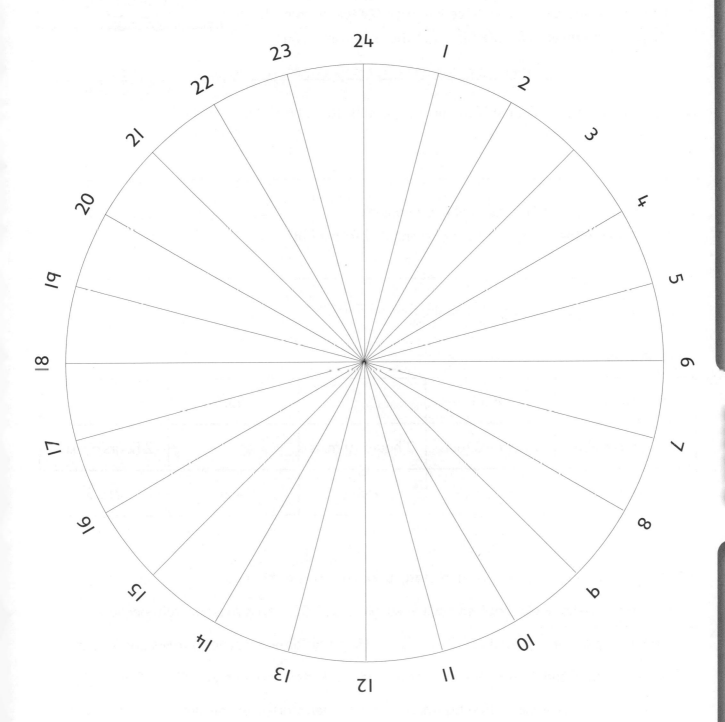

Calculating, measuring and understanding shape

Name _____   Date _____

Time and tide

1. Tim started watching Space Race Aliens on the television at 20:15. The programme lasts for 50 minutes. What time will it end?

_____

2. Ellen wants to go sailing at high tide. It is now 14:10 and high tide is at 17:30. How long will she have to wait?

_____

3. A fruit cake takes two and a half hours to cook. If I put it into the oven at 11:45, when should I take it out?

_____

4. Look at the chart below and fill in the missing times:

FILM TIMES

Time film starts:	18:35		12:45	
Duration of film:	1 hour 20 mins	2 hours 10 mins		2 hours 5 mins
Film ends at:		15:05	14:20	21:55

5. Fill in the missing times in this short story, using the clues to help you.

The time traveller looked at his watch. It said it was 17:55, which must be right because

ten minutes ago it had read _____ . He set his time machine to travel backwards

in time 8 hours and 25 minutes. He arrived and checked his watch again. Good! It read

_____ . He completed his transaction and then started to calculate how far forward

in time he must travel to be home in time for the news at 22:00. He needed to travel forwards

_____ .

Now make up some time questions of your own.

Calculating, measuring and understanding shape

BLOCK D

Name _____ Date _____

Steam train times

The following timetable is for a holiday steam train that runs up and down the coast.

Use the timetable to plan a day's excursion, visiting various places on the way.

Answer the questions below the timetable.

Sunnyville Steam Trains

Sunnyville	Depart	10:20	12:30	15:00
Theme park	Arrive	10:30	12:40	15:10
	Depart	10:35	12:45	15:15
Zoo	Arrive	11:25	13:35	16:05
	Depart	11:30	13:40	16:10
Beach	Arrive	11:55	14:05	16:35
	Depart	12:05	14:15	16:45
Quad bike centre	Arrive	12:20	14:30	17:00
	Depart	12:25	14:35	17:05
Bowling	Arrive	12:40	14:50	17:20
	Depart for Sunnyville	12:50	15:00	17:30
Sunnyville	Arrive	14:45	16:55	19:25

Plan your day out. Where would you like to go? Write down your expected arrival times, how long you will stay at each place and your return departure time.

Questions to answer

1. How long does it take the train to get from Sunnyville to the theme park? _____

2. How long does it take to get from the zoo to the quad bike centre? _____

3. How long is the entire outward journey to the bowling centre? _____

4. How long does it take to return to Sunnyville from the bowling centre? _____

5. What is the maximum amount of time I can spend at the beach if I am travelling by train from Sunnyville and back again? _____

Calculating, measuring and understanding shape

Lesson	Strands	Starter	Main teaching activities
1. Review	Measure Knowledge	**Draw and measure lines to the nearest millimetre; measure and calculate the perimeter of regular and irregular polygons; use the formula for the area of a rectangle to calculate the rectangle's area.**	• **Draw and measure lines to the nearest millimetre; measure and calculate the perimeter of regular and irregular polygons; use the formula for the area of a rectangle to calculate the rectangle's area.** • Recall quickly multiplication facts up to 10 × 10, use to multiply pairs of multiples of 10 and 100 and derive corresponding division facts. (Revision of Block B)
2. Review and teach	Use/apply Calculate	As for Lesson 1	• Solve one- and two-step problems involving whole numbers and decimals and all four operations, choosing and using appropriate calculation strategies, including calculator use. • Refine and use efficient written methods to multiply and divide HTU × U, TU × TU, U.t × U, and HTU ÷ U.
3. Review and teach	Use/apply Calculate	• As for Lesson 1 • Use a calculator to solve problems, including those involving decimals or fractions, eg to find ¾ of 150g; interpret the display correctly in the context of measurement.	As for Lesson 2
4. Practise	Use/apply Calculate	As for Lesson 1	As for Lesson 2
5. Apply	Use/apply Knowledge Calculate	As for Lesson 1	• Solve one and two-step problems involving whole numbers and decimals and all four operations, choosing and using appropriate calculation strategies, including calculator use. • Use knowledge of rounding, place value, number facts and inverse operations to estimate and check calculations. • Refine and use efficient written methods to multiply and divide HTU × U, TU × TU, U.t × U, and HTU ÷ U.
6. Teach	Shape Measure	Use understanding of place value to multiply and divide whole numbers and decimals by 10, 100 or 1000.	• Estimate, draw and measure acute and obtuse angles using an angle measurer or protractor to a suitable degree of accuracy; calculate angles in a straight line. • Interpret a reading that lies between two unnumbered divisions on a scale.
7. Teach and practise	Shape Measure	Solve one- and two-step problems involving whole numbers and decimals and all four operations, choosing and using appropriate calculation strategies, including calculator use.	• **Read and plot coordinates in the first quadrant; recognise parallel and perpendicular lines in grids and shapes; use a set-square and ruler to draw shapes with perpendicular or parallel sides.** • Estimate, draw and measure acute and obtuse angles using an angle measurer or protractor to a suitable degree of accuracy; calculate angles in a straight line. • Interpret a reading that lies between two unnumbered divisions on a scale.
8. Practise	Shape Measure	• Read, choose, use and record standard metric units to estimate and measure length, weight and capacity to a suitable degree of accuracy, eg the nearest centimetre; convert larger to smaller units using decimals to one place, eg change 2.6kg to 2600g. • Use a calculator to solve problems, including those involving decimals or fractions, eg to find ¾ of 150g; interpret the display correctly in the context of measurement.	• Estimate, draw and measure acute and obtuse angles using an angle measurer or protractor to a suitable degree of accuracy; calculate angles in a straight line. • Interpret a reading that lies between two unnumbered divisions on a scale.
9. Practise and apply	Calculate Shape Measure	**Draw and measure lines to the nearest millimetre; measure and calculate the perimeter of regular and irregular polygons; use the formula for the area of a rectangle to calculate the rectangle's area.**	• **Use efficient written methods to add and subtract whole numbers and decimals with up to two places.** • Estimate, draw and measure acute and obtuse angles using an angle measurer or protractor to a suitable degree of accuracy; calculate angles in a straight line. • Interpret a reading that lies between two unnumbered divisions on a scale.
10. Apply	Calculate Shape Measure	As for Lesson 9	As for Lesson 9

Unit 2 2 weeks

Speaking and listening objectives
● Understand and use the processes and language of decision making.

Introduction
This unit of work is in two main parts. The first part extends knowledge and confidence with multiplication and division, giving opportunities to use the written skills gained to solve a variety of word problems, briefly reviewing square numbers and relating this to finding the areas of squares. Emphasis is given to choosing an efficient method for the task, and decisions need to be made.

The second part of this unit explores all aspects of angles, measuring to a suitable degree of accuracy, calculating missing ones, angles of a straight line and solving problems involving angles. This encompasses other skills such as calculating and reading scales, as well as simply the language of angles. Again, children are encouraged to make decisions and to explain their thought processes to others.

Use and apply mathematics
● Solve one- and two-step problems involving whole numbers and decimals and all four operations, choosing and using appropriate calculation strategies, including calculator use.

Lessons 1–5

Preparation
Lesson 1: Make an OHT of the 'Multiplication square' resource sheet for display. Cut up a sheet of squared paper into squares.
Lesson 2: Prepare some examples of × calculations to hand out.
Lesson 3: Prepare some examples of ÷ calculations to hand out.

You will need
Photocopiable pages
'Making square numbers' (page 158), 'Written division skills' (page 159), one per child.
CD resources
Support and extension versions of 'Making square numbers', 'Written division skills' and 'Products of our times'. General resource sheets: 'Multiplication square', for display, and '0–9 digit cards', a few sets.
Equipment
Interactive whiteboard; a sheet of squared paper cut into 2 × 2 and 4 × 4 squares; coloured pens; scissors; adhesive; additional squared paper; rough paper and pencils (or individual whiteboards and pens if available); calculators.

Learning objectives

Starter
● Use a calculator to solve problems, including those involving decimals or fractions, eg to find ¾ of 150g; interpret the display correctly in the context of measurement.
● Draw and measure lines to the nearest millimetre; measure and calculate the perimeter of regular and irregular polygons; use the formula for the area of a rectangle to calculate the rectangle's area.

Main teaching activities
2006
● Solve one- and two-step problems involving whole numbers and decimals and all four operations, choosing and using appropriate calculation strategies, including calculator use.
● Use knowledge of rounding, place value, number facts and inverse operations to estimate and check calculations.
● Refine and use efficient written methods to multiply and divide HTU × U, TU × TU, U.t × U, and HTU ÷ U.
● Draw and measure lines to the nearest millimetre; measure and calculate the perimeter of regular and irregular polygons; use the formula for the area of a rectangle to calculate the rectangle's area.
● Recall quickly multiplication facts up to 10 × 10, use to multiply pairs of multiples of 10 and 100 and derive corresponding division facts. (Revision of Block B)
1999
● Use all four operations to solve simple word problems involving numbers and quantities based on 'real life', money and measures (including time), using one or more steps, including finding simple percentages.
● Choose and use appropriate number operations to solve problems, and appropriate ways of calculating: mental, mental with jottings, written methods, calculator.
● Check results of calculations.
● Extend written methods to HTU or U.t by U; long multiplication of TU by TU; HTU by U (integer remainder).
● Measure and draw lines to the nearest millimetre.
● Measure and calculate perimeters of rectangles and regular polygons.
● Understand area measured in square centimetres (cm²); use the formula for the area of a rectangle.

- Know by heart all multiplication facts up to 10 × 10; derive quickly division facts.
- Use known facts and place value to multiply and divide mentally.

Vocabulary

problem, solution, answer, method, strategy, operation, calculation, calculate, calculator, equation, add, subtract, multiply, divide, product, quotient, remainder, memory, display, key, enter, clear, place, place value, decimal, decimal point, decimal place, estimate, approximately, area, perimeter, square number, square root

Lesson 1 (Review)

Starter

Recall and rehearse: Ask the children to remind you of the formula for finding the area of a rectangle. Draw some rectangles on the board labelled with their length and breadth measurements. Use mixed units as well as simple measurements, such as 5m × 6m; 3.5m × 200cm, and so on. Ask the children to calculate the area on their whiteboard and hold them up when you say *Show me.*

Main teaching activities

Whole class: Display the 'Multiplication square' whiteboard resource (or use the 'Multiplication square' resource sheet on OHT). Explain that today you are going to look at special multiples: numbers that are multiplied by themselves, or square numbers.

Ask volunteers to highlight on the multiplication table numbers that are obtained by multiplying a number by itself - for example, 4 or 49. After the first few, ask: *Can you see the pattern on the grid?* (The square numbers form a diagonal line.) Explain that they are called square numbers because when one of these numbers is arranged as squares or dots, it makes a square. Demonstrate with squared paper squares showing 2 × 2 and 4 × 4. Ask the children to count the individual squares: 2 × 2 = 4 and 4 × 4 = 16. The inverse or opposite of a square is known as a square root - for example, 4 is the square root of 16. Explain that if they needed to find the side length of a square, given the area, they would need to find the square root, for example: *What is the side length of a square with an area of 25cm²?* (5cm – 5 is the square root of 25.) *And what is the perimeter of this shape?* (5cm × 4 = 20cm.)

Independent work: The children can use the 'Making square numbers' activity sheet to make and solve jigsaws of square numbers, count or calculate each square number and write the relevant multiplication fact and area in cm² beneath each jigsaw square. They can use the displayed 'Multiplication square' to check their answers.

Review

Check the results of the jigsaw puzzles and the square numbers calculated. Ask questions such as: *What is the square of 4? What is the square root of 25?* Invite the children to demonstrate the square numbers by using themselves to form a square 'grid' of bodies: 4 × 4, 5 × 5, and so on.

Differentiation

Less confident learners: Provide these children with the support version of the activity sheet. They may only find the square numbers of 2, 3, 4 and 5. They can count the squares on the jigsaw pieces to calculate the square numbers and areas.

More confident learners: These children should be able to complete the squares quickly. They can go on to calculate the squares of 11, 12 and 13 and, using squared paper, create the jigsaws for a friend.

Lesson 2 (Review and teach)

Starter

Refine and rehearse: Continue to explore area but this time, draw on the board rectangles showing the area not the dimensions. Ask: *If the area of this rectangle is 42m² what could the measurements of each side be? Could there be more than one answer? What if we used decimal numbers? Would you need to check with a calculator?* Repeat with other areas such as 50cm²; 100m².

Unit 2 ▌ 2 weeks

▷ ### Main teaching activities

Whole class: Explain to the children that you are going to revise the grid method for multiplying large numbers and also show them two more compact methods. Emphasise that no method is 'better': the children must choose the method with which they feel most comfortable and which gives the most accurate results. Provide opportunities for the children to attempt each method on their paper or board and hold it up to show you their calculations. Discuss the following methods of doing the calculation 134 × 5. Then try some further examples.

The grid method

```
134 × 5
  ×   |     5
 100  |   500
  30  |   150
   4  |    20
  ─────────────
      |   670
```

● Approximate first: 150 × 5 = 750. This will give you an idea of the size of the answer.
● Draw the grid and partition the number into H, T and U.
● Multiply each part carefully, aligning the place value of each answer.
● Add the numbers back up, starting with the most significant digit: '500 in your head, add 100, gives us 600, add 50 is 650, add 20 equals 670.'

The expanded vertical method

```
H T U
1 3 4
×   5
─────
5 0 0
1 5 0
  2 0
─────
6 7 0
```

This method is similar to the grid method and is a natural development from it. However, it relies on secure place value understanding.
● Write the calculation vertically.
● Multiply the most significant digit first (the hundreds): 100 × 5
● Multiply the tens: 30 × 5 = 150
● Multiply the units: 8 × 5 = 20
● Add up, counting on from the most significant digit as before.

It is possible to take the development onward another stage by using the expanded method above, but starting with the least significant digit (units) and thus inverting the recording. This prepares the children for:

The compact standard method

```
H T U
1 3 4
×   5
─────
6 7 0
1 2
```

This is vertical multiplication, but multiplying the smallest digit (units) first and carrying the next place value over. Not every child will be able to cope with this method, and you may choose to teach it only to one group in your group teaching time.
● Write the calculation vertically.
● Multiply the units first: 4 × 5 = 20. Write the 0 units in the units column and carry the 2 tens to underneath the tens column.
● Multiply the tens: 5 × 3 = 15. Add the extra 2 tens, making 17. Write 7 in the tens column and carry over 1 hundred.
● Multiply the hundreds: 1 × 5 = 5. Add the extra hundred, making 6.

Group work: Write three or four examples for groups to attempt using their (or your) chosen method. For example: 146 × 2; 231 × 5; 315 × 3; 336 × 4. The children should complete each calculation individually, but then share their answers with the group. The group can then discuss any differences in method or answer.

Review

Discuss the methods used and problems encountered. Make this more fun by dividing the class into three groups, each representing a different calculating method. The children have five minutes to jot down reasons why they believe their chosen method to be the best and most accurate one. They then present their reasons to the class, with opportunities for questioning and debate.

Differentiation

Less confident learners: The children could use the grid method only. They may only manage TU × U problems, such as 45 × 5; 23 × 5; 52 × 2; 43 × 2.
More confident learners: The children could work through the compact standard method, with more difficult multiples such as 319 × 8; 243 × 7; 745 × 9; 246 × 8.

BLOCK D

Lesson 3 (Review and teach)

Starter
Refine and rehearse: Continue exploring possible dimensions of rectangles from their given area. Ask the children to estimate first and then to use calculators to find possible measurements which are not whole numbers. For example, if the area is 42m² then the sides could be 6m × 7m or 3m × 14m or 1.5m × 28m. Discuss with the children the strategy for working this out.

Main teaching activities
Whole class: Explain that, since we have seen that multiplication and division are closely linked – one is the inverse or opposite of the other – we are now going to use multiplication facts we know to help us divide numbers that are bigger than our known table facts. For example: What is 62 ÷ 4? Encourage the children to estimate first: 4 ×10 is 40, too small. 4 × 20 is 80, too big. So we know the answer is between 10 and 20. Go on to demonstrate the 'chunking' method:

$$\begin{array}{r} 62 \ \div \ 4 \\ (10 \times 4=) \ \underline{40} \ - \\ 22 \\ (5 \times 4=) \ \underline{20} \\ 2 \end{array}$$

- Write the division question: 62 ÷ 4.
- Find a known × fact (10 × 4).
- Subtract that 'chunk', leaving 22.
- Find the next nearest × fact to 22 (5 × 4).
- Subtract that, leaving a remainder of 2.
- Answer: 15 (lots of 4) remainder 2

Repeat, asking the children to show you this method. Try 78 ÷ 5 and 56 ÷ 3.

Group work: The children can attempt more examples (such as 59 ÷ 3; 67 ÷ 4; 84 ÷ 5; 76 ÷ 5), individually in their books or on whiteboards, then discuss the results in groups.

Review
Check the children's understanding of the method by writing up one of the questions they have attempted on the board. For example, write 59 ÷ 3. Display the digit cards 3, 0, 2, 9, 2, 7, 2, 1, 9, 2 close by. Explain that all of these digits appear in the solution: the children have to decide where they fit and their appropriate place values, using the 'chunking' method of division. So a child might say: 'The first chunk is 10 × 3 = 30, so I need the 3 and the zero. Take 30 away from 59 and I'm left with 29, so I need a 2 for the tens and a 9 for the units. The next chunk is 9 × 3 = 27, so I need the 2 and the 7. Subtracting 27 from 29 leaves a remainder of 2, so the answer is 19 remainder 2.' Ask a volunteer to write up one of his or her calculations on the board, and to choose digit cards for the rest of the class to place.

Differentiation
Less confident learners: Children may find the activity very difficult if they do not know many multiplication facts. Try to create some division questions using only divisors 2 and 5 (for example, 27 ÷ 2 ; 35 ÷ 2; 39 ÷ 5; 68 ÷ 5).

More confident learners: Ask these children to attempt HTU division, using larger 'chunks'. For example: 124 ÷ 8; 129 ÷ 9; 131 ÷ 7; 327 ÷ 8. Remind them to estimate the range first.

Lesson 4 (Practise)

Starter
Refine and rehearse: Continuing the theme of area and perimeter, draw a rectangle on the board with a given area, such as 60m². Ask the children to calculate, using whole numbers only, all the possible dimensions for length × breadth. Then remind them that a perimeter is all the way around the outside of the shape, like a fence. From their side lengths, ask them to work out the possible perimeters, using calculators if helpful.

Main teaching activities
Whole class: Explain that the children will be using pencil and paper methods to solve division word problems. Read the questions on the 'Written division skills' activity sheet together. Work through the first example on the board with the children's help.

Individual work: Ask the children to complete the 'Written division skills' sheet.

Differentiation

Less confident learners: Provide the support version of the activity sheet, which involves dividing TU numbers by 2 and 5.
More confident learners: Provide the extension version, which involves dividing HTU numbers by numbers up to 9.

Review

Go through some of the questions and discuss the methods used. Ask children to explain which method they chose each time and why. Ask: *Is there someone who used a different method? Can you explain it?* Write up a calculation that has been solved incorrectly. Ask: *Can you see where the error has occurred? Can you explain what he/she has done wrong?*

Lesson 5 (Apply)

Starter

Refine: Tell the children this problem: *Farmer Jones wants to put his favourite goat, 'Daisy', into a pen with the area of 48m². However, he wants to use the smallest amount of wire and fencing for the perimeter that he can to save money. Work out the possible dimensions of the pen and their related perimeters to solve his problem.* Tell them that they will need to record and explain their methods of working.

Main teaching activities

Whole class: Explain that the children will be solving mixed multiplication and division problems. Read through the sheet 'Products of our times' activity sheet, highlighting the vocabulary that suggests or denotes whether the problem is to be multiplied or divided. Turn this into a game where you read the question and the children stand up if they hear a word suggesting multiplication and sit down if they hear a word suggesting division. Discuss also the fact that simpler calculations such as 6 × 5 do not need a written method.

Independent work: Distribute copies of the 'Products of our times' activity sheet for the children to complete.

Differentiation

Less confident learners: Provide the support version of the activity sheet, which uses simple word problems that involve multiplying and dividing by 2, 3, 5 and 10.
More confident learners: Provide the extension version, which involves multiplying and dividing by numbers to 9.

Review

Check some of the children's answers using inverse operations. Ask: *If the product is found by multiplying, what operation would you use to check the calculation?*

Lessons 6-10

Preparation

Lesson 7: Write on the board some questions for the starter.
Lesson 8: Draw on the board some angles for the main teaching activities.

You will need

CD resources

Support and extension versions of 'Round the bend' and 'What's the angle?'. General resource sheets: '0–9 digit cards' and 'Symbol cards' (decimal point card).

Equipment

Protractors; an OHP with a protractor or ICT equivalent; calculators; A4 card; felt pens.

Learning objectives

Starter

- Solve one- and two-step problems involving whole numbers and decimals and all four operations, choosing and using appropriate calculation strategies, including calculator use.
- Use understanding of place value to multiply and divide whole numbers and decimals by 10, 100 or 1000.
- Use a calculator to solve problems, including those involving decimals or fractions, eg to find ¾ of 150g; interpret the display correctly in the context of measurement.
- Read, choose, use and record standard metric units to estimate and measure length, weight and capacity to a suitable degree of accuracy, eg the nearest centimetre; convert larger to smaller units using decimals to one place, eg change 2.6kg to 2600g.
- Draw and measure lines to the nearest millimetre; measure and calculate the perimeter of regular and irregular polygons; use the formula for the area of a rectangle to calculate its area.

Main teaching activities
2006

- Solve one- and two-step problems involving whole numbers and decimals and all four operations, choosing and using appropriate calculation strategies,

including calculator use.
- Use knowledge of rounding, place value, number facts and inverse operations to estimate and check calculations.
- Use efficient written methods to add and subtract whole numbers and decimals with up to two places.
- Refine and use efficient written methods to multiply and divide HTU × U, TU × TU, U.t × U, and HTU ÷ U.
- Read and plot coordinates in the first quadrant; recognise parallel and perpendicular lines in grids and shapes; use a set-square and ruler to draw shapes with perpendicular or parallel sides.
- Estimate, draw and measure acute and obtuse angles using an angle measurer or protractor to a suitable degree of accuracy; calculate angles in a straight line.
- Interpret a reading that lies between two unnumbered divisions on a scale.

1999
- Use all four operations to solve simple word problems involving numbers and quantities based on 'real life', money and measures (including time), using one or more steps, including finding simple percentages.
- Choose and use appropriate number operations to solve problems, and appropriate ways of calculating: mental, mental with jottings, written methods, calculator.
- Check results of calculations.
- Extend written methods to: addition of more than two integers; addition or subtraction of a pair of decimal fractions (e.g. £29.78 + £53.34).
- Extend written methods to HTU or U.t by U; long multiplication of TU by TU; HTU by U (integer remainder).
- Read and plot co-ordinates in the first quadrant.
- Recognise perpendicular and parallel lines.
- Understand and use angle measure in degrees; identify, estimate and order acute and obtuse angles.
- Use a protractor to measure and draw acute and obtuse angles to the nearest 5°.
- Calculate angles in a straight line.
- Record estimates and readings from scales to a suitable degree of accuracy.

Vocabulary

angle degrees (°), angle measurer, protractor, set square, acute, obtuse, perpendicular, parallel

Lesson 6 (Teach)

Starter

Revisit: Create some two-digit decimal numbers using digit cards and the decimal point card. Hold them up and ask the children to multiply or divide each number by 10 or 100. Record their answers on the board. Revise the effect of these operations: the digits remain the same but move up one or two places, and the 'spaces' are filled by 0 to hold the place value.

Revise the effect of dividing by 10 or 100: the digits move down one or two places. If the digits move beyond the decimal point, the number becomes a decimal.

Main teaching activities

Whole class: Explain to the children that a protractor is used to measure the degrees of turn about a point. Display a protractor on the OHP. Explain that the main divisions are in tens and then subdivided into fives, and each small line is worth one degree. Remind the children about the work that they have previously done about reading unnumbered scales. Explain that the common semicircular protractors are for measuring between 0 and 180°, but a circular one is more useful for measuring up to 360° (a complete turn).

Explain that to measure an angle, you place the 'viewfinder' on the point of the angle and line up the straight line along the bottom of the protractor with one of the angle's lines. The inner and outer scales measure from zero from each end so that you can measure either a 'right-hand' or a 'left-hand' angle.

As an ICT link, you could use the Becta package (see the DfES training pack *Using ICT to support mathematics in primary schools*), which provides a demonstration protractor and many differentiated activities on angle measurement.

Independent work: Distribute the activity sheet 'Round the bend' and ask the children to measure the angles accurately (to the nearest 1°).

Review

Use an OHP to draw some angles. Ask for volunteers to come and measure them. Ask the children: *Is the protractor in the correct position? Which scale will we be using? Is the angle an exact measurement in line with the markings on the protractor? Which angle is it nearer? How big is the angle?* Check the children's measurements on the OHP. Discuss why there are minor variations (variable accuracy of lining up). Repeat using some different angles.

Differentiation

Less confident learners:
Provide the support version of the activity sheet, which uses simple angles. Children are asked to measure to the nearest 5°.

More confident learners:
Provide the extension version, with more demanding angles to measure, including some adjacent angles to make 180° on a straight line.

Lesson 7 (Teach and practise)

Starter

Refine and rehearse: Indicate the calculations shown below, written (in words) on the board. Ask the children what language clues are in each one to suggest what type of calculation is needed. Ask the children to find the answers and explain their methods.

- *Find the total of eighty-one and sixty-eight.*
- *What is the product of 25 and 3?*
- *Subtract seventeen from fifty.*
- *How many grams are there in two and a half kilograms?*

Main teaching activities

Whole class: Draw a horizontal line on the OHP. Talk about its properties: it is horizontal (level with the horizon); the angles on a straight line equal 180°; it will go on to infinity; and so on. Now draw a line at a 90° angle to the first one. Explain that any line at right angles with another line or surface is said to be perpendicular to it. In this case, the second line is vertical (at 90° to the horizon). Label the right angles on your diagram. Now draw and label two 45° angles on the same diagram.

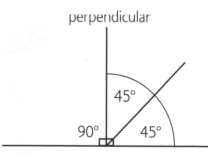

Ask the children how we know that these angle are 45°. (They are half of 90°.) Measure them with a protractor. Use these lines to demonstrate and discuss acute angles (less than 90°) and obtuse angles (more than 90°).

Independent work: Ask the children to draw and label their own perpendicular lines (one horizontal, one vertical) and use these to create acute and obtuse angles. Ask them to write a definition for each of these mathematical terms. Encourage them to draw and label another five obtuse angles and five acute angles, using the corner of a ruler as a right-angle guide.

Review

Draw several pairs of perpendicular lines on the board, using different orientations (so that there is not always a horizontal line). Ask:

- *What is the difference between a vertical line and a horizontal line?*

Differentiation
Less confident learners: Work with a group, providing support with vocabulary.
More confident learners: Expect more precise diagrams. Ask the children to make a list (with sketches) of acute and obtuse angles in the school environment.

● *Perpendicular lines are very important for the building industry. Can you think why?*
● *Can somebody draw another line on this diagram that is parallel to one of the lines shown? Is it perpendicular to the other line?*
● *What do we mean by 'parallel'?* Write a class definition on a piece of card and display it. *How many parallel lines can you see in this room?*

Lesson 8 (Practise)

Starter
Recall: Distribute calculators and ask the children to put 2750 into them. Ask: *What will you have to press to convert this number from grams to kilograms?* (÷ 1000) Repeat with other numbers and units of measure. Encourage the children to use the inverse .

Main teaching activities
Whole class: Draw two acute angles and two obtuse angles, jumbled up, on the board. Invite the children to identify which is which. Ask for four volunteers, one at a time, to come and measure the angles accurately with a protractor. Ask them to talk through what they are doing as they measure, saying which scale they intend to use (inside or outside) and why.
Independent work: Encourage the children to use a ruler to draw a pattern of six lines that cross each other. Then they should choose at least four angles they think are acute and four they think are obtuse, measure them carefully with a protractor, then label them with the angle (in degrees) and the code 'O' or 'A'. Ask them to count up the numbers of acute and obtuse angles created in the pattern: are there more of one type of angle than the other?

Differentiation
Less confident learners: Work with a group, providing support. Encourage the children to measure angles to the nearest 5°.
More confident learners: Challenge the children to create a pattern of straight lines where all the angles are obtuse.

Review
Share examples of drawings, including the extension challenge. Discuss why a drawing with only obtuse angles is difficult to achieve. (Whenever shapes are joined together, acute angles tend to appear.) Ask: *Do you think it is possible to draw a quadrilateral with only obtuse angles?* (No, because the angles of a quadrilateral equal 360°, which is 4 × 90°. If you have two angles over 90°, then inevitably the other two must be acute.)

Lesson 9 (Practise and apply)

Starter
Revisit and reason: Ask the children to tell you everything that they know about a regular pentagon. Say: *One of the sides of the regular pentagon is 2.5cm long, what is the perimeter of that shape?* The children can use a calculator to work this out. *Tell me what you pressed to work this out on a calculator.* Repeat with other regular shapes with decimal side lengths.

Main teaching activities
Whole class: Ask for a volunteer to draw a horizontal line on the board or OHP. Then ask him or her to add a vertical line and a slanting line crossing the horizontal line at the same point (see figure below). Explain that we are going to investigate the angles along a straight line. They add up to 180° (half a complete turn), so the three angles in the diagram must add up to 180°. Ask for a second volunteer to measure the three angles and add them up. Repeat this several times with other volunteers. Now draw a similar set of three lines and ask a child to measure two of the angles, then calculate the last angle.
Independent work: Explain that the children are going to check the accuracy of their angle measuring. Ask them to create three angles on paper by drawing three straight lines (see right),

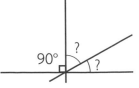

▷ then measure them as accurately as possible. Now ask them to add the angles together. Do they make 180º? If not, there has been an inaccurate measurement. Can they identify and correct it? Tell the children that they need to be accurate within at least 2° either way.

When the children have measured three angles that add up to 180°, ask them to label the angles on their diagram, and then to repeat the process several times with different angles.

Review

Compare the children's results. Discuss the variations in the angle totals (such as 178°–182°) as indicating the margin of error. Talk about why this might happen: lining up the protractor, thickness of pencil lines. Emphasise that angles on a straight line always add up to 180°.

Draw a horizontal line with two lines extending from it, as before. Ask for a volunteer to measure the angles. Extend one of the lines down below the horizontal, thus creating two more angles. Ask the children to use their knowledge of angles in a straight line to calculate the new angles without measuring. Are there any other patterns that the children can observe here? (Opposite angles are equal.) Explain that in this way we can calculate angles within a whole turn (360°).

Differentiation

Less confident learners: The children may need support when measuring. They could use calculators to find the totals.

More confident learners: Challenge the children to create three angles as before, measure two of them and predict the third by subtracting from 180°. Then they should extend the slanted line down below the horizontal line, and use it as a new base line of 180° to calculate the new angles created.

Lesson 10 (Apply)

Starter

Revisit: Say: *A rectangle has a perimeter of 24cm. What could the area be? Is there more than one answer? What could the various sides measure? Would they have the same area?* Repeat with a perimeter of 36cm.

Main teaching activities

Whole class: Draw two crossed lines. Label one of the angles as 110° (for example). Ask the children to use their knowledge of angles to find the other three angles. You might recap facts such as the angles in a straight line equal 180° and the angles in a complete turn add up to 360°. Also remind the children that opposite angles are equal. Talk the children through finding the missing three angles. Put in the opposite angle first, then count on to 180° to find the angle along the straight line. Remind them that this is good practice for their adding and subtracting skills too.

Independent work: Distribute the 'What's the angle?' activity sheet. Ask the children to use their knowledge to find the missing angles. Explain that they should show in their writing how they calculated the angles.

Review

Compare the children's results. Distribute A4 sheets of card and felt pens; ask each group to write a different 'angle fact' that they have learned and draw a diagram to show it. For example, they might write 'The angles in a triangle total 180°' and draw a triangle with the angles labelled. Ask the children: *What is the least amount of information you need to calculate a 'missing' angle? If I didn't have a protractor, how could I identify a right angle? If a straight line is crossed by two lines that are both perpendicular to it, what are the angles?*

Differentiation

Less confident learners: Provide the support version of 'What's the angle', where the children only have to find a missing angle on a straight line. They could use a calculator to work out the answers.

More confident learners: Provide the extension version, which includes finding a missing angle in a triangle. (The three internal angles of a triangle add up to 180°.)

Name _____ Date _____

Making square numbers

This sheet provides square jigsaws of different sizes. Each jigsaw shows a square number. Cut the jigsaws out carefully, then cut up each jigsaw along the thick lines.

Now put the jigsaws back together. Stick them down on another sheet of paper.

Label each jigsaw with the relevant table fact, for example 2 × 2 = 4, and the area, for example 4cm².

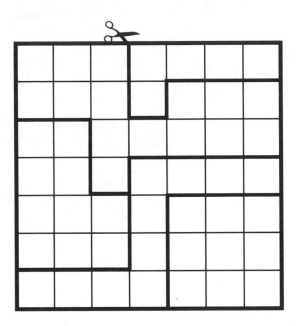

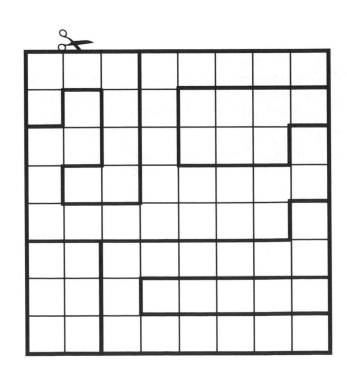

Name _____   Date _____

Written division skills

Solve these division problems.

You need to write out each problem in numbers on another sheet, and solve it using the 'chunking' method you have practised in class. You do not need to write out the words!

You can use a multiplication square to help you.

Here is an example:

Gloria has 26 stickers to put in an album.
She can fit 2 stickers on each page.
How many pages will she use?

$26 \div 2$
$$
\begin{array}{rl}
26 & \\
-\ 20 & \quad (10 \times 2) \\
\hline
6 & \\
-\ 6 & \quad (3 \times 2) \\
\hline
\text{Answer:} & \quad 13
\end{array}
$$

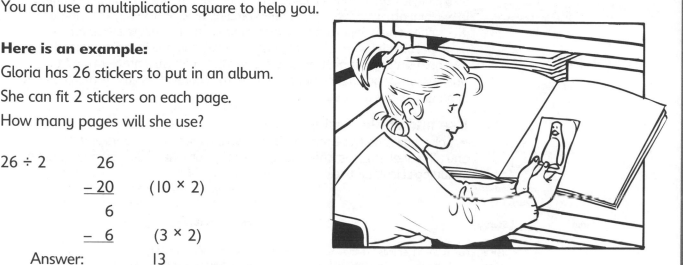

1. A class of 52 children sit in groups of 4. How many groups are there?

_____

2. Our class library has 78 group reading books. The books are in sets of 6. How many sets of group reading books do we have?

_____

3. Samir saves £3.00 of his pocket money every week, because he wants to buy a new computer game. He has saved £51 so far. How long has he been saving?

_____

4. Rolls are sold in packs of 4. The shop 'The Dusty Baker' has 88 rolls to sell on a Saturday morning. How many packs is that?

_____

5. A shoe shop has 54 shoes in its sale bin. How many pairs is that?

_____

6. 'There are 64 wheels in this car park,' says the attendant. How many 4-wheeled cars are parked there?

_____

7. Apple juice cartons are sold in boxes of 6 in the supermarket. The supermarket's computer says they have 84 cartons left to sell. How many boxes is that?

_____

8. Ann has earned £95 in 5 weeks. How much does she earn each week?

_____

9. The chairs in the hall have to be put into rows of 5. There are 89 chairs. How many rows will there be? Will there be any chairs left over?

_____

10. George has 83 football cards to stick into a book. He can fit 6 cards on each page. How many pages will he use?

_____

Unit 3 ▯ 2 weeks

Calculating, measuring and understanding shape

Speaking and listening objectives

- Understand different ways to take the lead and support others in groups.

Introduction

The first four lessons of this unit teach how to read and use the 24-hour clock and to apply it in real-life situations such as reading a timetable. It also includes the use of a calendar and how knowledge of numbers of days in each month is necessary to understanding how they work. This unit also gives children an opportunity to plan group activities using a scenario based on their calendar work, thus meeting the speaking and listening objective. The next set of lessons uses calculating skills to solve a problem, and the final lessons teach translations and how the coordinates can be manipulated in order to move a shape.

Use and apply mathematics

- Solve one- and two-step problems involving whole numbers and decimals and all four operations, choosing and using appropriate calculation strategies, including calculator use.

Lesson	Strands	Starter	Main teaching activities
1. Review	Measure	**Use efficient written methods to add and subtract whole numbers and decimals with up to two places.**	Read timetables and time using 24-hour clock notation; use a calendar to calculate time intervals.
2. Teach and practise	Measure	As for Lesson 1	As for Lesson 1
3. Teach and practise	Measure	Read timetables and time using 24-hour clock notation; use a calendar to calculate time intervals.	As for Lesson 1
4. Practise and apply	Measure	As for Lesson 3	As for Lesson 1
5. Teach and practise	Knowledge Calculate	Use a calculator to solve problems, including those involving decimals or fractions, eg to find ¾ of 150g; interpret the display correctly in the context of measurement.	• Use knowledge of rounding, place value, number facts and inverse operations to estimate and check calculations. • Refine and use efficient written methods to multiply and divide HTU × U, TU × TU, U.t × U, and HTU ÷ U.
6. Practise	Knowledge Calculate	Read, choose, use and record standard metric units to estimate and measure length, weight and capacity to a suitable degree of accuracy, eg the nearest centimetre; convert larger to smaller units using decimals to one place, eg change 2.6kg to 2600g.	As for Lesson 5
7. Review and practise	Use/apply Shape Measure	As for Lesson 6	• Solve one- and two-step problems involving whole numbers and decimals and all four operations, choosing and using appropriate calculation strategies, including calculator use. • Estimate, draw and measure acute and obtuse angles using an angle measurer or protractor to a suitable degree of accuracy; calculate angles in a straight line. • Interpret a reading that lies between two unnumbered divisions on a scale.
8. Teach	Shape	As for Lesson 6	**• Read and plot coordinates in the first quadrant; recognise parallel and perpendicular lines in grids and shapes; use a set-square and ruler to draw shapes with perpendicular or parallel sides.** • Complete patterns with up to two lines of symmetry and draw the position of a shape after a reflection or translation.
9. Teach and practise	Shape	**Draw and measure lines to the nearest millimetre; measure and calculate the perimeter of regular and irregular polygons; use the formula for the area of a rectangle to calculate the rectangle's area.**	As for Lesson 8
10. Apply	Shape	As for Lesson 9	As for Lesson 8

Lessons 1–4

Preparation
Lesson 1: Write on the board some examples of incorrect column addition. Copy the '24-hour clock' resource sheet onto OHT.
Lesson 2: Write on the board some examples of incorrect column subtraction. Make a copy of an excerpt from a calendar for each child and prepare some questions based on the excerpt.
Lesson 3: Make copies of one month from a calendar. Prepare some questions related to the calendar month you have displayed.

You will need
CD resources
General resource sheet: '24-hour clock', for display and for support.
Equipment
Calendars (whole, or pages from).

Learning objectives

Starter
● Use efficient written methods to add and subtract whole numbers and decimals with up to two places.
● Read timetables and time using 24-hour clock notation; use a calendar to calculate time intervals.

Main teaching activities
2006
● Read timetables and time using 24-hour clock notation; use a calendar to calculate time intervals.
1999
● Read the time on a 24-hour digital clock and use 24-hour clock notation, such as 19:53. Use timetables.
● Solve word problems involving time.
● Use a calendar (Year 4).

Vocabulary
days of the week, months of the year, second (s), minute (min), hour (h), day, month, calendar, timetable, 12-hour clock, 24-hour clock, am and pm

Lesson 1 (Review)

Starter
Refine and reason: Write up on the board three written addition calculations which have been incorrectly completed, for example:

```
H T U . t h
1 4 3 . 7 8
+ 3 6 7 . 3 5
4 1 1 . 0 3
```

Ask the children to spot the mistakes in calculating. Ask: *Can anybody suggest some rules that this person might follow to avoid these silly mistakes?* Repeat with other examples.

Main teaching activities
Whole class: Display the OHT of the '24-hour clock' resource sheet. Revise reading time in 24-hour notation. For example, ask: *What time is 20:30? … 18:15? … 21:45? Tell me the time you go to bed/get up/watch your favourite soap in 24-hour notation.*
  Remind the children that during 24 hours of every day, the hands of an analogue clock travel twice round the clock face. Hence in 24-hour digital notation, the first circuit is written using the first 12 hours – 10:15, 08:20 and so on, and the second set of 12 hours continue the counting, ie 13:25. Remind the children that in the 12-hour clock, 'am' stands for 'antemeridian' or 'before midday' and 'pm' means 'post meridian' or 'after midday'; hence morning or afternoon. Write some times up on the board and invite the children to translate them into the 24-hour clock equivalent times: 9.45pm (add 12 to the hour time for the second time around the clock) = 21:45; 8.10am = 08:10; 7.10pm = 19:10. Demonstrate the difference in notation for the 24-hour clock, including the : (colon) between the hours and minutes.
Paired work: In pairs, create an ideal day of television viewing using 24-hour digital notation. Write the start and finish times and the length of each programme.

Programme	Start	End	Duration
Football Focus	07:45	08:15	30 minutes

Review

Using the children's ideal television planners, ask questions such as: *What would you be watching at 08:50, 11:25, 13:18, 02:30?* From this create a class ideal viewing plan and ask related questions such as:
● *If a programme started at 13:20 and ended at 14:10, how long was the programme?*
● *A film starts at 16:25 and lasts for 2 hours and 50 minutes - what time does it end?*

Lesson 2 (Teach and practise)

Starter

Refine and review: Repeat the starter from Lesson 1, but this time use three examples of subtraction calculations which have been completed incorrectly, for example:

```
H T U . t h
7 0 2 . 4 6
- 2 3 5 . 4 3
5 3 3 . 0 3
```

Main teaching activities

Whole class: Show the children the OHT or flipchart of a timetable. Spend some time asking the children to read the times and calculate travelling times, etc. Ensure that everyone understands how a timetable works.
Independent work: Using the given timetables, ask the children to answer the questions and pose some of their own.

Review

Share answers to some of the timetable questions and correct misconceptions. Ask the children to volunteer some questions of their own and ask the others to solve them. Ask: *What is the longest/shortest journey?* Now ask some mental time calculations, for example:
● *A car arrives at its destination at 14:18. It had been travelling for 2 hours and 45 minutes. What time did it set off?*
● *Our postman says it took him 5 hours and 15 minutes to complete his round today. He left the sorting office at 06:35. What time did he finish his round?*
Discuss ways of counting on and counting back to solve these questions.

Lesson 3 (Teach and practise)

Starter

Rehearse: Ask if any of the children have a strategy for remembering how many days there are in each month. Some children may know the old rhyme:
'30 days has September, April June and November,
All the rest have 31 except February which has 28 days clear and
29 each Leap year.'
Another strategy is as follows: Hold out a clenched hand in front of you with the four knuckles uppermost. The knuckles represent months with 31 days, and the spaces in between represent the months with 30 days or less. Start at the knuckle of your index finger 'January' (31), then the space between that and the next knuckle 'February' (28/29 - ie not 31). Continue until you reach knuckle of your little finger 'July' and then start back at your

Differentiation
Less confident learners: Support this group with a 24-hour clock face to help with the hours and calculating the duration of programmes.
More confident learners: Stipulate that this group must allow for advertisement breaks, trailers, etc. Hence, no programme will end exactly as another starts: ie Coronation Street 19:30–19:58.

Differentiation
Less confident learners: Provide a simplified timetable.
More confident learners: Use a larger, more complex timetable to pose questions for a partner to answer.

Calculating, measuring and understanding shape — BLOCK D

index finger for 'August' and carry on.

Main teaching activities

Whole class: Explain to the children that knowledge of the numbers of days in each month will be useful when using calendars to solve problems. Indicate the excerpt of a calendar that you have displayed on the board. Ask some questions to enable the children to become used to the layout: *How many Sundays are there in this month? How many complete weeks? What day of the week will the first of next month fall?*

Independent work: Explain to the class that they are to use this calendar to answer further questions which you have prepared, some of which will relate to the previous or next month. For example:

● *Jim's birthday is on the 23rd May. His sister's birthday is 13 days later. What day and date is that?*
● *Annie arranged her party on the first Sunday of the month although her birthday was nine days before this. What day and date was Annie's birthday?*
● *We are going on holiday for two weeks, we return on the second of May. When do we leave?*

Review

Ask the children how their knowledge of days in each month helped them to solve these questions. Say: *If I left for a three week holiday on the 27th of this month, what day would I return? How did you work it out?* Remind them to be careful about counting on from the day of departure, which is included in the holiday dates.

Differentiation

Less confident learners: These children might feel more comfortable working with an adult using a separate calendar page to find the answers to simpler questions.
More confident learners: Further challenge these children to work out questions such as 'What day of the week will Christmas Day be on?', working forward from the calendar page you have supplied.

Lesson 4 (Practise and apply)

Starter

Rehearse: Use the strategies learned in Lesson 3 to answer some days in a month questions such as: *How many more days are there in July than February when it's not a leap year? Which two months have the most days, June and July or July and August?*

Whole class: Distribute whole month pages of the calendars that you have collected, one between a pair of children. It is immaterial if children have different pages. Ask them to make statements using information from the calendar to their talk partner. Discuss any difficulties or anomalies in the calendar layout.

Paired work: Working independently, ask the children to make up six of their own questions related to the calendar they had in the previous lesson. Then they should swap the questions to challenge their friend. At the end of the session they should check and verify each other's answers.

Review

Say: *I want you to work in groups of five to study one month represented by the calendar. Pretend that you are all on holiday in a cottage for one month and you need to make plans for sharing the jobs and chores for your time there so that no one person is doing all the work. Start by deciding what jobs will need doing and how you are going to share them out. Use your calendar to show what you have decided.*

Differentiation

Less confident learners: These children should work in a small group with an adult to gain confidence at asking questions.
More confident learners: These children should be able to ask more ambitious questions which go beyond a three-month period.

Lessons 5-6

Preparation
Lesson 6: Write on the board the word problems for the main teaching activities.

You will need
Photocopiable pages
'Round, estimate and multiply' (page 169), one per child.
CD resources
Support and extension versions of 'Round, estimate and multiply'. General resource sheets: '0-9 digit cards', one set per child.
Equipment
Calculators; dice (1-10 and 1-6).

Learning objectives

Starter
● Use a calculator to solve problems, including those involving decimals or fractions, eg to find ¾ of 150g; interpret the display correctly in the context of measurement.
● Read, choose, use and record standard metric units to estimate and measure length, weight and capacity to a suitable degree of accuracy, eg the nearest centimetre; convert larger to smaller units using decimals to one place, eg change 2.6kg to 2600g.

Main teaching activities
2006
● Use knowledge of rounding, place value, number facts and inverse operations to estimate and check calculations.
● Refine and use efficient written methods to multiply and divide HTU × U, TU × TU, U.t × U, and HTU ÷ U.
1999
● Check results of calculations.
● Extend written methods to HTU or U.t by U; long multiplication of TU by TU; HTU by U (integer remainder).

Vocabulary
problem, solution, answer, method, strategy, compare, order. explain, predict, reason, reasoning, pattern, relationship, operation, calculation, calculate, calculator, divide, difference, remainder, estimate, approximate, approximately

Lesson 5 (Teach and practise)

Starter
Reason: Distribute calculators. Say: *Tell me how you would use your calculator to help you solve these problems: I made three fruit cakes using 5.1kg of dried fruit. How many grams of dried fruit did I need for one cake? How many grams would I need for two cakes? What key sequence did you use?* Repeat with a similar question such as: *I used 3.25 litres of paint to cover five walls. How much paint would I need for just one wall? In millilitres?*

Main teaching activities
Whole class: Explain to the children that they are going to use their written multiplication skills to solve problems involving decimals.
   Write up on the board 89 × 5. Ask the children which method they would choose to solve this calculation. Then write up 8.9 × 5. Ask: *What have you got to remember about the place value and the position of the decimal point when multiplying decimal numbers? What does the 9 in this calculation represent?* Estimate the approximate size of this answer. Repeat using a number of other decimal examples: 6.3 × 7 or 8.3 × 8.
Independent work: Ask the children to generate some U.t × U questions using dice or digit cards. They must estimate the general size of the answers and then solve them.

Review
Ask the children to estimate the relative size of the following: 3.8 × 7; 7.2 × 12. Ask them to explain how this is helpful when solving decimal multiplications. Ask two different children to demonstrate how they would calculate 83.9 × 4, one using the grid method and one using a standard written method. Discuss how a thorough knowledge of place value is essential in each case to avoid mistakes.

Differentiation
Less confident learners: Only give these children a 1-6 dice or digit cards of a low value to assist their multiplying.
More confident learners: These children should be able to multiply bigger numbers such as TU.t × U or numbers with two decimal places. They should be given higher value digit cards.

Lesson 6 (Practise)

Starter

Revisit: Ask measurement questions: *What unit of measurement would you use to measure the amount of liquid in: a bath; a drinking glass; a teaspoon; a bucket? Explain your choice. If you knew that a drinking glass held 300ml, and a bath held 120 litres of water, how many glasses would it take to fill the bath? How did you calculate that?*

Main teaching activities

Whole class: Write up onto the board the following question: *If one box of chocolates weighs 645g, what would be the mass of six boxes? Give your answer in kg.* Remind the children that they should round and estimate first before calculating this. Ask for someone to explain how to solve this calculation and then how to convert it into a decimal number to give the answer in kilograms. Repeat with another example such as: *My journey to school is 9.1km. How far do I travel in a school week?* Ask: *What is the estimate? Did you recognise whether to round up or down?* Now calculate.

Independent work: Distribute the activity sheet 'Round, estimate and multiply'. Remind the children that they must choose whether to round up or down and estimate before calculating, in order to ensure that their answers have accurate place value. Also tell them that they must make up some decimal word problems of their own, to demonstrate that they can decode multiplication questions.

Review

Take a few examples from the worksheet and ask individuals to talk you through their methods. Write up the following calculation and ask the children to tell you at a glance if it is incorrect and why it must be so: $54.8 \times 6 = 3288$. Ask them to explain to you the misconception about the place value.

Differentiation

Less confident learners:
Provide the support version of the activity sheet, which uses lower values.
More confident learners:
Provide the extension version, which uses higher values and requires unit conversions.

Lessons 7–10

Preparation

Lesson 8: Draw on the board or an OHT a table for the equivalent measures in the starter. Copy the 'Blank axes' resource sheet onto OHT. Prepare a 2D shape to use in conjunction with the 'Blank axes' to demonstrate translation.
Lesson 9: 'Blank axes' on OHT.

You will need

Photocopiable pages
'Translations' (page 170), one per child.
CD resources
Support and extension versions of 'Translations'. General resource sheet: 'Blank axes', for children's use and for display.
Equipment
Card; a protractor; adhesive; scissors.

Learning objectives

Starter

● Read, choose, use and record standard metric units to estimate and measure length, weight and capacity to a suitable degree of accuracy, eg the nearest centimetre; convert larger to smaller units using decimals to one place, eg change 2.6kg to 2600g.
● Draw and measure lines to the nearest millimetre; measure and calculate the perimeter of regular and irregular polygons; use the formula for the area of a rectangle to calculate the rectangle's area.

Main teaching activities

2006

● Solve one- and two-step problems involving whole numbers and decimals and all four operations, choosing and using appropriate calculation strategies, including calculator use.
● Read and plot coordinates in the first quadrant; recognise parallel and perpendicular lines in grids and shapes; use a set-square and ruler to draw shapes with perpendicular or parallel sides.
● Complete patterns with up to two lines of symmetry and draw the position of a shape after a reflection or translation.
● Estimate, draw and measure acute and obtuse angles using an angle measurer or protractor to a suitable degree of accuracy; calculate angles in a straight line.
● Interpret a reading that lies between two unnumbered divisions on a scale.

1999

● Use all four operations to solve simple word problems involving numbers

BLOCK D

▷

and quantities based on 'real life', money and measures (including time), using one or more steps, including finding simple percentages.
● Choose and use appropriate number operations to solve problems, and appropriate ways of calculating: mental, mental with jottings, written methods, calculator.
● Read and plot coordinates in the first quadrant.
● Recognise perpendicular and parallel lines.
● Recognise where a shape will be after a translation.
● Understand and use angle measure in degrees; identify, estimate and order acute and obtuse angles.
● Use a protractor to measure and draw acute and obtuse angles to the nearest 5°.
● Calculate angles in a straight line.
● Record estimates and readings from scales to a suitable degree of accuracy.

Vocabulary
position, direction, reflection, reflective symmetry. Line of symmetry, mirror line, translation, coordinates, x-coordinate, y-coordinate, origin, x-axis, y-axis, problem, solution, answer, method, strategy, compare, order, explain, predict, reason, reasoning, pattern, relationship

Lesson 7 (Review and practise)

Starter
Revisit: More measures.
● *How would I write 6 kilograms and 40 grams as a decimal? Check using your calculator. Were you right?*
● *How would I write 3kg 600g as a decimal?*
● *Tell me something that you would measure using kilograms. What about grams?*
● *Which is bigger 50g or 0.5kg? Explain your answer.*
● *What unit of measurement would you use for weighing a dog? If the dog wouldn't sit still on the scales, how could you weigh it, knowing your own weight was 42kg? What calculation would you have to do?*

Main teaching activities
Whole class: Explain to the class that you are going to provide them with a puzzle and that they must follow the instructions very carefully and compare their results with others in their group. It is designed to aid their understanding of angles and to help them remember some rules about angles of a straight line and angles of a triangle.
Group work: Distribute pieces of card, a protractor, adhesive and scissors to each member of a group of five or six children. Ask each person to carefully draw a triangle, no less than 8cm tall, of any sort, onto the card and to label the angles A, B, and C. Then ask them to measure each angle carefully and to label accordingly. Cut out the triangles with great care and then tear off each of the three corners, including the labelling. Place the angles A,B, and C together; they should form a straight line. Stick down onto a group display piece of card and compare the results of the whole group. Use a calculator to add the three angles of each triangle together; they should add up to 180°.

Review
Compare the findings of different groups. Ask: *What have we shown? What will it help us to remember? If our calculations did not add up to exactly 180, what does that tell us about our accuracy? What margin of accuracy do we think is acceptable? Was everybody able to follow the instructions? Did you support other members of your group?*

▷

Lesson 8 (Teach)

Starter
Revisit: Ask the children to raise their hands to answer these equivalence questions. Have a scribe to fill in the table for you. Ask questions such as: *How many grams in a kilogram? How many centimetres in a metre? How many millimetres in a metre? How many millilitres in half a litre?*

Main teaching activities
Whole class: Define translations or translated shapes as shapes that slide up or down, or left or right, as opposed to reflected shapes which turn over as they cross a mirror line. Demonstrate this using the 'Blank axes' resource sheet on the OHP and a 2D shape. Slide the shape along from coordinate to coordinate.

Revise the use of coordinates, reminding the children that the x-coordinate is always given first and that coordinates are written using brackets, for example (2, 6).

Ask for three children to name a coordinate. Mark each one and join it up to create a triangle. Ask the children: *If I translated this shape two squares to the right what would be its coordinates now?* (The x-coordinates plus 2, the y-coordinates as before.) Repeat with another shape.

Independent work: Distribute the 'Blank axes' resource sheet. Indicate the negative numbers that continue along the line beyond zero. Explain that we can use these to move our shape into another quadrant.

Write up the following coordinates on the board: (2, 4), (2, 7), (5, 5). Ask the children to mark these points and join them up using a ruler. Label the points A, B and C. Now ask them to translate the whole shape six squares to the left, into a different quadrant. Re-label the points A1, B1, and C1 and list the coordinates. Repeat the process by translating the original shape downwards by seven squares. Label A2, B2 C2 and record the coordinates. Emphasise that when translating the shape to the left or right it is the x-coordinate that will change, and when translating a shape up or down the y-coordinate is affected. A point translated left crossing the y axis line will become negative. Likewise a point translated down the y-axis and crossing to the x-axis will become negative.

Review
Ask the children to look at the coordinates of the original and translated shapes. Ask: *What pattern can you see in these coordinates? How many squares did we move the shapes? What has happened to the coordinates?* (For the first translation the x-coordinate has had 6 taken away from it and for the second, the y-coordinate has had 7 subtracted from it.)

Now ask: *What do you think we would have to do to this shape to translate it into the empty quadrant?* (Move 6 to the left and 7 down or (x - 6, y - 7).) Do so on the OHT, by counting squares and marking the points A3, B3, C3 and recording the coordinates.

Differentiation
Less confident learners: This group might need help to ensure that points move only in one direction along a line.
More confident learners: This group should be able to draw and translate an additional shape of their own.

Lesson 9 (Teach and practise)

Starter
Revisit: Ask the children to estimate area. For example, say: *Tell me something that has an approximate area of 30m². How did you work that out? What did you need to know?* Repeat with other areas such as 310cm² (an exercise book).

Main teaching activities
Whole class: Remind the children about their observations about how coordinates change to match the number of spaces moved left or right, up or down, of a point. On an OHT of 'Blank axes' draw a square with coordinates (-2, 1), (-6, 1), (-2, 4), (-6, 4). Ask the children: *If I want to translate this shape to the right, which coordinates will change?* (The x-coordinates.)

Say: *I want to translate this shape seven spaces to the right, how will the coordinates change?* (Add 7 to each *x*-coordinate.) Write the coordinates like this:

A (–2,1)	→	A1 (5,1)
B (–6,1)	→	B1 (1,1)
C (–2,4)	→	C1 (5,4)
D (–6,4)	→	D1 (1,4)

Explain that this can be written as a formula ($x + 7$, y), which means add 7 to the *x*-number whilst the *y*-number stays the same.

Ask for a volunteer to plot these new points and draw the translated shape. Do the children think it is accurate? Count the squares to check.
Independent work: Distribute more copies of the 'Blank axes' resource sheet. Ask the children to draw a shape such as a rectangle or a triangle to translate, starting at point (-7, 1) for point A. Keep the shape within one quadrant. Ask the children to label and list the points with their coordinates. Now ask them to calculate the new coordinates if they were to apply the formula ($x + 8$, y). Draw the new shape and label and list the coordinates. Now ask them to apply a new formula to the original shape (x, $y - 6$). Repeat the process as before.

Review

Say to the children, *We have one quadrant with no shape in it. What do we have to do to our coordinate numbers to translate our original shape into that quadrant?* (Add to the *x*-coordinate and subtract from the *y*-coordinate at the same time, ie ($x + 8$, $y - 6$).) Ask the children to calculate the new coordinates for translated shape: A3, B3, C3, etc. Ask for a volunteer to test the theory by drawing the shape based on the new coordinates. Ask: *Why are these translated shapes not reflections?* (They have moved by sliding and have not 'turned over' or been reflected in a mirror line.)

Differentiation

Less confident learners: These children will need adult support to ensure accuracy.
More confident learners: This group could draw an irregular 2D shape (see below) and translate each point.

Lesson 10 (Apply)

Starter

Refine: Ask the children to estimate the approximate area of a window pane. Ask: *How can you work this out? What do you have to estimate first? What mathematical rule are you applying?* Repeat with other rectangular shapes or composite shapes made up of rectangles.

Main teaching activities

Whole class: Revise with the children the effect of adding numbers to or subtracting numbers from coordinates. Ask: *If I want to move a shape to the right, what must I do to the formula?* (Add to *x*) *What about moving to the left?* (Subtract from *x*-coordinate.) *What about moving a shape downwards?* (Subtract from the *y*-coordinate.) *And upwards?* (Add to the *y*-coordinate.) Ask: *In what direction would a shape move if I applied this formula ($x + 4$, $y - 2$)?* (Right and down.)
Independent work: Distribute the activity page 'Translations' to the children. Explain that there are some shapes which need formulas applying to them to translate them to elsewhere on the grid. The formula ($x + 2$, $y - 1$) means add 2 to the *x*-coordinate number and take 1 from each *y*-coordinate number. Remind them that they must label each point and record the coordinates.

Review

Ask: *Can anybody explain the difference between a translation and a reflection? What is the formula used for, when translating points?* (A shortcut way of finding the position of a translated shape without counting squares.) Compare and share translations. Ask the children to check each other's work for accuracy.

Differentiation

Less confident learners: Use the support version of the activity sheet, which contains simple shapes to translate, initially in one direction only.
More confident learners: Use the extension version, which uses more complex shapes for translation.

Name _____   Date _____

Round, estimate and multiply

I have eight jugs. Each holds 3.1 litres of water. How much water do I have altogether? **My estimate =**	I make some apple cakes. Each cake uses 0.67kg of apples. I make seven cakes. How many kilograms of apples have I used? **My estimate =**
My pond takes 65.4 litres of water to top up every month. I think it has sprung a leak! How much water will I have wasted over six months? **My estimate =**	My brother cycles 18.9km every day to keep fit. How far will he have cycled in one week? **My estimate =**
My baby sister weighed 3.18kg when she was born. She has put on 1.2kg every week for six weeks. How heavy is she now? **My estimate =**	James saved £38.60 every month for six months. How much has he saved altogether? **My estimate =**
Now make up two questions of your own:	

SCHOLASTIC PHOTOCOPIABLE

Name _____

Date _____

Translations

Apply these formulae to translate the shapes. Record the coordinates here:

1. (x + 11, y)	2. (x + 12, y − 5)	3. (x − 2, y − 12)
A (−9,8) → AI (2,8)	E (−5,2) → EI (7,−3)	I (−4,8) → II (−6,−4)
B (−7,8) → BI (,)	F (,) → FI (,)	J (,) → JI (,)
C (−9,2) → CI (,)	G (,) → GI (,)	K (,) → KI (,)
D (−7,2) → DI (,)	H (,) → HI (,)	

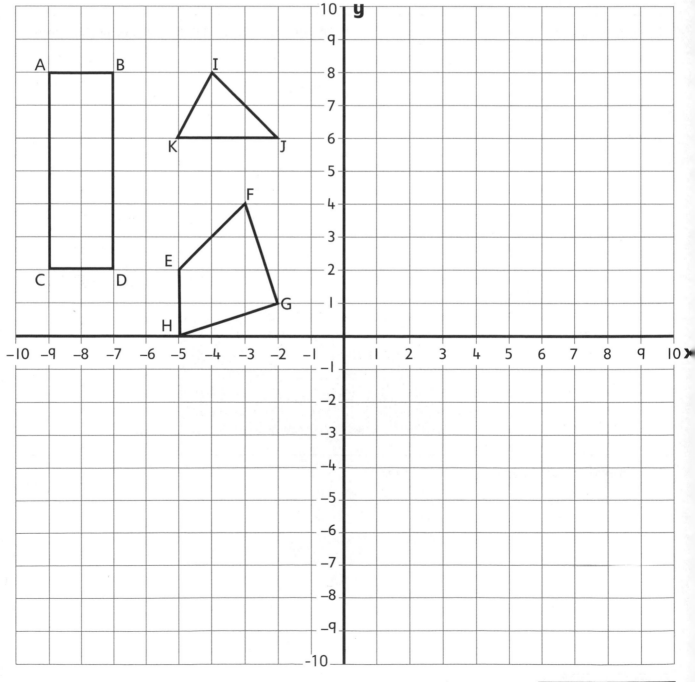

Securing number facts, relationships and calculating

Key aspects of learning
- Problem solving
- Communication
- Reasoning

Expected prior learning

Check that children can already:
- use diagrams to identify equivalent fractions, eg $^6/_8$ and $^3/_4$, or $^7/_{100}$ and $^7/_{10}$; interpret mixed numbers and position them on a number line, eg $3^1/_2$
- use decimal notation for tenths and hundredths and partition decimals; position one- and two-place decimals on a number line
- know the equivalence between decimal and fraction forms of one half, one quarter, tenths and hundredths
- double and halve two-digit numbers
- use written methods to record, support and explain multiplication and division of two-digit numbers by a one-digit number, including division with remainders, eg 15×9, $98 \div 6$
- use the vocabulary of ratio and proportion.

Objectives overview

The text in this diagram identifies the focus of mathematics learning within the block.

Representing and solving one- and two-step problems with whole numbers and decimals, all four operations

Interpreting solutions

Explaining reasoning

Equivalence of fractions

Percentages

Fractions and percentages of quantities

Tables to 10 × 10; multiplying multiples of 10 and 100

Sums, differences, doubles and halves of decimals

Block E: Securing number facts, relationships and calculating

Mental methods: TU × U, TU/U

Written methods: HTU × U, TU/U, U.t × U, HTU/U

Scaling numbers up and down

Finding proportions of quantities

Using a calculator

BLOCK E

Securing number facts, relationships and calculating

Lesson	Strands	Starter	Main teaching activities
1. Review and teach	Knowledge Calculate	• Recall quickly multiplication facts up to 10 × 10 and use them to multiply pairs of multiples of 10 and 100; derive quickly corresponding division facts. • Identify pairs of factors of two-digit whole numbers and find common multiples, eg for 6 and 9.	• Identify pairs of factors of two-digit whole numbers and find common multiples, eg for 6 and 9. • Refine and use efficient written methods to multiply and divide HTU × U, TU × TU, U.t × U and HTU ÷ U.
2. Teach	Knowledge Calculate	As for Lesson 1	As for Lesson 1
3. Teach and practise	Knowledge Calculate	As for Lesson 1	As for Lesson 1
4. Review and practise	Knowledge Calculate	As for Lesson 1	As for Lesson 1
5. Practise and apply	Use/apply Knowledge Calculate	Extend mental methods for whole-number calculations, eg to multiply a two-digit number by a one-digit number, to multiply by 25, to subtract one near multiple of 1000 from another.	• Solve one- and two-step problems involving whole numbers and decimals and all four operations, choosing and using appropriate calculation strategies... • Refine and use efficient written methods to multiply and divide HTU × U, TU × TU, U.t × U and HTU ÷ U. • Identify pairs of factors of two-digit whole numbers and find common multiples, eg for 6 and 9.
6. Teach	Use/apply Counting Calculate	As for Lesson 5	• Explain reasoning using diagrams, graphs and text; refine ways of recording using images and symbols. • Express a smaller whole number as a fraction of a larger one, eg recognise that 5 out of 8 is $^5/_8$; find equivalent fractions eg $^7/_{10} = ^{14}/_{20}$ or $^{19}/_{10} = 1^9/_{10}$; relate fractions to their decimal representations. • Find fractions using division, and percentages of numbers and quantities...
7. Teach and practise	Use/apply Counting Calculate	Identify pairs of factors of two-digit whole numbers and find common multiples, eg for 6 and 9.	As for Lesson 6
8. Teach and practise	Use/apply Counting Calculate	Recall quickly multiplication facts up to 10 × 10 and use them to multiply pairs of multiples of 10 and 100; derive quickly corresponding division facts.	As for Lesson 6
9. Teach and practise	Counting Calculate	As for Lesson 8	• Express a smaller whole number as a fraction of a larger one, eg recognise that 5 out of 8 is $^5/_8$; find equivalent fractions eg $^7/_{10} = ^{14}/_{20}$ or $^{19}/_{10} = 1^9/_{10}$; relate fractions to their decimal representations. • Find fractions using division, and percentages of numbers and quantities... • Use a calculator to solve problems, including those involving decimals or fractions; interpret the display correctly in the context of measurement.
10. Teach	Counting Calculate	As for Lesson 8	• Express a smaller whole number as a fraction of a larger one, eg recognise that 5 out of 8 is $^5/_8$; find equivalent fractions eg $^7/_{10} = ^{14}/_{20}$ or $^{19}/_{10} = 1^9/_{10}$; relate fractions to their decimal representations. • Find fractions using division, and percentages of numbers and quantities...
11. Practise	Counting Calculate	Find fractions using division, eg $^1/_{100}$ of 5kg, and percentages of numbers and quantities, eg 10%, 5% and 15% of £80.	As for Lesson 10
12. Teach and practise	Calculate	As for Lesson 8	Use a calculator to solve problems, including those involving decimals or fractions, interpret the display correctly in the context of measurement.
13. Apply	Use/apply Calculate	Express a smaller whole number as a fraction of a larger one, eg recognise that 5 out of 8 is $^5/_8$; find equivalent fractions eg $^7/_{10} = ^{14}/_{20}$ or $^{19}/_{10} = 1^9/_{10}$; relate fractions to their decimal representations.	• Solve one- and two-step problems involving whole numbers and decimals and all four operations, choosing and using appropriate calculation strategies... • Extend mental methods for whole-number calculations, eg to multiply a two-digit number by a one-digit number, to multiply by 25, to subtract one near multiple of 1000 from another.
14. Teach and practise	Use/apply	As for Lesson 13	Represent a puzzle or problem by identifying and recording the information or calculations needed to solve it; find possible solutions and confirm them in the context of the problem.
15. Apply	Use/apply	As for Lesson 8	As for Lesson 14

Unit 1 ▮ 3 weeks

BLOCK E

Speaking and listening objectives

- Present a spoken argument, sequencing points logically, defending views with evidence and making use of persuasive language.

Introduction

The first five lessons of this unit teach a variety of different approaches to multiplication leading towards partitioning for larger multiplication questions, with plenty of opportunities for practice along the way. The next set of lessons introduces fractions and percentages in a fairly simple way, with some practical applications to help children understand the basic principles. The final block of lessons looks at number patterns, using a calculator for rounding and ordering numbers. This is rounded off by an investigation into number patterns, where children have to consider and discuss their findings, persuading others with their presentation of evidence and explaining their way of working.

Use and apply mathematics

- Represent a puzzle or problem by identifying and recording the information or calculations needed to solve it; find possible solutions and confirm them in the context of the problem.
- Solve one- and two-step problems involving whole numbers and decimals and all four operations, choosing and using appropriate calculation strategies, including calculator use.

Lessons 1-11

Preparation

Lesson 6: Write fractions on the board for the independent work.
Lesson 8: For the starter, draw the table of multiples on the board. Copy 'Blank 100 square' onto OHT. Prepare the 'Fractions, decimals and percentages' cards.
Lesson 9: Copy 'Blank 100 square' onto OHT.
Lesson 11: Draw a number line 0-1 with the fractions 0.5, 0.8, 0.25, 0.3, 0.75, incorrectly positioned along it.

You will need

Photocopiable pages
'Tricky times' (page 185), 'Different ways to multiply' (page 186), 'Bits and pieces' (page 187), one for each child.
CD resources
Support and extension versions of 'Tricky times', 'Different ways to multiply', 'Bits and pieces'; 'Percentages to find'. General resource sheets: 'Blank multiplication square', for extension; 'Number cards 1-100' (cards 10-99); 'Number fans 0-9'; '0-9 digit cards'; 'Fractions, decimals and percentages' cards, various uses. 'Multiplication square' interactive resource.
Equipment
Interactive whiteboard; calculators and an OHP calculator or similar for display; dice for each group; three or four paper circles to represent cakes (or use real cakes); Multilink cubes; counters; sticky tack; a long strip of card; a marker pen; 1cm squared paper.

Learning objectives

Starter

- Recall quickly multiplication facts up to 10 × 10 and use them to multiply pairs of multiples of 10 and 100; derive quickly corresponding division facts.
- Extend mental methods for whole-number calculations, eg to multiply a two-digit by a one-digit number (eg 12 × 9), to multiply by 25 (eg 16 × 25), to subtract one near multiple of 1000 from another (eg 6070 − 4097).
- Identify pairs of factors of two-digit whole numbers and find common multiples, eg for 6 and 9.
- Recall quickly multiplication facts up to 10 × 10 and use them to multiply pairs of multiples of 10 and 100; derive quickly corresponding division facts.
- Find fractions using division, eg $1/100$ of 5kg, and percentages of numbers and quantities, eg 10%, 5% and 15% of £80.

Main teaching activities
2006

- Solve one- and two-step problems involving whole numbers and decimals and all four operations, choosing and using appropriate calculation strategies, including calculator use.
- Explain reasoning using diagrams, graphs and text; refine ways of recording using images and symbols.
- Express a smaller whole number as a fraction of a larger one, eg recognise that 5 out of 8 is $5/8$; find equivalent fractions eg $7/10 = 14/20$ or $19/10 = 1\frac{9}{10}$; relate fractions to their decimal representations.
- Identify pairs of factors of two-digit whole numbers and find common multiples, eg for 6 and 9.
- Refine and use efficient written methods to multiply and divide HTU × U, TU × TU, U.t × U and HTU ÷ U.
- Find fractions using division, eg $1/100$ of 5kg, and percentages of numbers and quantities, eg 10%, 5% and 15% of £80.
- Use a calculator to solve problems, including those involving decimals or fractions, eg to find $3/4$ of 150g; interpret the display correctly in the context of measurement.
1999
- Use all four operations to solve simple word problems involving numbers and quantities based on 'real life', money and measures (including time), using one or more steps, including finding simple percentages.

- Choose and use appropriate number operations to solve problems, and appropriate ways of calculating: mental, mental with jottings, written methods, calculator.
- Explain methods and reasoning, orally and in writing.
- Relate fractions to their decimal representations: that is, recognise the equivalence between the decimal and fraction forms of one half, one quarter, three quarters... and tenths and hundredths (eg $\frac{7}{10}$ = 0.7, $\frac{27}{100}$ = 0.27).
- Recognise when two simple fractions are equivalent, including relating hundredths to tenths (eg $\frac{70}{100} = \frac{7}{10}$).
- Change an improper fraction to a mixed number (eg change $\frac{13}{10}$ to $1\frac{3}{10}$).
- Find all the pairs of factors of any number up to 100.
- Extend written methods to HTU or U.t by U; long multiplication of TU by TU; HTU by U (integer remainder).
- Relate fractions to division, and use division to find simple fractions, including tenths and hundredths, of numbers and quantities (eg $\frac{3}{4}$ of 12, $\frac{1}{10}$ of 50, $\frac{1}{100}$ of £3.
- Find simple percentages of small whole-number quantities (eg 25% of £8).
- Develop calculator skills and use a calculator effectively.

Vocabulary

problem, solution, calculator, calculate, calculation, equation, operation, symbol, inverse, answer, method, explain, predict, reason, reasoning, pattern, relationship, add, subtract, multiply, divide, sum, total, difference, plus, minus, product, quotient, remainder, multiple, common multiple, factor, divisor, divisible by, decimal fraction, decimal place, decimal point, percentage, per cent (%), fraction, proper fraction, improper fraction, mixed number, numerator, denominator, unit fraction, equivalent, cancel

Lesson 1 (Review and teach)

Starter

Rehearse: Display the 'Multiplication square' whiteboard resource. Highlight the final five columns and click 'hide'. Ask children to look for division facts, ie the inverse of multiplication facts. Ask: *What is 28 divided by 4?* Highlight 28 on the grid, then find its factors (4 and 7) by highlighting the 4 row and the 7 column or vice versa. Invite individuals to challenge the class with a variety of division fact questions.

Main teaching activities

Whole class: Continuing to use the 'Multiplication square', explain that since we already know some multiplication facts, we can use them to find more difficult ones. Explain how we can double the 2-times table to find the 4-times table. Demonstrate that if 6 × 2 = 12, then 6 × 4 = 24. Repeat with some examples of 3× doubled to make 6× or 4× doubled to make 8×. Ask for ways to find multiples of 7 and 9 (for example, 3× + 4× = 7× and 10× – 1× = 9×). For each times table reveal a few examples by highlighting squares and clicking 'reveal'. Ask the children to remind you how to find the remaining tables (6 to 10). Write a list of their suggestions on the board.

Independent work: Give each child a copy of the 'Tricky times' activity sheet. Ask the children to complete the blank times-tables grid (part 1), using tables facts they know and the rules you have just discussed.

Differentiation

Less confident learners: Use the support version of 'Tricky times', with paired grids for 2× and 4×, 5× and 10×, 3× and 6×.

More confident learners: Use the extension version, where the multiples include HTU numbers. Ask children to look for further patterns. Can they suggest any alternative methods using known table facts? (For example, the 9× could be made by tripling the 3×.)

Review

Challenge the children to think of questions using a variety of multiplication and division vocabulary. Ensure that the various words are understood and used correctly, for example: *How many 6s in 54? How many lots of 8 in 56? What is the product of 4 and 5?* Use the children's answers to complete the displayed multiplication square. This will get harder as more questions are needed. Now ask: *Can you think of a method of finding multiples larger than 10 that we might try? How might this help us when we multiply bigger numbers?* (Partitioning and recombining allows us to solve more difficult multiplications using known facts.)

Lesson 2 (Teach)

Starter

Recall: Ask quick-fire times-tables questions such as: *5 × 3, 7 lots of 2, double 9.* Ask the children to make the answers with their number fans and hold them up when you say *Show me.*

Main teaching activities

Whole class: Display the 'Multiplication square' interactive resource. Explain that the children are going to use the methods they used in Lesson 1 to help them multiply bigger numbers that are not usually in the times tables they know. They will also write down how the answer was found, using brackets. Ask the children to use the grid to help them find 15 × 8. Write on the board: 15 × 8 = (10 × 8) + (5 × 8) = 80 + 40 = 120. Explain that 10, 8 and 5 are factors of 120 and can be multiplied in any order. The brackets make it clear what should be multiplied, what should be added and in what order (whatever is in the brackets should be done first). Now try 18 × 7, 23 × 7 and 29 × 6.

Independent work: Ask the children to complete part 2 of 'Tricky times', using the completed grid.

Review

Share some answers and ask the children to explain the strategies they used. Ask individuals to demonstrate their methods on the board. These may include:

● Partitioning and adding known times tables
eg 14 × 4 = (10 × 4) + (4 × 4) = 40 + 16 = 56
● Using a multiple of 10 and adjusting
eg 18 × 9 = (20 × 9) – (2 × 9) = (10 × 9) + (10 × 9) – (2 × 9) = 90 + 90 – 18 = 180 – 18 = 162
● Doubling known times tables
eg 7 × 12 = (7 × 6) + (7 × 6) = 42 + 42 = 84

   Ask: *How could we use this method for HTU numbers?* Work out 179 × 5 on the board. Take suggestions for methods. Explain that sometimes partitioning creates such a long string of calculations that errors are likely, and so we need to find a better way of organising the calculations (such as using a multiplication grid).

Differentiation

Less confident learners: Use the support version of the activity sheet, which has smaller numbers and multiples of 2, 3, 4, 5 and 10 only. This group may need support in using brackets.
More confident learners: Use the extension version and/or a 'Blank multiplication grid' to include more challenging numbers. The children could double 6×, 7×, 8× and 9× to find 12×, 14×, 16× and 18×. Could they extend their grid to include multiples of 100?

Lesson 3 (Teach and practise)

Starter

Recall and rehearse: Use a range of vocabulary to test the children's recall and understanding of multiplication and division facts. Ask questions such as: *How many 6s in 42? How many is 4 lots of 3? If I know 10 × 4 is 40, what is 20 × 4 or 40 × 4? Divide 18 by 3. What is the product of 8 and 6?* Ask the children to find the answers on their number fans and hold them up when you say *Show me.*

Main teaching activities

Whole class: Explain that you are going to build together on your knowledge from Lessons 1 and 2. You are going to partition numbers and use doubling to solve TU × U problems. Ask: *How can we double 47?* Explain that you can partition it into 40 and 7, double each part, then recombine by adding. Demonstrate using brackets:
47 × 2 = (40 × 2) + (7 × 2) = 80 + 14 = 94.

   Practise with some more examples. Now ask: *If we know this, how could it help us to multiply by 4?* Explain that this means doubling and doubling again:
47 × 4 = (47 × 2) × 2 = 94 × 2 = (90 × 2) + (4 × 2) = 180 + 8 = 188.

Independent work: Ask the children to generate their own doubling problems by picking cards from a set of two-digit number cards (10–99) and doubling the numbers. You might want to give some children numbers less than 50 and other children numbers greater than 50. The children should record their work by writing number sentences, using brackets.

Review

Ask individuals appropriately differentiated questions, such as: *How would you double 26? … 58? … halve 54… halve 96?*

Revise the children's multiplication strategies. *How would you work out 27 × 4?* (partition into 20 × 4 and 7 × 4, then add) *…36 × 6?* (partition into (10 × 6) × 3 and 6 × 6, then add) *…16 × 7?* (find 8 × 7, then double).

Ask the children: *Look at the following calculation and decide which method has been used. Is the method correct? If not, can you explain where it has gone wrong?*
16 × 8 = (8 × 8) × 2 = 64 × 2 = 124 .

Lesson 4 (Review and practise)

Starter

Read and refine: Ask the children to write down a two-digit number, apply a rule you will tell them and pass it on. Say: *Multiply by 10; add 10; divide by 100; add 100; divide by 10.* Record the operations on the board so the children can check their calculations. Ask: *How big a number have you got? Who has a decimal number?* Check that the numbers are all in the same range.

Main teaching activities

Whole class: Following on from the work on partitioning, review the grid method as a means of avoiding having long, confusing strings of brackets. Write on the board:

94	× 3
×	3
90	270
4	12
=	282

Remind the children about place value in relation to multiplying by 10 and 100: 90 × 3 is the same as 9 × 3 × 10. The children will use multiples of 10 and 100 when partitioning. Remind them that extra care is needed when recombining the numbers: *It's no use getting the multiplying correct if your adding is wrong.* To add the numbers, look at the most significant digit (the one with the highest place value) first. So to add 270 and 12: Keep 270 in your head, add 10, then add 2.

Independent work: Ask the children to create TU x U problems, using a six-sided dice to generate the numbers. Solve them by using the grid method. They should check each answer by dividing, using a calculator.

Differentiation

Less confident learners: The children could double only multiples of 5 and 10 to begin with.
More confident learners: The children could try multiplying numbers by 4.

Differentiation

Less confident learners: The children can multiply numbers 20–25 and 30–35 by 2 or 5, as defined by the teacher.
More confident learners: The children can create their own examples where the target answer is between 800 and 1000 (for example, 41 × 20 or 274 × 3). This requires them to estimate first.

174	× 6
×	6
100	600
70	42
4	24
=	672

Review

Invite individuals to demonstrate some examples on the board. Write on the board an example containing some errors. Ask: *Can you spot the mistakes and put it right?*
Place value forgotten: 42 has not been × by 10.
The 6 should be used to multiply, not added in with the answer.

Lesson 5 (Practise and apply)

Starter

Refine and rehearse: Ask the children to consider the subtraction calculation, 3001 – 1000. It does not pose too many difficulties. Near multiples of 1000 are quite easy to subtract mentally. Say: *Think about how you would calculate the following: 8090 – 2001. Explain your strategy. Did you round and adjust or count on from 2000 and adjust. What about 4989 – 2006. What would you do in this instance?*

Main teaching activities

Whole class: Give each child a copy of the 'Different ways to multiply' activity sheet. Read through some of the problems together. Talk about the methods of multiplication you have tried in the previous few lessons. Remind the children about using known table facts and doubling. Revise partitioning and using brackets for TU × U, and using the grid method for more difficult numbers. Explain that knowing a variety of methods is better than relying on one. Go through the questions on the sheet, identifying together the method that is most suitable in each case and marking it on the sheet.

Independent work: Ask the children to work through the problems on the sheet. Encourage checking using inverse calculations, with a calculator if necessary.

Review

Work through a selection of the problems from the activity sheet. Choose an example of each multiplication method and discuss why some methods are more appropriate for a given calculation than others. For example:

● 6 × 5 is a mental calculation using known facts.
● 18 × 4 is a mental calculation using doubling. It may be helpful to use informal jotting.
● 28 × 7 is best done using partitioning with brackets as an informal jotting, since the numbers are too big and unwieldy to hold in your head.
● 176 × 6 should be done using the grid method, because there are several parts to the calculation and they need to be presented in an organised way to avoid errors.

Differentiation

Less confident learners: Use the support version of the activity sheet, which reinforces multiplying by 10 and partitioning two-digit numbers, using TU × U examples.

More confident learners: Use the extension version, which includes HTU × U and TU × TU examples. Then challenge the children to write some word problems of their own. Can they write both a one-step problem and a two-step problem? (For example: 'Jane saves £1.50 pocket money for six weeks. How much has she saved?' or 'Fred has 38 football stickers. He buys a new pack of five every week. How many stickers will he have after six weeks?')

Lesson 6 (Teach)

Starter

Refine and rehearse: Continue to calculate near multiples of 1000 from Lesson 5. Ensure that each volunteer is able to verbalise the steps they went through. Record for all to consider.

Main teaching activities

Whole class: Display a small cake or cake shape and cut it in half. Hold up one half and ask the children how much of the cake you have in your hand. Explain that one half is written as ½ because it is one piece out of a possible two.

Repeat this process with another cake, using the same language, for ¼, $^1/_3$ and $^1/_6$. Write up the fraction ½; explain that the top number is called the numerator (the number of pieces you have) and the bottom number is called the denominator (the total number of pieces there are). Hold up $^2/_3$, $^3/_4$, $^5/_6$ and so on, repeating the same language.

Ask what fraction has a numerator of 3 and a denominator of 5. Now ask how much you would be holding if you had $^5/_4$. Show this using the 'cake'. Explain that this is called an improper fraction, because it is more than a whole. Demonstrate wholes such as $^2/_2$ and $^4/_4$. Explain that $^5/_4$ is one whole cake and one quarter, so it can be written as 1¼ . This is called a mixed number, since it combines a whole number and a fraction.

Independent work: Give each child a sheet of 1cm squared paper. Explain that the children need to shade, draw and label the fractions you have

▷

written onto the board, including improper fractions. Write up: $^3/_5$; $^1/_2$; $^1/_4$; $^3/_4$; $^1/_{10}$; $^3/_{10}$; $^4/_5$; $^6/_5$; $^4/_4$; $^9/_4$.

Review

Hold up $^2/_4$ and $^1/_2$ of a 'cake'. Ask what the children notice. (They are equivalent.) Ask them which fraction they would prefer. Now ask: *Would you rather have $^1/_2$ or $^1/_3$? $^1/_{10}$ or $^1/_5$? What helps you decide? If I cut one cake into ten pieces, what fraction would each piece be? If I cut it into five pieces, what fraction would each piece be? How do you know which fraction is bigger?* Invite the observation that the bigger the denominator, the smaller the fraction (if the numerator is the same). *If I divided this cake up so that everybody can have a piece, what fraction would each person get?* Share the 'cakes'.

Lesson 7 (Teach and practise)

Starter

Recall: Play 'Factor facts'. Give each child a set of 0-9 digit cards. Call out a number such as 12, 10, 16, 64, 21, 36... Ask the children to hold up all the factors of that number below 10.

Main teaching activities

Whole class: Revise how many fractions there are in a whole: $^2/_2$, $^3/_3$ and so on. Discuss how $^6/_5$ must be more than a whole. Demonstrate this using Multilink cubes. Make a tower of five red cubes and say this is a whole chocolate bar. Now make a tower of six red cubes, compare it to the original and record it as '$^6/_5$ or $1\frac{1}{5}$'.

Write $^{11}/_{10}$ on the board. Count out 11 counters and stick them to the board with sticky tack. Explain that each counter is $^1/_{10}$ of a packet of sweets, so we must have more than one whole packet. Draw a circle around 10 counters, then write '$1\frac{1}{10}$'. Ask the children to enter 11 ÷ 10 into a calculator. The display will show 1.1. Explain that the first decimal place represents tenths, so the calculator shows that $^{11}/_{10}$ is greater than 1 whole.

Now write $^{15}/_6$. Use the counters to illustrate that this improper fraction contains 2 wholes or lots of $^6/_6$. Demonstrate that this can be calculated by dividing the numerator by the denominator: 15 ÷ 6 = 2.5 = $2\frac{1}{2}$. Repeat, using $^{13}/_4$.

Independent work: Distribute copies of the 'Bits and pieces' activity sheet. Explain that this sheet gives practice in changing improper fractions to mixed numbers and vice versa.

Review

Ask the children to convert $3\frac{3}{4}$ to an improper fraction. ($^{15}/_4$) Ask: *How did you do that? What about $5\frac{2}{3}$? What do you have to multiply? What must you remember to add? Can anyone come and write a rule saying how to do this, so we can display the rule to remind us what to do?* (Provide the card strip and marker pen for this.) Ask: *Which is bigger, $^{10}/_3$ or $^{12}/_4$?* ($^{10}/_3 = 3\frac{1}{3}$ and $^{12}/_4 = 3$.) *Can you explain how you worked it out? Can you convert $^{82}/_{10}$ to a mixed number? Can anyone draw this on the board as cakes?*

Lesson 8 (Teach and practise)

Starter

Invite two children to complete the prepared grid and explain their thinking as they do so. They should observe that the digits remain the same but move up a place value, and a zero fills the space to 'hold' or 'mark' the place value. As they work, ask the rest of the class: *What do you notice about the place value? What is the job of the zero? How is the number of zeros in the multiple related to the number of zeros in the answer?* Continue the grid horizontally, using other numbers (such as 70 and 900) to multiply by.

Differentiation

Less confident learners: Ask the children to colour simple fractions up to one whole, for example $^1/_4$; $^1/_2$; $^3/_4$; $^4/_4$; $^1/_5$; $^2/_5$; $^3/_5$; $^4/_5$; $^5/_5$.

More confident learners: These children should be able to demonstrate equivalent fractions such as: $^3/_2 = 1\frac{1}{2} = ^6/_4$ or $^3/_4 = ^6/_8 = ^{12}/_{16}$ or $1\frac{3}{5} = ^8/_5 = ^{16}/_{10}$.

Differentiation

Less confident learners: Use the support version of 'Bits and pieces', which provides diagrams for the children to shade before they write the answers.

More confident learners: Use the extension version, with larger numerators to provide multiple whole numbers and more challenging calculations.

▷

	×3	×30	×300
6	18	180	1800
4			
7			

Main teaching activities

Whole class: Talk about the word equivalent, meaning the 'same value as'. Give an example, such as $^2/_4$ and $^1/_2$. Demonstrate this using Multilink cubes or drawing a circle on the board and dividing it. Look at $^{70}/_{100}$. Explain that this number could be simplified by dividing both the numerator and the denominator by 10 to make them smaller. The total amount stays the same. So $^{70}/_{100}$ is equivalent to $^7/_{10}$. Use the 'Blank 100 square' resource sheet to demonstrate: colour in 70 squares, then overshade seven lots of ten. You use the same number of squares. Write $^{30}/_{100}$ and $^{90}/_{100}$ on the board and invite simplification to equivalent fractions ($^3/_{10}$ and $^9/_{10}$).

Hand out calculators. Now explain that we can sometimes find a decimal equivalent to a fraction, because decimal numbers show tenths and hundredths. Ask the children to put 70 ÷ 100 into the calculator and say what the answer (0.7) means. Now ask them to put in 7 ÷ 10. The answer is the same, showing that $^{70}/_{100}$ and $^7/_{10}$ are equivalent. Repeat this with $^3/_{10}$ and $^{30}/_{100}$. Explain that in a decimal everything has to be written as tenths or hundredths, though fractions can have any numbers. Ask the children to put 1 ÷ 2 into the calculator. The answer is 0.5. Can they explain why? Use the calculator to show that $^1/_2 = ^2/_4 = ^3/_6 = ^4/_8 = ^5/_{10} = 0.5$.

Paired work: Remove the percentage cards from the 'Fractions, decimals and percentages' cards and give a set to each pair. Ask the children to look at each fraction, use the calculator to discover the equivalent decimal, then arrange their cards in pairs on the table.

Review

Compare the children's sets of paired cards. Ask each pair of children to hold up the fraction and decimal cards representing one half. Say: *We know ½ = 0.5 and ¼ = 0.25. What do you think ¾ is? How can we work it out? How many lots of 0.25 do we need?* Count together in 0.25s: 0.25, 0.50, 0.75... *What comes next? What fraction is 1 equivalent to?* Play 'Fraction Snap': call out a fraction or decimal and the children hold up the equivalent card. Alternatively, split the class into two teams: one team holds up fraction cards, the other team holds up decimal cards. Call out fractions and decimals alternately.

Differentiation

Less confident learners: Ask the children to match up only the 'tenths' fractions and decimals.
More confident learners: Ask the children to generate further fractions and their decimal equivalents, for example $^3/_4$, $^4/_5$, $^2/_5$, $^7/_8$...

Lesson 9 (Teach and practise)

Starter

Recall: Play 'Multiplication challenge'. All the children stand in a circle. Explain that one child challenges another with a quick-fire times table question. The second child either answers immediately or sits down. If the answer given is correct, the challenger sits down and the second child becomes the new challenger. If there is no answer or an incorrect answer, the rest of the class call out the answer and the challenger asks another child a new question. The last child standing is the winner. You could produce a 'handicap' system to level up the abilities: ask some groups about the 2, 5 and 10 times tables and others about the 7, 8 and 9 times tables.

Main teaching activities

Whole class: Revise tenths and hundredths, asking for equivalent decimals: $^1/_{10} = 0.1$; $^2/_{10} = 0.2$... Introduce the concept of percentages as parts of 100. Display the 'Blank 100 square' resource sheet. Shade in ten squares (= 10% or 10 out of 100). Show that 35 out of 100 = 35%. Show how percentages are linked to fractions and decimals: $^1/_{10}$ = 0.1 = $^{10}/_{100}$ = 10%. Use the 'Fractions, decimals and percentages' cards to start a class table of equivalents on the board:

Fraction	Decimal	Out of 100	Percentage
$^1/_{10}$	0.1	$^{10}/_{100}$	10%

Paired work: Ask the children to work through a set of fractions cards, finding the equivalent decimals with a calculator, then write the percentages.

Review

Ask: *How would you obtain $^1/_{10}$ of a cake?* (Cut it into 10 pieces.) *What would $^1/_{10}$ be equivalent to? How would you find 10% of a cake? What about 50% of a cake, or 25% of a bag of sweets?* Repeat the 'Pairs' game from Lesson 8, with one team holding up the fraction card and the other team holding up the percentage card as you call out each decimal.

Lesson 10 (Teach)

Starter

Recall: Play 'Division challenge'. This is the same as 'Multiplication challenge' in Lesson 9, but the children ask division questions based on times-tables facts. As before, a 'handicap' system may be operated.

Main teaching activities

Whole class: Explain that finding a percentage of a number is also linked to division, and it can be helpful to remember the equivalent fraction. Demonstrate by saying: *What is 100% of 50? What is 10% of 50? Remember that from our table in the last lesson, 10% is equivalent to $^1/_{10}$. To find $^1/_{10}$ of a number we divide by 10. So to find 10% of a number we divide by 10. So 10% of 50 = 5. From this, I can find 20%* (twice as much). *What is 20% of 50?* Now ask whether anyone can remember the equivalent fraction for 50%. *This can help us to find 50% of a number. How can this help us find 25%?* (25% = ¼, so we can divide by 4.)

Explain that any percentage can be found by using fractions. 75% of 36 can be found by adding 50% (18) and 25% (9) to get 27. We can find harder percentages: 13% of 30 can be made up by finding 10% (3) and 3 lots of 1% (0.3 × 3) and adding them to get 3.9.

Independent work: Ask the children to complete the 'Percentages to find' activity sheet, using the equivalents table from Lesson 9. Remind them to record which fraction they used each time, and show how they calculated the answers.

Review

Ask questions that link fractions and percentages, such as: *Which is greater, 50% of 60 or half of 60? Which would you prefer, 25% of £10 or $^1/_5$ of £10? Why?* (Because 25% is equivalent to ¼, which is bigger than $^1/_5$.) Ask the children to think of a comparison question that uses equivalents they have learned. Split the class into two teams to challenge each other. Keep the score, and ask the children to explain their reasoning.

Lesson 11 (Practise)

Starter

Read and rehearse: Indicate the number line you have drawn on the board. Ask the children to look carefully at the fractions placed along it. *Are they correct? Why not?* Ask for volunteers to reposition them and explain how they decided where to place them.

Main teaching activities

Provide each child with a number of small 'Blank 100 square' resource

Differentiation

Less confident learners: The children could work only with tenths.
More confident learners: The children could include $^1/_4$, $^1/_5$, $^1/_8$, $^3/_4$ and so on.

Differentiation

Less confident learners: Provide the support version of the sheet, which involves finding only 10% and 50%.
More confident learners: Provide the extension version, which involves finding percentages such as 13% by calculating them in parts.

sheets. For each one ask them to colour a number of the squares and then express the shaded area as both a fraction and a percentage. More confident learners might be able to go on and use small blocks of squares and still see the fraction/percentage relationship. For example, colouring $^2/_4$ squares = $^1/_2$ = 50%.

Review
Ensure understanding of the relationship between finding a fraction and turning it into a percentage. Ask: *How would I find $^1/_3$ of a number? What would I key into my calculator? What is the equivalent percentage of ½? How do you know? Can you prove it as a fraction?* ($^{50}/_{100}$) *If I coloured 23 squares on my 100 square, what fraction would that be? Why can't I make it any smaller?*

Lessons 12-15

Preparation
Lesson 13: Write up the calculations for the main teaching activities.

You will need
CD resources
Core, support and extension versions of 'Nearest and next'. General resource sheets: '0–9 digit cards' and a decimal point card from 'Symbol cards', for display purposes.
Equipment
Calculators.

Learning objectives
Starter
● Recall quickly multiplication facts up to 10 × 10 and use them to multiply pairs of multiples of 10 and 100; derive quickly corresponding division facts.
● Express a smaller whole number as a fraction of a larger one, eg recognise that 5 out of 8 is $^5/_8$; find equivalent fractions eg $^7/_{10}$ = $^{14}/_{20}$ or $^{19}/_{10}$ = 1$^9/_{10}$; relate fractions to their decimal representations.

Main teaching activities
2006
● Represent a puzzle or problem by identifying and recording the information or calculations needed to solve it; find possible solutions and confirm them in the context of the problem.
● Solve one- and two-step problems involving whole numbers and decimals and all four operations, choosing and using appropriate calculation strategies, including calculator use.
● Use a calculator to solve problems, including those involving decimals or fractions, eg to find $^3/_4$ of 150g; interpret the display correctly in the context of measurement.
● Extend mental methods for whole-number calculations, eg to multiply a two-digit by a one-digit number (eg 12 × 9), to multiply by 25 (eg 16 × 25), to subtract one near multiple of 1000 from another (eg 6070 – 4097).
1999
● Use all four operations to solve simple word problems involving numbers and quantities based on 'real life', money and measures (including time), using one or more steps, including finding simple percentages.
● Choose and use appropriate number operations to solve problems, and appropriate ways of calculating: mental, mental with jottings, written methods, calculator.
● Develop calculator skills and use a calculator effectively.
● Use mental calculation strategies (several objectives).

Vocabulary
problem, solution, calculator, calculate, calculation, equation, operation, symbol, inverse, answer, method, explain, predict, reason, reasoning, pattern, relationship

Lesson 12 (Teach and practise)

Starter
Revisit: Play 'Place value shuffle'. Use the digit cards 0–9 and a decimal point card to create a two-digit whole number such as 79. Ask two children to hold up these cards, then ask the rest of the class to predict where these

Securing number facts, relationships and calculating

BLOCK E

digits would move to if 79 were multiplied by 100. Ask: *What should we put in the 'spaces' left when the digits 'shuffle' up the place value?* (Zeros to hold the place value: 7900.) Repeat using different numbers such as 8.2 and 168. Include dividing by 10 or 100.

Main teaching activities
Whole class: Ask the children to enter 0.6 into their calculators. Ask them: *How far is this from the next integer or whole number?* (0.4, because the next integer is 1.) Discuss the difference between the 'next integer' (which means that you are counting on) and the 'nearest integer' (which means that you need to round up or down, depending on whether the decimal fraction is larger or smaller than 0.5). Ask: *What would you add to 1.4 to reach the next integer?* Encourage the children to use their calculators. (The answer is 0.6, because the next integer is 2.) Repeat using 0.6, 1.8, 3.7 and so on, until everyone is comfortable with the term 'next integer'.

Independent work: Distribute the 'Nearest and next' activity sheet. Explain that some of these decimal numbers need rounding up to the next integer, and some need rounding up or down to the nearest integer.

Review
Explain that you are going to ask some questions. They may involve rounding up or down to the nearest integer, or counting on to the next integer. Discuss the difference. Ask:

● *Is 2.45 rounded to 2 or to 3? Why?*
● *I started with a number and rounded it to the nearest integer. The answer was 31. What number could I have started with? What is the smallest number I could have started with? How do you know?*
● *I started with a number and rounded it to the next whole number. The answer was 8. What could I have started with?*

Differentiation
Less confident learners: Provide the support version of 'Nearest and next', which includes number lines to assist counting.
More confident learners: Provide the extension version of 'Nearest and next', which includes some numbers with two decimal places to be rounded.

Lesson 13 (Apply)

Starter
Refine: Split the class into groups of six. Ask them each to write down a fraction between 6 and 7 (such as 6⅓). Ask the group to order their fractions, the smallest first. Ask: *How do you know which is bigger, ¹/₅ or ¹/₈?* (The larger the denominator, the smaller the fraction.) Ask each group to read out their list for the class to check. Correct any errors.

Main teaching activities
Whole class: Indicate the calculations on the board: 1000 ÷ 5; 25 × 5; 1045 – 745; 1204 + 1094; 29.85 × 7; 23 × 7; (25 × 5) + (6 × 4). Now write four column headings: Mental, Jottings, Written, and Calculator. Ask the children to sort the calculations into the various headings giving reasons for their choice. Some interesting conflicting views may arise since some children will have greater confidence with mental calculations and others will need the security of a written method. Talk about what we mean by choosing an 'efficient' method. That is one that a child can do reasonably quickly but accurately. Use the example of £400.01 – £10.00. Discuss how this calculation would take much too long as a written calculation since it would require a lot of decomposition or redistributing and adjusting, leaving a considerable margin for error, whereas it is possible to do the calculation mentally or with jottings much more efficiently. Talk through also how two-step problems can be made clearer by the use of brackets. Ask the class to write down some suggestions of calculations to fit under each category. Choose two or three to write up underneath the appropriate headings.

Paired work: Ask the children to work along the categories choosing two or three of the problems to solve. Use the method suggested by the category heading but then discuss if any of the other methods might be suitable, or if not, why not. Ask the children to note down their thoughts as they work through the questions.

Differentiation
Less confident learners: These children will need adult guidance as to the most efficient method to choose since they may rely heavily on one type of calculating method. The adult helper may be able to demonstrate some alternatives as they work as one group together.

More confident learners: These children may be the group least flexible in their choices of methods to solve problems since they will choose a mental calculation the most often. They too may need guidance as to the most efficient method and how they need an alternative calculation to check their results.

Review

Draw together all the opinions discussed in this lesson. Ask: *Did we all have the same ideas or use the same methods? Does this matter? How can an alternative method help us to check our answers?* Write up the following calculation: (24 × 4) × 60. Ask: *How would you choose to solve this calculation, if a calculator was unavailable? What order would you do it in?* Change the numbers in the problem to ones where you would choose a mental method.

Lesson 14 (Teach and practise)

Starter

Refine: Continue the work on ordering fractions from Lesson 13. Each group of six children can order the fractions belonging to another group. Work with the whole class to order all of the fractions. Discuss equivalent fractions as they arise (for example, 6⅑ = 6⅔).

Main teaching activities

Whole class: Explain to the children that they are going to investigate patterns in number. Draw a triangle on the board and ask for volunteers to suggest any number to put at each vertex or corner. Then put a dot at the midpoint of each side and join up the dots to make a new shape. At each dot, write the number which is the difference between the numbers either side of it. Ask the children to notice any special relationship between the resulting differences. (With triangles, two of the difference numbers add up to the third.)

Paired work: Explain to the children that they are going to test this theory with other starting numbers and then go on to explore the same test with a quadrilateral starting shape. (For quadrilaterals, two results occur: either the two opposite midpoint numbers equal each other when added together, eg 6 + 3 = 8 + 1 or 8 - 6 = 3 - 1; alternatively, three of the resulting numbers add up to the fourth one. 8 = 5 + 1 + 2 or 8 - 5 = 2 + 1. It seems that both of these situations can occur with the same starting digits in different positions, so warn the children that they should not be satisfied with only one relationship or pattern.)

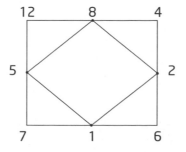

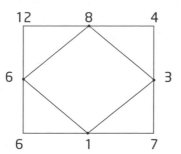

Differentiation

Less confident learners: These children will require a lot of support to organise their work and their thinking in a logical way. They may find spotting a pattern difficult. They should use small starting numbers to make this easier.

More confident learners: These children should relish this open-ended task and be able to investigate lots of different starting points, building up a good bank of evidence.

Review

Collate patterns and relationships that the children have found. Invite some pairs to put forward their ideas, and discuss methods and practices.

Lesson 15 (Apply)

Starter

Recall: Play 'Square root bingo'. Split the class into groups of six and give each group six different digit cards from 2 to 9. Call out questions such as: *What is the square root of 36?* The groups who have the correct digit (6) turn it face down. The winning group is the first to turn over all its cards.

Main teaching activities

Continue the investigations from Lesson 14. Encourage the more confident learners to find a similar relationship between the midpoint numbers created by regular pentagons or hexagons.

Review

Continue to encourage the children to explain the relationships that they have found.

Name _____   Date _____

Tricky times

1. Complete this multiplication grid, using the times table facts you know to help you with the more difficult ones. Some answers have been put in to help you.

×	2	3	4	5	6	7	8	9	10
2	4		8						
3									
4				20					40
5									
6		18							
7									
8									
9			36						
10									

2. Use the completed grid above to help you partition these multiplication problems and write the answers. Don't forget to use brackets.

18 × 3 = (10 × 3) + (8 × 3) = 30 + 24 = 54

16 × 4 = (____ × ____) + (____ × ____) = _____

17 × 5 = _____

15 × 9 = _____

23 × 4 = _____

26 × 7 = _____

34 × 6 = _____

41 × 8 = _____

Securing number facts, relationships and calculating

BLOCK E

Name _____   Date _____

Different ways to multiply

Can you solve these multiplication questions?

Before you try, decide which is the best method for each question. Record the code letter of your chosen method in the box. Do your working out on another sheet of paper if necessary.

Write **M** for mental calculation, **XD** for known times tables that you can double, **P** for partitioning with brackets or **G** for a written method such as the grid method.

Problem	Method
16 × 8 =	
70 × 6 =	
47 × 7 =	
78 × 3 =	
6 × 7 =	
Andrew is sponsored 5p for every length of the swimming pool he swims. If he does 25 lengths, how much money will he collect?	
Andrew has nine sponsors. How much money will he make altogether?	
My car does 17 miles for every litre of petrol. If I put in 8 litres, how far can I travel?	
There are 48 tables in a restaurant. Six people can sit at each table. How many people can sit in the restaurant at the same time?	
There are six biscuits in each packet and six packets on the shelf. How many biscuits are there on the shelf?	
The school cook can fit nine pudding dishes on one tray. If she has 34 trays, how many puddings has she made?	
I have 14 goldfish, but Liam has 4 times as many. How many fish does Liam have in his pond?	

Securing number facts, relationships and calculating

BLOCK E

Name _____ Date _____

Bits and pieces

1. Change these improper fractions to mixed numbers – that is, whole numbers and fractions. Draw them first if it helps you to visualise them.

| $\frac{3}{2}$ | $\frac{5}{3}$ | $\frac{6}{4}$ |

| $\frac{7}{5}$ | $\frac{8}{7}$ | $\frac{6}{5}$ |

| $\frac{9}{4}$ | $\frac{6}{3}$ | $\frac{7}{3}$ |

2. Now change these mixed numbers to improper fractions.

| $1\frac{1}{2}$ | $1\frac{1}{3}$ | $1\frac{2}{3}$ |

| $1\frac{2}{5}$ | $1\frac{3}{4}$ | $2\frac{1}{4}$ |

| $2\frac{3}{4}$ | $2\frac{4}{5}$ | $2\frac{2}{6}$ |

3. Write four equivalent improper fractions and mixed numbers of your own.

| | |
| | |

■ **SCHOLASTIC** **PHOTOCOPIABLE**

Securing number facts, relationships and calculating

BLOCK E

Securing number facts, relationships and calculating

Lesson	Strands	Starter	Main teaching activities
1. Teach	Counting	Express a smaller whole number as a fraction of a larger one, eg recognise that 5 out of 8 is $\frac{5}{8}$; find equivalent fractions, eg $\frac{7}{10} = \frac{14}{20}$ or $\frac{19}{10} = 1\frac{9}{10}$; relate fractions to their decimal representations.	Use sequences to scale numbers up or down; solve problems involving proportions of quantities, eg decrease quantities in a recipe designed to feed six people.
2. Teach	Counting	As for Lesson 2	As for Lesson 1
3. Teach and practise	Counting	As for Lesson 2	As for Lesson 1
4. Apply	Use/apply Calculate	As for Lesson 2	As for Lesson 1
5. Teach	Use/apply Counting	• Find fractions using division, eg $\frac{1}{100}$ of 5kg, and percentages of numbers and quantities, eg 10%, 5% and 15% of £80. • Understand percentage as the number of parts in every 100 and express tenths and hundredths as percentages.	• Explain reasoning using diagrams, graphs and text; refine ways of recording using images and symbols. • Express a smaller whole number as a fraction of a larger one, eg recognise that 5 out of 8 is $\frac{5}{8}$; find equivalent fractions, eg $\frac{7}{10} = \frac{14}{20}$ or $\frac{19}{10} = 1\frac{9}{10}$; relate fractions to their decimal representations.
6. Teach and practise	Counting	**Use knowledge of place value and addition and subtraction of two-digit numbers to derive sums and differences, doubles and halves of decimals, eg 6.5 ± 2.7, halve 5.6, double 0.34.**	Express a smaller whole number as a fraction of a larger one, eg recognise that 5 out of 8 is $\frac{5}{8}$; find equivalent fractions, eg $\frac{7}{10} = \frac{14}{20}$ or $\frac{19}{10} = 1\frac{9}{10}$; relate fractions to their decimal representations.
7. Review and practise	Counting	As for Lesson 6	As for Lesson 6
8. Practise	Counting Calculate	As for Lesson 6	• Express a smaller whole number as a fraction of a larger one, eg recognise that 5 out of 8 is $\frac{5}{8}$; find equivalent fractions, eg $\frac{7}{10} = \frac{14}{20}$ or $\frac{19}{10} = 1\frac{9}{10}$; relate fractions to their decimal representations. • Use a calculator to solve problems, including those involving decimals or fractions, eg to find $\frac{3}{4}$ of 150g; interpret the display correctly in the context of measurement.
9. Practise	Counting Calculate	As for Lesson 6	• Express a smaller whole number as a fraction of a larger one, eg recognise that 5 out of 8 is $\frac{5}{8}$; find equivalent fractions, eg $\frac{7}{10} = \frac{14}{20}$ or $\frac{19}{10} = 1\frac{9}{10}$; relate fractions to their decimal representations. • Find fractions using division, eg $\frac{1}{100}$ of 5kg, and percentages of numbers and quantities, eg 10%, 5% and 15% of £80.
10. Practise	Counting	As for Lesson 6	Express a smaller whole number as a fraction of a larger one, eg recognise that 5 out of 8 is $\frac{5}{8}$; find equivalent fractions, eg $\frac{7}{10} = \frac{14}{20}$ or $\frac{19}{10} = 1\frac{9}{10}$; relate fractions to their decimal representations.
11. Teach and practise	Counting Calculate	As for Lesson 6	• Express a smaller whole number as a fraction of a larger one, eg recognise that 5 out of 8 is $\frac{5}{8}$; find equivalent fractions, eg $\frac{7}{10} = \frac{14}{20}$ or $\frac{19}{10} = 1\frac{9}{10}$; relate fractions to their decimal representations. • Understand percentage as the number of parts in every 100 and express tenths and hundredths as percentages. • Find fractions using division, eg $\frac{1}{100}$ of 5kg, and percentages of numbers and quantities, eg 10%, 5% and 15% of £80.
12. Apply	Counting Calculate	As for Lesson 6	• Understand percentage as the number of parts in every 100 and express tenths and hundredths as percentages. • Find fractions using division, eg $\frac{1}{100}$ of 5kg, and percentages of numbers and quantities, eg 10%, 5% and 15% of £80.
13. Apply	Counting Calculate	Find fractions using division, eg $\frac{1}{100}$ of 5kg, and percentages of numbers and quantities, eg 10%, 5% and 15% of £80.	As for Lesson 12
14. Apply	Use/apply Calculate	As for Lesson 13	• Represent a puzzle or problem by identifying and recording the information or calculations needed to solve it; find possible solutions and confirm them in the context of the problem. • Explain reasoning using diagrams, graphs and text; refine ways of recording using images and symbols. • Find fractions using division, and percentages of numbers and quantities.
15. Apply	Use/apply Calculate	As for Lesson 13	As for Lesson 14

Unit 2 ▪ 3 weeks

Speaking and listening objectives
● Understand and use the processes and language of decision making.

Introduction
This unit is principally about fractions, decimals, percentages, and ratio and proportion. There are many links between this topic and times tables and division, and children will rely heavily on this knowledge. It culminates with a designing exercise that gives opportunities for the decision making required by the speaking and listening objective but also gives children a chance to apply their knowledge acquired in the unit.

Use and apply mathematics
● Represent a puzzle or problem by identifying and recording the information or calculations needed to solve it; find possible solutions and confirm them in the context of the problem.

Lessons 1-13

Preparation
Lesson 1: Make up four or five Multilink sticks in different ratios, such as two blue to three red and one green to four pink. Make up the 'Fractions questions and answers' cards.
Lesson 2: Draw 'sweet bags' with various ratios of sweets for the individual work.
Lesson 4: Write some fraction word problems on the board or OHT.
Lesson 7: Prepare some 'fraction of' questions for independent work.
Lesson 11: Prepare some 'percentage of' questions for independent work.

You will need
Photocopiable pages
'Ratio and proportion problems' (page 200), 'Improper fractions and mixed numbers' (page 201), 'Fraction and decimal equivalents' (page 202), 'What's the percentage?' (page 203), one per child.
CD resources
Support and extension versions of 'Ratio and proportion problems', 'What's the percentage?', and 'Sally's Sports'; extension version of 'Improper fractions and mixed numbers'. General resource sheets: 'Number fan cards 0-9', one per child; '0-9 digit cards', one per child; 'Fractions questions and answers', for whole-class use; 'Fractions, decimals and percentages', for class use.
Equipment
A six-sided or ten-sided dice for each pair of children; Multilink cubes in different colours; circles of paper for folding; calculators; Blu-Tack.

Learning objectives

Starter
● Express a smaller whole number as a fraction of a larger one, eg recognise that 5 out of 8 is ⅝; find equivalent fractions, eg ⁷⁄₁₀ = ¹⁴⁄₂₀, or ¹⁹⁄₁₀ = 1⁹⁄₁₀; relate fractions to their decimal representations.
● Understand percentage as the number of parts in every 100 and express tenths and hundredths as percentages.
● Use knowledge of place value and addition and subtraction of two-digit numbers to derive sums and differences, doubles and halves of decimals, eg 6.5 ± 2.7, halve 5.6, double 0.34.
● Find fractions using division, eg ¹⁄₁₀₀ of 5kg, and percentages of numbers and quantities, eg 10%, 5% and 15% of £80.

Main teaching activities
2006
● Explain reasoning using diagrams, graphs and text; refine ways of recording using images and symbols.
● Express a smaller whole number as a fraction of a larger one, eg recognise that 5 out of 8 is ⅝; find equivalent fractions, eg ⁷⁄₁₀ = ¹⁴⁄₂₀, or ¹⁹⁄₁₀ = 1⁹⁄₁₀; relate fractions to their decimal representations.
● Understand percentage as the number of parts in every 100 and express tenths and hundredths as percentages.
● Use sequences to scale numbers up or down; solve problems involving proportions of quantities, eg decrease quantities in a recipe designed to feed six people.
● Find fractions using division, eg ¹⁄₁₀₀ of 5kg, and percentages of numbers and quantities, eg 10%, 5% and 15% of £80.
● Use a calculator to solve problems, including those involving decimals or fractions, eg to find ¾ of 150g; interpret the display correctly in the context of measurement.
1999
● Explain methods and reasoning, orally and in writing.
● Relate fractions to their decimal representations: that is, recognise the equivalence between the decimal and fraction forms of one half, one quarter, three quarters... and tenths and hundredths (eg ⁷⁄₁₀ = 0.7, ²⁷⁄₁₀₀ = 0.27).
● Recognise when two simple fractions are equivalent, including relating hundredths to tenths (eg ⁷⁰⁄₁₀₀ = ⁷⁄₁₀).
● Change an improper fraction to a mixed number (eg change ¹³⁄₁₀ to 1³⁄₁₀).
● Begin to understand percentage as the number of parts in every 100.
● Express one half, one quarter, three quarters, and tenths and hundredths, as percentages (eg know that ¾ = 75%).
● Solve problems involving ratio and proportion (Year 6).
● Relate fractions to division, and use division to find simple fractions,

Unit 2 — 3 weeks

including tenths and hundredths, of numbers and quantities (eg ¾ of 12, ¹⁄₁₀ of 50, ¹⁄₁₀₀ of £3).
● Find simple percentages of small whole-number quantities (eg 25% of £8).
● Develop calculator skills and use a calculator effectively.

Vocabulary

decimal fraction, decimal place, decimal point, percentage, per cent (%), fraction, proper fraction, improper fraction, mixed number, numerator, denominator, unit fraction, equivalent, cancel, ratio, proportion, in every, for every, to every

Lesson 1 (Teach)

Starter

Refine and rehearse: Split the class in half. Using the 'Fractions questions and answers' cards, distribute the questions to one group and the answers to the other. The groups take turns to read out a question. The child with the answer responds and the pair are matched. Either pair up the children or stick the pairs of cards up on the board.

Main teaching activities

Whole class: Introduce the word 'ratio' as meaning 'one for every...'. Say: *If I have one blue cube for every three red ones, then the ratio is 1:3. That means one blue for every three red.* Display a suitable Multilink stick. *What fraction of this stick is blue?.... red?* (¼, ¾.) Explain that a fraction expressed in this way is called a 'proportion'. Demonstrate several examples with Multilink to help the children see the relationship between ratio and proportion. Encourage them to use cubes to produce the ratios visually. Ask them to consider a ratio of two blue cubes for every four red ones. *What is the proportion of blue cubes?* (²⁄₆) Remind the children what they already know about simplifying fractions: ²⁄₆ could also be expressed as ¹⁄₃.
Paired work: Ask the children to look at the Multilink patterns that you have prepared and to identify the ratio and then the proportion of each colour. It may help them to draw and colour each pattern on squared paper, then record the ratio and proportions.

Review

Discuss the results of the paired work to assess the children's level of success. Play 'Human ratios' to consolidate the ideas of ratio and proportion. Ask four boys and three girls (or four children with brown hair and three with fair hair) to stand up. Ask: *What is the ratio? What is the proportion of boys?* Add four more boys and three more girls, then repeat the questions. Add one more boy and girl, two more and so on. Keep asking about the ratio and the proportions, and simplify the fractions as appropriate. You could have a 'scribe' to keep a record of the ratios and proportions you have created.

Differentiation

Less confident learners: The children will probably need adult support. They could use cubes to build the examples for themselves.
More confident learners: The children could go on to create examples of their own and record the ratios and proportions.

Lesson 2 (Teach)

Starter

Rehearse: Ask some simple fraction questions, such as ¹⁄₃ of 30; ¼ of 24... Then ask: *If we know ¹⁄₃ of 30 is 10, what is ²⁄₃ of 30? How did you work it out?* (two lots of ¹⁄₃.) Ask some similar questions: ¹⁄₅ of 25, ²⁄₅ of 25; ¹⁄₃ of 27, ²⁄₃ of 27; ¼ of 24, ¾ of 24.

Main teaching activities

Whole class: Explain that just as fractions have equivalents, so do ratios. Distribute paper and pencils or individual whiteboards and pens. Show a stick of two yellow and three green cubes. Explain that these represent a packet of five sweets. The manufacturer always produces sweets in this ratio. Ask the children to draw this packet. Now say that the manufacturer has decided to bring out a bumper packet, double the size. Ask: *How many yellow and* *green sweets are in each packet? Draw what you think and show me.* (Four yellow and six green.) *How many would be in a giant packet that had ten yellow sweets?* (15.) Show how the answers can be multiplied up, as with fractions.

Independent work: Draw some sweet bags and give the total number of sweets and the ratio of colours for the children to identify by drawing and shading the correct number in each packet.

▷

Differentiation

Less confident learners: The children can use Multilink cubes to build the ratios before recording on the sheet.
More confident learners: Ask the children to draw three sizes of bags of sweets, using the same ratio of colour that provides an opportunity to explore equivalent ratios.

Review

Set a problem: *There are 30 children in a class. There is a ratio of 2:1 girls to boys. How many girls and how many boys are there?* (20 girls, 10 boys.) *What strategies did we use to solve this?* (Working out that $1/3$ of the class are boys and $1/3$ of 30 is 10.) *As well as the ratio, what other information did we need?* (The number of children in the class.)

Play 'Human Ratios' again. This time, have a group of 12 children: six boys and six girls. Ask the rest of the class to suggest ratios and proportions that they could make from this group, and all the different ways that they could represent these (using 2, 4, 6, 8, 10 or all of the children). Repeat this using different numbers.

Lesson 3 (Teach and practise)

Starter

Refine and rehearse: Play 'What's the question?' Arrange the children into teams of 4 or 5. Hold up a single-digit card and ask the children to suggest a fraction question with this answer. Give one point (a counter or Multilink cube) for a simple fraction and two points for a multiple fraction. For example, the answer 6 could match the question *What is $1/5$ of 30?* (1 point) or *What is $2/3$ of 9?* (2 points.)

Main teaching activities

Whole class: Say that you are going to discuss problems using ratio and proportion. Say: *In a tea shop, there are seven cakes or biscuits on each plate. They are in a ratio of 3:4 biscuits to cakes. Draw the plate to demonstrate this.* Ask: *What is the fraction or proportion of cakes?* ($3/7$.) Now show how the calculation can be reversed: *In another teashop, the proportion of cakes on each plate is $5/7$. What is the ratio of cakes to biscuits?* Ask for a volunteer to draw them. Repeat using different proportions and ratios, such as: 3:4; 4:6; $3/8$; $5/9$.

Paired work: The children work in pairs with a ten-sided dice to generate more ratios of biscuits to cakes, draw them and write the proportion of cakes on each plate.

Differentiation

Less confident learners: The children can use a six-sided dice to generate ratios and draw them.
More confident learners: The children can use a ten-sided dice to generate proportions of cakes, putting the smaller number as the numerator and the larger number as the denominator. They can then work out the ratio of cakes to biscuits in each case (for example, $2/9 \rightarrow$ 2 out of 9 items are cakes $\rightarrow$ the ratio is 2:7 cakes to biscuits.

Review

Say: *I have 15 cakes. Two-thirds of them are iced buns, the rest are gingerbread men. What is the ratio of gingerbread men to iced buns?* (5:10 or 1:2.) Remind the children that some ratios can be simplified.

Play 'Human Ratios', using groups of 6 or 8 children (mixed boys and girls). Say a ratio that needs simplifying, such as 4:6, 5:10 or 15:3, and ask the children in each group to arrange themselves into the simplest form of that ratio. (Some children may sit down, leaving the required number standing.) Each time, ask one of the groups to explain how they simplified the ratio and another to name the proportion of girls (or boys).

▷

Lesson 4 (Apply)

Starter

Refine and reason: Ask fraction word problems:

● *There are 33 children in a class. $^1/_3$ of them have brown hair. What fraction does not have brown hair? How many children is that?*
● *There are 40 children at a youth club. $^1/_4$ wear sweatshirts, the rest wear T-shirts. How many children wear T-shirts?*
● *There are 55 people at a meeting. $^2/_5$ of them have lace-up shoes. How many do not?*
● *Out of the 108 children in a cross-country race, $^1/_9$ finish in less than 20 minutes. How many children took longer than that? Discuss the strategy of finding a simple fraction and then multiplying by the numerator to find a multiple fraction such as $^2/_3$ or $^3/_4$. Talk about alternative strategies, such as finding $^1/_9$ and subtracting it from the total to find $^8/_9$.*

Main teaching activities

Whole class: Continue the discussion of ratio and proportion problems. Say: *I have 20 cakes on a plate and $^1/_5$ of them are chocolate. The rest are plain. How many cakes are plain?* ($^1/_5$ of 20 = 4, 20 – 4 = 16.) *What is the ratio of chocolate to plain cakes?* (4:16 = 1:4.) *If I have 30 cakes in a ratio of 1:4 chocolate to plain, how many of each do I have?* ($^1/_5$ are chocolate, which is 30 ÷ 5 = 6 cakes, so there are 30 – 6 = 24 plain cakes.)
Independent work: Ask the children to complete the 'Ratio and proportion problems' activity sheet.

Review

Ask the children to give you a definition of ratio ('one for every…') and proportion ('one in every…'), and to tell you how they are linked (add the ratio numbers together to find the denominator of the proportion fraction, and each ratio number can be the numerator). For example, 3:4 → 3 biscuits for every 4 cakes → proportions of $^3/_7$ biscuits and $^4/_7$ cakes. Ask: *If I have a bag of sweets with a ratio of 3:2 toffees to fruit gums and nothing else, how many sweets might there be in the bag?* (Any multiple of 5.) Ask for a volunteer to demonstrate some possibilities on the board by drawing the sweets. Repeat this question with different ratios, such as 6:7, 4:3 and 3:8.

Differentiation

Less confident learners:
Provide the support version of the activity sheet, which suggests using cubes to support making ratios.
More confident learners:
Provide the extension version, with more challenging calculations. The children could create further ratio questions to challenge a friend.

Lesson 5 (Teach)

Starter

Ask quick-fire percentage questions such as: *10% of 30; 20% of 60; 15% of 40; 25% of 24; 50% of 32; 11% of 120.* Ask children to show the answers on their number fans.

Main teaching activities

Whole class: Ask the children to identify some simple fractions, using folded paper circles and cubes: *Two cubes are green and three are blue. What fraction is blue?* ($^3/_5$) Then show them shapes or cube towers that are all one colour: *Six cubes are blue. What fraction is that?* (6 or 1 whole.) Now hold up $^7/_6$ using your circles. Ask: *How many sixths is that?* Write it on the board and explain that this is called an improper fraction. *How else could we say this fraction?* (1 whole and $^1/_6$.) Repeat using $^5/_3$ and $^{13}/_5$.

Indicate a prepared number line, divided into fifths. Count the fifths out loud together: *one fifth, two fifths… 1 whole or five fifths.* Demonstrate that we can then count on in fifths (*six fifths, seven fifths…*) or in whole numbers and fifths (*one and one fifth, one and two fifths…*). Use the number line to find more equivalent fractions, such as: *What is the same as $^7/_5$?* (1 and $^2/_5$.)
Independent work: Distribute copies of the 'Improper fractions and mixed numbers' activity sheet . Explain that it presents shapes and number lines for the children to identify as improper fractions and mixed numbers. (For an ICT link, look at the similar examples on www.visualfractions.com.)

Differentiation

Less confident learners: The children could use Multilink cubes to model the number lines shown on the activity sheet.
More confident learners: The children could complete the extension version of the activity sheet, which involves converting written improper fractions to mixed numbers and vice versa, and suggesting a rule for the conversion. (For example: $^{33}/_5 = 33 \div 5 = 6^3/_5$.)

Review

Ask the children to convert some improper fractions (such as $^{15}/_6$) to mixed numbers ($2^3/_6$). Ask: *Do you notice anything about that fraction?* Remind them that sometimes fractions can be further simplified because they are equivalent: $^3/_6 = \frac{1}{2}$, so $^{15}/_6 = 2\frac{1}{2}$.

Divide the class into groups of four to six children and play 'Speedy equivalents'. Call out a mixed number, such as 2 and $^4/_8$, and ask the groups to write down as many equivalent fractions as they can in two minutes. Compare their answers, which may include $2\frac{1}{2}$, $^{20}/_8$, $^{10}/_4$, $^{15}/_6$, $2^3/_6$ and so on. Ask the children to explain how they decided on some of the more unusual fractions. Repeat with $1\frac{3}{4}$.

Lesson 6 (Teach and practise)

Starter

Rehearse: Play 'Doubling around the room', with the groups passing on a number and doubling it each time. When you call 'change', change from doubling to halving. Start with 0.5, 1.5 or 3.2... Repeat a few times, starting from 3.1, 4.5, 0.7 or 1.2.

Main teaching activities

Whole class: Explain that this lesson is about ordering mixed numbers. Draw a number line labelled 0–5. Ask: *How can we mark different numbers and fractions on this line? Where on this number line would we place 2½? What about 3½? How would I know where to place 1¼ or 1¾?* Explain that we need some 'markers' to help us place numbers correctly on a line. In this instance, it would be helpful to mark the whole numbers 1–5 first. These in turn will enable us to find the 'half' numbers. Finally, we can mark in the quarters by halving each half. Demonstrate this on the number line, asking individuals to mark the numbers and fractions. Repeat with a number line from 10 to 20, asking the children to mark mixed numbers such as 13½, 15¼ and 17¾.
Independent work: Ask the children to draw a number line 10cm long on squared paper and label it 0–5, marking in the integers (whole numbers) every 2cm. Now ask them to label the line with the following: 1½, 3¼, 3¾, 2¼, 4½, 4¾, ½ , ¼ , 2½ , $3^1/_8$, $4^1/_8$.

Differentiation

Less confident learners: The children could write in all the halves first (½, 1½, 2½...) and then the quarters (¼, 1¼, 2¼...) to encourage logical division of the lines. Ask them to mark the ¾ if you feel it is appropriate.
More confident learners: Include more challenging fractions that require different divisions of the line, such as $1^1/_3$, $3^2/_3$, $4^1/_8$ and $4^3/_8$, to test the children's understanding of these divisions.

Review

Discuss how the children have placed mixed numbers on a number line by dividing up the line between each two successive integers into the appropriate fraction of a whole. Ask questions such as: *On a number line 0–1, where would you place $^1/_3$? How would you divide up the line? What about finding $^1/_8$?... $^1/_{16}$?*

Discuss how repeated halving of the line can give quarters, eighths and sixteenths. In theory you could use this method to find $^1/_{64}$, but in practice it would be difficult to do that on paper. Now discuss how it is possible to mark multiples of a fraction (such as ¾) on a number line. Ask: *Where should we place $^3/_8$ or $2^3/_{16}$?* Invite volunteers to demonstrate this using a 0–5 number line on the board.

Lesson 7 (Review and practise)

Starter

Revisit: Play 'Pairs' with the children. You write a decimal number on the board; the children write the complementary decimal number to make 1.0 on their whiteboards and hold these up when you say *Show me*. Repeat several times.

Main teaching activities

Whole class: Revise finding a simple fraction of a number. For example, we can find a half by dividing by 2, a quarter by dividing by 4 and so on. Ask the

children to find a half of 18, 22, 24, 32. Ask: *What is a half of 7, 17, 23?* (3.5 or 3½ and so on.) Extend this process by asking the children to find one-third of a number such as 12, 9, 18, 30. Ask: *If we can find ¹/₃ of a number, can anyone explain how we might find ²/₃?* (Find ¹/₃ and double it.) *What is ²/₃ of 15? 24? 36?* Repeat this process, finding ¼ and then ¾ of 32, 24, 40.
Independent work: Provide the children with questions that ask for simple and multiple fractions of numbers. These could include: ¼ of 32; ½ of 16; ¾ of 24; ¹/₅ of 35; ³/₅ of 35; ¹/₇ of 42; ³/₇ of 42, and so on.

Review

Write the number 5 on the board and ask the children to tell you some division facts that give this answer. Write these up around the number. Repeat for 2, 10 and 12. Encourage the children to use a wide range of times-table facts. Ask: *How did you work this out?*

Now ask the children to tell you some fractions of numbers that give the answers above. Add these to the facts already recorded on the board. Discuss how fractions are closely related to division: the denominator is the divisor and the numerator is the multiple. Ask the children to tell you ¾ of 24, ²/₃ of 9 and so on.

Differentiation

Less confident learners:
Provide questions which only ask for simple fractions (such as ½ of 8, ¹/₃ of 27, ¼ of 16, etc) and multiple fractions using tenths only (such as ³/₁₀ of 50; ⁷/₁₀ of 30; ⁹/₁₀ of 60).
More confident learners:
Provide questions which ask for more complex fractions such as ³/₈ of 64, ⁴/₉ of 63 and ¹/₅ of 45.

Lesson 8 (Practise)

Starter

Revisit: Write a decimal number such as 6.3 on the board. Ask the children to identify the number that goes with this number to make 10, ie 3.7. Repeat with 2.3, 4.9, 7.1, 8.2, 6.8, 9.9, 1.7, 0.2. Encourage the children to think in terms of 'pairs to make 10'.

Main teaching activities

Whole class: Give each child a calculator. Explain that a calculator can be very helpful for converting a fraction to its decimal equivalent. Discuss some familiar real-life examples of decimals, such as half of £1 (£0.50 = 50p) or temperatures such as 9.5°C.

Explain that a fraction such as ½ implies 1 ÷ 2. That is the numerator divided by the denominator. Ask the children to key this into their calculators and press =. They should be able to tell you that ½ = 0.5. Select the matching pair from the set of fraction and decimal cards (use the relevant cards from the 'Fractions, decimals and percentages' cards) and fix them to the board. Explain that we can find all other decimal equivalents of fractions in the same way. Ask the children to find the decimal equivalents of ¹/₁₀ and ¼. Fix the matching pairs of cards to the board.

Now explain that some fractions have long and complicated decimal equivalents. Ask the children to key in ⅓. Explain that this number can be rounded to 0.33. Alternatively, the complete fraction can be shown as 0.33̇, using a dot to show the recurring digit (which would continue into infinity). Repeat for ⅐ and demonstrate that the decimal can be rounded to 0.14, but there is no single recurring digit.
Independent work: Encourage the children to use their calculators to find the decimal equivalents of the fractions on the 'Fraction and decimal equivalents' activity sheet. When they have finished, ask them to highlight with a small star the pairs they think will be useful to learn, and then to try to learn them.

Review

Ask the children to share their findings. Record their answers by displaying the pairs of equivalent fraction and decimal cards on the board. Ask: *Did anyone notice that some of the fractions had the same decimal equivalents? Can you explain why?* Draw two circles, dividing one into tenths and one into fifths to show that ²/₁₀ is the same as ¹/₅. *Are there any other decimals that are equal to both a tenths fraction and a fifths fraction?* Discuss an example, such as ⁴/₁₀ = ²/₅ = 0.4. Explain that the numerator and denominator of ²/₅

Differentiation

Less confident learners: The children may need some help to read the calculator display accurately and to round the numbers to two decimal places.
More confident learners: Challenge the children to identify some more numbers as fractions or decimals and find their equivalents – for example, ²/₃, ²/₅ and 0.2.

are both multiplied by 2 to give $^4/_{10}$. Repeat this to show that $^8/_{20}$ is another equivalent. Ask the children to check this with their calculators. Ask for a volunteer to suggest a rule for finding equivalents such as $^2/_{10} = 0.2$.

Lesson 9 (Practise)

Starter
Revisit and refine: Explain that the children are going to double decimal numbers. Start with a familiar example such as double 2.5 = 5. Ask the children to double 7.5, 9.5, 11.5, 15.5. Ask: *Why do these numbers always double to a whole number?* Ask the class what happens when we double ¼ or 0.25. For example, double 2.25 = 4.5, which can be doubled again to make 9. Repeat with starting points of 3.25, 1.25, 8.25 and so on to build confidence and familiarity.

Main teaching activities
Whole class: Write $^7/_{10}$ on the board. Ask the children: *What does this mean? Is it more or less than 1? How would I write it as a decimal?* (0.7) Repeat the questions for $^7/_{100}$.

Now write $^7/_{100}$. *How would I write this as a decimal?* (0.70 or 0.7) Point out that $^7/_{10}$ and $^7/_{100}$ are equivalent. Explain this by saying: *I have two identical cakes. I cut one into 10 pieces and the other into 100 pieces. Which would be more: 7 of the 10 pieces or 70 of the 100 pieces?* (They are the same amount.) Ask the children to put both fractions into the calculator to check that they are equivalent. Demonstrate that the larger-numbered fraction can be divided by 10 to simplify it: $^{70}/_{100} = ^7/_{10} = 0.7$.

Recap by reminding the children that the size of a fraction is determined by two things:
● how many pieces a whole (number, cake and so on) is divided into (the denominator);
● how many of the pieces you are given (the numerator).

Group work: Distribute two packs of the completed 'Fraction and decimal equivalents' cards (see Lesson 8) to each group and tell them that they are going to play equivalent snap. They will have to keep their wits about them to recognise equivalent decimals and fractions.

Review
Ask the children to use their knowledge of hundredths to write the fraction equivalents of the following decimals on their whiteboards: 0.7, 0.4, 0.6, 0.65, 0.25. Then ask: *Which of those decimals cannot be represented as tenths?* (The ones not divisible by 10.) Demonstrate this on the board – for example, $^{70}/_{100} = ^7/_{10}$, but $^{65}/_{100}$ does not have a tenths equivalent.

Ask the children to use their calculators to investigate whether other fractions have tenths equivalents – for example, ask them to try $^2/_5$ and $^6/_{20}$. Discuss the relationship between tenths and fifths, and between tenths and twentieths.

Differentiation
Less confident learners: Encourage the children to put each fraction into the calculator in order to check the equivalent decimal value.
More confident learners: Aim for speed of recognition.

Lesson 10 (Practise)

Starter
Revisit: Ask the children to use their number fans to display the answer to these decimal sums and differences and to hold up the fans when you say *show me:*
4.6 + 3.9; 9.7 – 2.5; 3.8 + 7.5; 2.9 + 5.6; 11.3 – 5.9; 9.1 – 4.3

Main teaching activities
Whole class: Explain to the children that since we can quickly and easily write the decimal equivalents of tenths and hundredths, it is helpful if we can see that other fractions can be converted to tenths if we want to convert them to decimals. For example, $^1/_5$ can be converted to tenths by multiplying the numerator and the denominator by 2: $^1/_5 = ^2/_{10} = 0.2$.

Securing number facts, relationships and calculating

BLOCK E

Likewise, $^2/_5$ can be converted to $^4/_{10}$ = 0.4. Ask: *Can anyone think of any other fractions that can be multiplied up to make tenths?* The children may suggest halves: ½ = $^5/_{10}$ = 0.5. *What about dividing? Can you divide $^5/_{50}$ down to a tenths fraction?* (Divide the top and bottom by 5: $^5/_{50}$ = $^1/_{10}$ = 0.1) *What about $^6/_{20}$?* (Divide the top and bottom by 2: $^6/_{20}$ = $^3/_{10}$ = 0.3)

Independent work: The children can continue to investigate fractions that can be simplified to make tenths or hundredths in order to reveal their decimal equivalent. Encourage them to use both division and multiplication, and to record their findings in this way:

- $^6/_{20}$ divide both numbers by 2 = $^3/_{10}$ = 0.3
- $^4/_5$ multiply both numbers by 2 = $^8/_{10}$ = 0.8
- $^{50}/_{100}$ divide both numbers by 10 = $^5/_{10}$ = 0.5.

Review

Ask: *What is the decimal equivalent of $^4/_5$... $^{30}/_{100}$... $^{20}/_{20}$...? What other fraction/decimal equivalents do we know?* The children may suggest: ¼ = 0.25; ½ = 0.5; ¾ = 0.75. *How can these help us to find some other equivalents?* Discuss how some fractions can be simplified to ¼ or ½ so that the decimal can easily be found (for example, $^4/_{16}$ = ¼ = 0.25). Write the fractions ¼, ½ and ¾ on the board, then ask the children to contribute as many equivalents as they can. For example: ¼ = 0.25 = $^2/_8$ = $^4/_{16}$ = $^8/_{32}$ and so on.

Differentiation

Less confident learners: Give this group easier starting fractions to convert, such as $^2/_{20}$, $^4/_{20}$, $^2/_5$, $^1/_5$, $^4/_5$, $^{10}/_{20}$, $^{10}/_{50}$, $^5/_{50}$, $^{30}/_{100}$, $^{60}/_{100}$.

More confident learners: Encourage this group to convert fractions with low numerators and higher denominators, such as $^4/_{200}$ and $^6/_{100}$.

Lesson 11 (Teach and practise)

Starter

Rehearse: Ask the children to use their number fans to display the following decimal doubles when you say *Show me:*

Double 6.7; 4.9; 2.9; 7.4; 0.23; 0.47; 1.36; 2.35

Say: *A number when doubled gives 9.2. What was the number? What about 11.6?*

Main teaching activities

Whole class: Explain to the children that we can use our knowledge of decimal equivalents to find percentages. 'Per cent' means 'out of 100', so 75% is the same as $^{75}/_{100}$ or 0.75 and 25% is the same as $^{25}/_{100}$ or 0.25. Use a set of 'Fractions, decimals and percentages' cards to play a matching game, as they did in a previous lesson to play decimal snap. Spread the cards face up on the floor or table, so that all the children can see them. Invite the children to look for trios of equivalent cards (for example: ½, 0.5, 50%). Attach each trio to the board with sticky tack. Explain that knowing these equivalents means we can either find fractions of numbers from percentages or vice versa, since they are interchangeable. Demonstrate by asking: *What is half of 60?* Most children should be able to answer '30'. Now ask: *What is 50% of 60?* Repeat this with other fraction/percentage equivalents, such as: ¼ and 25%; $^1/_{10}$ and 10%.

Independent work: Ask the children to find percentages of numbers and amounts of money using even amounts and percentages in multiples of 10, and 25%.

Review

Ask some simple percentage questions such as 50% of 90 and 25% of 16. Then ask: *Can we find all percentages, from 1 to 100%, by using fractions? What about 20% or 75%?* Discuss what fraction/percentage equivalents the children know. They can find 20% of a number if they remember that 20% = 0.2 = $^1/_5$, so they can divide the number by 5. Likewise 67% is just over $^2/_3$ (0.66). 75% of a number is ¾, so it can be worked out by finding ¼ and multiplying by 3 (or finding 50% and 25% and adding them).

Differentiation

Less confident learners: The children may need adult support to link finding percentages and fractions of numbers to using division. Ask questions such as *How can we find ¼ of 8?* (8 ÷ 4.)

More confident learners: Give the children harder problems which require working out percentages that have decimal number answers (for example, 25% of 49).

Lesson 12 (Apply)

Starter

Rehearse: As for Lesson 11, ask children to use number fans to show answers to decimal halves. Say:
Halve 4.8; 2.4; 2.5; 6.8; 15.6; 23.2; 18.7
Ask: *Explain how you would find half of the number 38.78.*

Main teaching activities

Whole class: Explain to the children that to find some percentages, we need to use two or more stages. For example, to find 5% we could find 10% and then halve it:
5% of 60   →   10% of 60 = 6
So   5% of 60 = 3
Ask the children to suggest ways of finding 15%, 75%, 30%, 90% and so on. Demonstrate some examples of methods on the board.
Independent work: Distribute the activity sheet 'What's the percentage?'. Ask the children to calculate the percentages and show how they found them.

Review

Ask: *How would I find 35% of 70?* Demonstrate a method:
1. Find 10% of 70 = 7
2. Multiply by 3 to find 30% = 7 × 3 = 21
3. Halve 7 to find 5% = 3.5
4. Add 30% and 5 % = 21 + 3.5 = 24.5
   Ask similar questions, encouraging the children to explain their answers:
- *How would you find 12% of 96?*
- *How would you calculate 5% of 150?*
- *If a pair of trainers costing £55 has been reduced in price by 8%, how would you calculate the new price? Can anyone suggest a different method?*
- *How could I quickly calculate 95% of 300?*

Differentiation

Less confident learners: The children can use the support version, where the percentages are multiples of 10.
More confident learners: The children can use the extension version, with more complex numbers and percentages.

Lesson 13 (Apply)

Starter

Rehearse: Use number fans to 'show me' quick-fire percentages such as 25% of 32 or 20% of 70.

Main teaching activities

Whole class: Remind the children that shops often use percentages when they advertise their price reductions in sales. Distribute the 'Sally's Sports' activity sheet. Explain that the prices in a sports shop have been reduced by the percentages shown. The children have to find the new sale price for each item. Work through one example. Remind the children that to find the sale price, they have to subtract the discount from the original price.
Independent work: Ask the children to use the activity sheet to work out the sale prices.

Review

Ask: *Can anyone suggest some different ways I might calculate 70% of a number, or 35%, or 12%?* Methods for finding 70% might include: find 10% and multiply by 7; find 50% and 20% and add them; find 50%, add 10%, then add 10%; find 75% and subtract 5%.
   Play 'Percentage consequences'. Give each child a whiteboard and pen. Ask them to write a number smaller than 100 on their board. Now write on the classroom board a series of percentage additions or subtractions for them to apply to the number – for example: *Add 10%. Add 25%. Add 60%. Take off 5%. Add 100%* (and so on). After each new percentage has been added or taken away, they should pass their board to the next child, who continues. The first player to pass 500 holds up their board for the class to check.

Differentiation

Less confident learners: The children can use the support version of 'Sally's Sports', with simpler prices.
More confident learners: The children can use the extension version with more complex prices and percentages.

Lessons 14-15

Securing number facts, relationships and calculating

BLOCK E

Preparation
Lessons 14-15: 'Blank 100 square' enlarged to A3 size.

You will need
CD resources
General resource sheets: 'Blank 100 square', one per pair, enlarged to A3 size; 'Fractions, decimals and percentages'.
Equipment
Card; coloured pencils; Blu-Tack; adhesive; scissors; other game-making equipment.

Differentiation
Less confident learners: This group may need guidance to model their game on one they know well such as 'Snakes and Ladders'.
More confident learners: Expect questions or challenges of a higher quality and remind them about time management.

Learning objectives

Starter
● Find fractions using division, eg $\frac{1}{100}$ of 5kg, and percentages of numbers and quantities, eg 10%, 5% and 15% of £80.

Main teaching activities
2006
● Represent a puzzle or problem by identifying and recording the information or calculations needed to solve it; find possible solutions and confirm them in the context of the problem.
● Explain reasoning using diagrams, graphs and text; refine ways of recording using images and symbols.
● Find fractions using division, eg $\frac{1}{100}$ of 5kg, and percentages of numbers and quantities, eg 10%, 5% and 15% of £80.
1999
● Explain methods and reasoning, orally and in writing.
● Relate fractions to division, and use division to find simple fractions, including tenths and hundredths, of numbers and quantities (eg $\frac{3}{4}$ of 12, $\frac{1}{10}$ of 50, $\frac{1}{100}$ of £3).
● Find simple percentages of small whole-number quantities (eg 25% of £8).

Vocabulary
decimal fraction, decimal place, decimal point, percentage, per cent (%), fraction, proper fraction, improper fraction, mixed number, numerator, denominator, unit fraction, equivalent, cancel

Lesson 14 (Apply)

Starter
Recall and reason: Use 'Fractions, decimals and percentages' to play a 'pelmanism' matching game. As the children turn over the trios of cards ask questions such as: *Are they an equivalent trio? What fraction/decimal/percentage would match this card? Can you remember where the 0.5 card was?*

Main teaching activities
Whole class: Explain to the children that they are going to make a game to test other people's knowledge of fractions, decimals and percentages. They have already played a matching card game so their version is to be a board game. It must test equivalence and also knowledge of fractions and percentages of numbers.
Paired work: Distribute an enlarged 'Blank 100 square' to each pair of children. Explain that they may use any of the other materials that you have provided but they have a time limit for their production of this lesson and the next. At the end of the time they must explain their game to others and talk about the decisions that they needed to make.

Review
Ask for some sample questions from each pair without giving too much detail away about the layout or plan for their game. Ask: *How do you think your game will help children to use and remember fractions, decimals and percentages? How has it furthered your understanding?*

▷ Lesson 15 (Apply)

Starter

Recall and reason: Ask a range of decimal, fraction and percentage questions to remind the children of the sort of questions that could be used in their game.

Main teaching activities

Continue with the production of the fraction, decimal, percentage board games from Lesson 14.

Review

Ask the children to explain their game and the decision-making processes that they went through. If possible, display all of the games and ask the children questions such as: *Which game do you think would be the hardest? Why? Which would be easier? Is there a game that you think would help you to remember equivalent fractions, decimals and percentages? Why do you think that?*

Name _____   Date _____

Ratio and proportion problems

1. To make a profit, a tea shop needs to provide more plain biscuits than chocolate ones.
   They experiment with various ratios.
   For each ratio of chocolate to plain biscuits, draw the biscuits and write the proportion of
   chocolate biscuits.

   | 2:3 | | 3:4 | | 2:5 | | 3:5 | |

   Proportion of biscuits that are chocolate:

   ▢   ▢   ▢   ▢

2. Different shades of green are mixed at the paint shop. The higher the ratio of
   yellow to blue, the paler the shade is.
   Look at these ratios of yellow to blue. For each one, work out the proportions.
   Write the ratios in order from the palest shade to the darkest. Are any the same?

Ratio yellow: blue	2:3	1:4	2:5	3:5	1:2
Proportions: yellow					
Proportions: blue					
Ratios in order:					

3. To make purple paint, red and blue paint are
   mixed in the ratio of 3 tins of red to 4 tins of blue.

   > 3 red + 4 blue = 7 tins of purple paint

   How many tins of each colour do I need to make 14 tins of purple paint?

   _____ red + _____ blue

   I decide to change the proportion of red paint to $\frac{2}{5}$. I need 25 tins of purple paint in this new

   shade. What is the ratio of red to blue? _____

   How many tins of red and blue do I need? _____ red + _____ blue

Name _____   Date _____

Improper fractions and mixed numbers

1. Write the fraction shown in the circles as an improper fraction and a mixed number.

          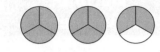

_____   _____

   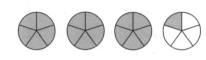

_____   _____

2. Look at the number lines below. Write the improper fraction and the mixed number shown by each letter.

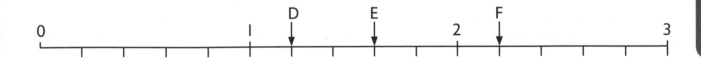

A = _____   B = _____   C = _____

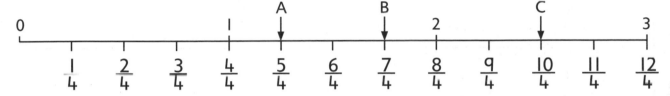

D = _____   E = _____   F = _____

G = _____   H = _____   I = _____

Securing number facts, relationships and calculating

BLOCK E

Name _____   Date _____

Fraction and decimal equivalents

Securing number facts, relationships and calculating

BLOCK E

Fraction	Decimal equivalent	Fraction	Decimal equivalent
$\dfrac{1}{3}$		$\dfrac{2}{3}$	
$\dfrac{1}{4}$		$\dfrac{3}{4}$	
$\dfrac{1}{2}$		$\dfrac{1}{5}$	
$\dfrac{2}{5}$		$\dfrac{1}{6}$	
$\dfrac{1}{7}$		$\dfrac{1}{8}$	
$\dfrac{1}{9}$		$\dfrac{1}{10}$	

Can you spot the relationship between these symbols?

$\dfrac{1}{2}$ %   ÷

Name _____   Date _____

What's the percentage?

Percentage	Answer	Percentage	Answer
50% of 90		25% of 160	
30% of 60		75% of 200	
10% of 80		20% of 40	
15% of 30		30% of 70	
15% of 80		35% of 60	
11% of 80		11% of 90	
5% of 60		3% of 120	

Securing number facts, relationships and calculating

BLOCK E

Securing number facts, relationships and calculating

Lesson	Strands	Starter	Main teaching activities
1. Review	Use/apply	Solve one- and two-step problems involving whole numbers and decimals and all four operations, choosing and using appropriate calculation strategies, including calculator use.	Represent a puzzle or problem by identifying and recording the information or calculations needed to solve it; find possible solutions and confirm them in the context of the problem.
2. Teach	Use/apply Calculate	As for Lesson 1	• Solve one- and two-step problems involving whole numbers and decimals and all four operations, choosing and using appropriate calculation strategies, including calculator use. • Refine and use efficient written methods to multiply and divide HTU × U, TU × TU, U.t × U, and HTU ÷ U.
3. Teach and practise	Use/apply Calculate	Express a smaller whole number as a fraction of a larger one, eg recognise that 5 out of 8 is $^5/_8$; find equivalent fractions, eg $^7/_{10}$ = $^{14}/_{20}$, or $^{19}/_{10}$ = $1^9/_{10}$; relate fractions to their decimal representations.	As for Lesson 2
4. Teach and practise	Use/apply Calculate	As for Lesson 3	As for Lesson 2
5. Apply	Use/apply Calculate	As for Lesson 3	As for Lesson 2
6. Apply	Use/apply Calculate	• Express a smaller whole number as a fraction of a larger one, eg recognise that 5 out of 8 is $^5/_8$; find equivalent fractions, eg $^7/_{10}$ = $^{14}/_{20}$, or $^{19}/_{10}$ = $1^9/_{10}$; relate fractions to their decimal representations. • Find fractions using division, eg $^1/_{100}$ of 5 kg, and percentages of numbers and quantities, eg 10%, 5% and 15% of £80.	As for Lesson 2
7. Apply	Use/apply Calculate	As for Lesson 6	As for Lesson 2
8. Apply	Use/apply Calculate	Find fractions using division, eg $^1/_{100}$ of 5kg, and percentages of numbers and quantities, eg 10%, 5% and 15% of £80.	As for Lesson 2
9. Teach	Counting	As for Lesson 8	Use sequences to scale numbers up or down; solve problems involving proportions of quantities, eg decrease quantities in a recipe designed to feed six people.
10. Teach and practise	Counting	As for Lesson 8	As for Lesson 9
11. Teach and practise	Counting	Express a smaller whole number as a fraction of a larger one, eg recognise that 5 out of 8 is $^5/_8$; find equivalent fractions, eg $^7/_{10}$ = $^{14}/_{20}$, or $^{19}/_{10}$ = $1^9/_{10}$; relate fractions to their decimal representations.	As for Lesson 9
12. Apply	Counting	Represent a puzzle or problem by identifying and recording the information or calculations needed to solve it; find possible solutions and confirm them in the context of the problem.	As for Lesson 9
13. Teach and practise	Counting	As for Lesson 12	• Use sequences to scale numbers up or down; solve problems involving proportions of quantities, eg decrease quantities in a recipe designed to feed six people. • Understand percentage as the number of parts in every 100 and express tenths and hundredths as percentages.
14. Teach	Use/apply Counting	• Use sequences to scale numbers up or down; solve problems involving proportions of quantities, eg decrease quantities in a recipe designed to feed six people. • Represent a puzzle or problem by identifying and recording the information or calculations needed to solve it; find possible solutions and confirm them in the context of the problem.	• Use sequences to scale numbers up or down; solve problems involving proportions of quantities, eg decrease quantities in a recipe designed to feed six people. • Represent a puzzle or problem by identifying and recording the information or calculations needed to solve it; find possible solutions and confirm them in the context of the problem.
15. Apply	Use/apply Counting	As for Lesson 14	As for Lesson 14

Unit 3 ⬛ 3 weeks

Speaking and listening objectives
- Present a spoken argument, sequencing points logically, defending views with evidence and making use of persuasive language.

Introduction
In this unit there is a strong element of using and applying skills learned in earlier units in this block. The first five lessons develop multiplication and division skills and then children use them in the next three lessons in problem-solving situations involving measures and money. There is a strong element of decision making in Lesson 8, and children may need to use their powers of persuasion to get their first choices. Lessons 9–13 further develop confidence with ratio, proportion and percentages. Finally the children apply their understanding to make a simple 'exchange' game.

Use and apply mathematics
- Represent a puzzle or problem by identifying and recording the information or calculations needed to solve it; find possible solutions and confirm them in the context of the problem.
- Solve one- and two-step problems involving whole numbers and decimals and all four operations, choosing and using appropriate calculation strategies, including calculator use.

Lessons 1-8

Preparation
Lesson 2: Prepare a grid of multiples of 2, 4, 5 and 10 and some dice labelled 2, 4, 5, 10, blank, blank.
Lesson 3: Write up some short division questions.
Lesson 4: Write up some short division questions.
Lesson 5: Separate the fractions and decimals cards from the 'Fractions, decimals and percentages'

You will need
Photocopiable pages
'Division word problems' (page 217), 'DIY at Number 32' (page 218) and 'Shopping list' (page 219), one per child.
CD resources
Support and extension versions of 'Division word problems' and 'DIY at Number 32'. General resource sheets: 'Number fan cards 0-9', one for each child; 'Fractions, decimals and percentages' cards.
Equipment
Six-sided and ten-sided dice; coloured pens; calculators; OHP calculator or similar for display.

Learning objectives

Starter
- Solve one- and two-step problems involving whole numbers and decimals and all four operations, choosing and using appropriate calculation strategies, including calculator use.
- Express a smaller whole number as a fraction of a larger one, eg recognise that 5 out of 8 is $\frac{5}{8}$; find equivalent fractions, eg $\frac{7}{10} = \frac{14}{20}$, or $\frac{19}{10} = 1\frac{9}{10}$; relate fractions to their decimal representations.
- Find fractions using division, eg $\frac{1}{100}$ of 5 kg, and percentages of numbers and quantities, eg 10%, 5% and 15% of £80.

Main teaching activities
2006
- Represent a puzzle or problem by identifying and recording the information or calculations needed to solve it; find possible solutions and confirm them in the context of the problem.
- Solve one- and two-step problems involving whole numbers and decimals and all four operations, choosing and using appropriate calculation strategies, including calculator use.
- Refine and use efficient written methods to multiply and divide HTU × U, TU × TU, U.t × U, and HTU ÷ U.
1999
- Use all four operations to solve simple word problems involving numbers and quantities based on 'real life', money and measures (including time), using one or more steps, including finding simple percentages.
- Choose and use appropriate number operations to solve problems, and appropriate ways of calculating: mental, mental with jottings, written methods, calculator.
- Round up or down after division, depending on the context.
- Extend written methods to HTU or U.t by U; long multiplication of TU by TU; HTU by U (integer remainder).

Vocabulary
problem, solution, calculator, calculate, calculation, equation, operation, symbol, inverse, answer, method, explain, predict, reason, reasoning, pattern, relationship, add, subtract, multiply, divide, sum, total, difference, plus, minus, product, quotient, remainder, multiple, common multiple, factor, divisor, divisible by

Lesson 1 (Review)

Starter

Reason: Ask a child to provide a three-digit number. Indicate the numbers 3, 6, 30, 5 and 8 written on the board. Ask the children to use only these numbers and any or all of the four operations to get as close as possible to the three-digit number. Less confident learners could use calculators. Ask the child with the closest answer to explain his or her calculation, so that everyone can try it. Repeat, asking for a new three-digit number.

Main teaching activities

Whole class: Revise the idea of an inverse (opposite) operation – for example, division is the inverse of multiplication. Remind the children that they can do many two-digit calculations mentally, using their known multiplication facts and place value. For example, ask: *What is 60 × 8?; 60 × 80? How did you calculate that? What knowledge did you use? Are there any other calculations that knowing 6 × 8 might help you to solve?* (For example, 12 × 8 or 6 × 16.)

Ask questions to elicit a variety of number facts related to 6 × 8, such as: *What number sentence could I make if I doubled each of the factors?... if I multiplied each factor by 100? What about using the inverse operation to create division facts: how are they related?* Display the related facts as a 'tree' diagram:

eg $48 \div 6 = 8$ ⟵ $6 \times 8 = 48$ ⟶ $6 \times 16 = 96$
    $48 \div 8 = 6$ ⟵⟶ $12 \times 8 = 96$
    $60 \times 8 = 480$ ⟵⟶ $6 \times 80 = 480$

   $600 \times 8 = 4800$ $60 \times 80 = 4800$ $6 \times 800 = 4800$

Independent work: Ask the children to create their own 'known facts' tree diagram, based on a known multiplication fact such as 8 × 3, 6 × 7 or 5 × 6. They should use a calculator to check their facts when they have finished.

Review

Write 400 × 800 on the board. Ask: *Can you calculate 400 × 800 mentally? How?* (By using a known fact and increasing the place value by four places.) *How did you know the approximate size of the answer?* (By the number of zeros in the question.) *What other number facts did 4 × 8 help you to find?* (Inverses and doubles, such as 40 × 80, 40 × 800, 32,000 ÷ 80.)

Now write the number 320 in the middle of the board. Invite the children to use their knowledge of numbers and place value to find number facts with this answer (such as 32,000 ÷ 100, 8 × 40, 80 × 4, 3.2 × 100).

Differentiation

Less confident learners: The children can start with a simple table fact such as 2 × 3 or 4 × 2.
More confident learners: The children can extend their tree diagram to a third or fourth layer, exploring numbers into the thousands.

Lesson 2 (Teach)

Starter

Refine: Draw a number line labelled 5–6. Ask the children what number should be placed at the midpoint (5.5), then at ¼ and ¾ of the way along the line (5.25 and 5.75). Ask for volunteers to place 5.1, 5.95, 5.4 and so on, and to explain how they decided where to place each number.

Main teaching activities

Whole class: Revise short division of a three-digit number by a single digit. Depending on your school calculation policy, some of your children may be confident with written short division and others may just be starting to use it. You may choose to use this lesson to focus on children who need extra help in this area.

Demonstrate a division such as 137 ÷ 3:

$$3\overline{)1\,\overset{1}{3}\,\overset{1}{7}} \\ 4\,5^{r2}$$

Relate this method to the times-table facts the children looked at in Lesson 1. Explain that the remainder can be expressed as a fraction - in this case, we have 2 left over out of the 3 that we were dividing by. This can be expressed as $^2/_3$. So $137 \div 3 = 45^2/_3$. Repeat this demonstration with other examples, such as $129 \div 4$, $208 \div 5$, $211 \div 2$.

Independent work: Explain that the children are going to practise short division by generating numbers (with a 2, 4, 5, 10 dice) to use as divisors. If the division has a remainder, this should be expressed as a fraction. For example, the children can generate a three-digit number (such as 533) by throwing one ordinary dice three times, then generate the divisor by throwing once the prepared dice, then work out the division (for example, $533 \div 4 = 133$ remainder 1, which is 133 and $^1/_4$).

Review

Check the children's understanding of how remainders can be expressed as fractions by asking for volunteers to demonstrate these examples: $151 \div 2$, $216 \div 5$, $418 \div 10$. Ask: *How do you know what the numerator will be? How do you know what the denominator will be?* (The numerator is the number remaining; the denominator is the divisor.)

$$151 \div 2 = 75\,r1 \rightarrow 75\frac{1}{2}$$

remainder

divisor

Draw the children's attention to $418 \div 10$. Ask: *Did we need to use a calculator to solve this? What answer would we have got?* (41.8) *What answer did we get when we used short division?* ($41^8/_{10}$) *Can anybody spot a link between these two answers?* ($^8/_{10}$ is the same as 0.8)

Differentiation

Less confident learners: The children can use the prepared dice to generate numbers and divisors. They may need adult support with short division, and express leftovers as a remainder only.
More confident learners: The children can use a ten-sided dice to generate higher numbers.

Lesson 3 (Teach and practise)

Starter
Refine and rehearse: Ask the children to compare fractions and tell you which is bigger. Say: *Which would you prefer, half a cake or $^4/_6$ of a cake? One and $^1/_3$ cakes or $^3/_3$?* Each time, ask the children to explain their answer. Repeat with other examples.

Main teaching activities
Whole class: Tell the children that today, they will continue to use short division and express the remainders as fractions - but they are also going to change the fractions into decimals. Explain that they already know some fraction and decimal equivalents, for example $^1/_{10} = 0.1$, $^1/_5 = 0.2$, $^8/_{10} = 0.8$. Revise other known equivalents such as those of ¼, ¾, $^1/_3$ and $^2/_3$. Record these on the board for reference.

Independent work: Indicate the following short division questions on the board: $157 \div 3$; $649 \div 10$; $213 \div 4$; $126 \div 4$; $419 \div 2$; $418 \div 8$; $586 \div 8$; $139 \div 4$. Explain that all of the questions will generate answers with fraction remainders, which the children should be able to convert to decimals using the equivalents listed on the board. Some of the calculations may need simplifying first.

Review
Explain to the children that we need a way to check our division calculations. Sometimes the inverse calculation is straightforward – for example, we can check $48 \div 6 = 8$ using $6 \times 8 = 48$. However, some calculations involving fractions might be difficult to check, especially if we want to use a calculator. Ask: *How could we check this calculation using a calculator?* Write on the board: $118 \div 4 = 29^2/_4 = 29½$. *What knowledge do we have to have that will help us to put this into the calculator?* (The knowledge of equivalent fractions and decimals.) $29½ = 29.5$ and $29.5 \times 4 = 118$.

Revise known fraction/decimal equivalents such as ½ = 0.5 and ¼ =

Differentiation

Less confident learners: The children may still need adult support with short division. Provide them with simple TU ÷ U questions which give a fraction remainder, for example: 82 ÷ 2; 73 ÷ 2; 49 ÷ 3; 66 ÷ 5; 78 ÷ 5; 39 ÷ 4; 59 ÷ 2.

More confident learners: Provide these children with ThHTU ÷ U questions, such as: 5126 ÷ 4; 2213 ÷ 4; 1157 ÷ 3; 6649 ÷ 10; 4419 ÷ 2; 4418 ÷ 5; 5586 ÷ 8; 4136 ÷ 4.

0.25. Use a calculator to demonstrate that $137 ÷ 3 = 45\frac{2}{3} = 45.666666$. Write this as $45.\dot{6}$. Ask: *What does the dot above the last digit mean?* (A recurring number. The actual division goes on to infinity.) *Will this inverse be accurate?* $45.67 × 3 = 137.01$. (Not quite, because 45.66 is the original answer rounded to two decimal places.)

Ask the children to try the following calculations, using a calculator, and check which inverse operations give an accurate answer: $122 ÷ 7$; $131 ÷ 5$; $241 ÷ 8$; $126 ÷ 9$. Ask: *Why did some of these not give an exactly correct answer when reversed?* (Because the original answer had to be rounded up or down.)

Lesson 4 (Teach and practise)

Starter

Refine and rehearse: Have a random selection of fractions displayed on the board. Ask the children to order them, starting with the smallest. Ask: *Can you explain how you decide which fraction is the smallest?* The children may suggest looking for the largest denominator. *What else do you have to consider when you are comparing fractions?* Make sure the children understand that the size of the numerator is also important – for example, $^7/_{10}$ is a larger fraction than $^3/_5$. If in doubt when comparing two fractions, they can convert them to decimals.

Main teaching activities

Whole class: Explain that today, the children will continue to use short division and express the answer as a decimal. Point out that some fraction/decimal equivalents are difficult to remember. Ask: *What can we do if we get a fraction remainder where we don't know the decimal equivalent?* (Use a calculator.) Explain that any fraction can be changed into a decimal by dividing the numerator by the denominator. Key into the calculator: $3 ÷ 10 = 0.3$. Try with other known equivalents before trying unknown fractions such as $^5/_6$ or $^4/_7$. Explain that some recurring decimals, such as $^4/_7$, have a recurring group of digits (0.57142857…). These decimals can be rounded to two decimal places (0.57). So, for example, $281 ÷ 7 = 40\frac{1}{7} = 40.14$. Remind the children that they cannot use the inverse operation for accurate checking if they have rounded an answer to two decimal places.

Independent work: Display the following short division problems. Some of the answers may need rounding: $189 ÷ 5$; $866 ÷ 5$; $986 ÷ 6$; $724 ÷ 7$; $369 ÷ 5$; $365 ÷ 7$. Remind the children to use short division first, only using a calculator to determine an unknown decimal.

Review

Ask the children:
● *Which fractions created recurring decimals? What do we have to remember when we check these?*
● *Have you learned any new equivalents that you think you will remember?*
● *What did you notice about $^2/_4$? … $^2/_{10}$?*

Provide each pair of children with a calculator. Call out a fraction or a decimal and ask the children to use their calculators to find the equivalent. Fractions are easier: they can simply be keyed into the calculator. Finding a fraction for a given decimal is more a matter of trial and error. To earn a point, the children must give the correct answer and explain what they did to find it. Give extra points at your own discretion for clear explanations and reasoning. The pair with the highest number of points are deemed the 'winners'.

Differentiation

Less confident learners: Provide similar division problems with TU ÷ U questions and simple or no remainders, for example: 23 ÷ 2; 33 ÷ 2; 65 ÷ 4; 46 ÷ 5; 87 ÷ 6.

More confident learners: Provide similar division problems with ThHTU ÷ U questions, such as: 2185 ÷ 5; 5866 ÷ 5; 3986 ÷ 6; 1724 ÷ 7; 2369 ÷ 5; 7365 ÷ 7.

Lesson 5 (Apply)

Starter

Refine and rehearse: Write a mixed selection of decimal and fraction pairs on the board. Ask for volunteers to match and link them with a coloured line (for example: $^2/_{10}$ = 0.2, $^{29}/_{100}$ = 0.29, ¼ = 0.25, ¾ = 0.75, $^1/_5$ = 0.2). Present a selection of fraction and decimal cards (from the 'Fractions, decimals and percentages' set) and ask the children to order them on a 0–1 number line. Discuss how the cards can be ordered, and especially how knowing equivalents can help. For example: *I have to decide which is smaller, 0.25 or $^1/_3$. I can recall that 0.25 = ¼, so it is less than $^1/_3$.*

Main teaching activities

Whole class: Explain that the children are going to apply their skills to solving word division problems that use money and measures. Remind them how to convert a word problem into a number sentence and then calculate the answer, perhaps generating a fraction or decimal remainder. For example, Mrs Smith has 1945 centimetres of wood to make into four equal-length bookshelves. How long will each shelf be?

$$0\ 4\ 8\ 6\ \text{r}1 = 486¼\text{cm or } 486.25\text{cm each}$$
$$4)1\ ^19\ ^34\ ^25$$

Independent work: Distribute the 'Division word problems' activity sheet. Ask the children to solve the word problems using their division skills.

Review

Share some of the children's answers with the class and iron out any difficulties or misconceptions that occur. Then ask: *What is the practical reason for rounding long decimal numbers to two decimal places when we are talking about money or measures?* (We usually cannot measure to any more than two decimal places, and money is only available in two decimal places. *Why do we convert fractions of numbers into decimals for money and measures?* (¼ of 1cm or £1 doesn't mean much, and isn't easily measurable until converted to mm or pence by using the decimal form.)

Ask: *Tell me a word problem that might use the calculation 204 ÷ 3.* This could be any practical problem. Repeat with 274 ÷ 8. Now ask: *Tell me a division word problem that has the answer 12 … 25.* Go through the steps necessary to go backwards from an answer to a calculation and then to a word problem. This is useful for reinforcing the solving of word problems.

Differentiation

Less confident learners: Provide the support version of 'Division word problems', with simpler problems.
More confident learners: Provide the extension version, with two-step problems.

Lesson 6 (Apply)

Starter

Revisit: Use a set of 'Fractions, decimals and percentages' cards to play 'trios' as the children did in the previous unit. Place all the cards face down (or stuck loosely to the board). Ask for volunteers to come and turn over three cards, so that everyone can see them. If they are a matching trio (such as 0.25, ¼, 25%) then they can be removed from the board. If not, they are turned face down and another child attempts to find a trio.

Main teaching activities

Whole class: Explain that weights and measures are important to our daily lives and we cannot avoid using them, whether shopping or doing home decoration. Introduce the concept of a house, Number 32, which is in need of some redecoration before the new owners can move in.

Distribute activity sheet 'DIY at Number 32' and go through the various measurements. Explain that sometimes the measurements may need converting to smaller units in order to calculate. For example: *Sally wants three new shelves in her room. Her shorter wall measures 2.8m. Shelving*

Securing number facts, relationships and calculating

BLOCK E

▶

is sold in 300cm or 10m lengths. Which is the best buy for Sally's shelves? How much would be wasted?

Ask: *If we have measurements in both metres and centimetres, what must we do to calculate the problems? How many centimetres in a metre?*
Independent work: Use the measurements on activity sheet 'DIY at Number 32' to calculate the home improvements needed at Number 32. Think carefully about standardising measurements before calculating.

Review
Go through some of the questions, asking individuals what operation they chose and how they created a calculation to solve the problem. Work through some of the examples on the board to iron out misconceptions and confusion. Encourage the children to draw a diagram of anything they cannot visualise.

Differentiation
Less confident learners: Provide the support version of the activity sheet, with simplified numbers and questions.
More confident learners: These children can work independently and then create more measurement questions and calculations of their own.

Lesson 7 (Apply)

Starter
Ask fraction questions related to division, such as $\frac{1}{4}$ of 32 or $\frac{1}{5}$ of 35, 48 sweets divided into eighths, one half of 90, and so on. The children hold up the answers on their number fans when you say *Show me*.

Main teaching activities
Whole class: Explain to the children that mixed units can sometimes be used in 'real-life' problems. Floors might be measured in m^2 whereas tiles are measured in cm^2. In order to calculate how many tiles may be needed, a common unit of measure needs to be used. Ask: *If a floor area measures 3m × 4m, how do you calculate how many 30 × 30cm tiles you need?* Convert the area to 300cm × 400cm. You can fit 10 × $30cm^2$ tiles across and $13\frac{1}{3}$ down. Since you have to buy whole tiles, the calculation would look like this: 10 × 14 = 140 tiles.
Independent work: Continue problem solving from Lesson 6. Ask the children to calculate the area of carpet needed for each room. Calculate the number of tins of paint needed for each room. A tin of paint covers $1\frac{1}{2}$ walls and costs £9.80. Sally wants one wall pink and the rest green. Mum wants the kitchen to have a different colour on each wall. Dad wants their bedroom all cream and the sitting room has one wall covered in wallpaper which Mum doesn't want to change. How much in total will they spend on paint?

Differentiation
Less confident learners: Use the support version of the 'DIY at Number 32' activity sheet. These children may experience difficulty in visualising the problem and may need added adult support. They should be encouraged to sketch out the different aspects of the problem, for example draw the tin of paint per room or draw a sketch of the floor area.
More confident learners: These children might like to sketch and redecorate an imaginary bedroom of their own, making up the dimensions. The computer simulation of painting a room on the 'Dulux' website might be a starting point.

Review
Ask questions such as: *What are the clues in these questions to help you decide on the operation to use? What formula did you use to calculate area? Why can't you calculate using mixed units?* Ask: *Think of a question, linked to Number 32, which could be solved using this number question: (4.1 × 2.8) ÷ 2.* (Sally wants half of her bedroom floor carpeted.)

Ask the group of children who made up their own measures questions related to number 32 to challenge the rest of the class.

Lesson 8 (Apply)

Starter
Revisit: Ask questions about fractions of quantities, such as $\frac{3}{4}$ of 1 litre or $\frac{2}{3}$ of 300g. The children raise their hands to answer.

Main teaching activities
Whole class: Explain to the class that as an extension to their 'real-life' word problem activities they are going to plan a barbeque for an end-of-term treat for the whole class. They must calculate what and how much food they need to buy and how much it will cost. They might have to reduce the amount of food and drink if the costs are too high. They must also work out how much to charge per person to cover their costs. This will involve them discussing

▷

Differentiation

Less confident learners: This group of children may need guidance in the art of negotiation as well as having adult support to calculate their shopping list. It may be a good idea for this group to use a calculator, as long as they can demonstrate what they had to press to obtain their answers.

More confident learners: These children might use their ICT skills to go 'virtual' shopping on a supermarket's internet shopping site. Remind them that this is only hypothetical and not to place any actual orders!

how much people can afford or would be willing to pay. Provide the children with the 'Shopping list' photocopiable sheet, which gives a unit cost for each item.

Group work: The children must work together to plan their menu and use their calculating skills to work out costs. Tell them that you need a detailed costing and evidence of their calculations. Tell them that they have to work democratically and that individuals may have to use their most persuasive language in order to get their choice of menu. Remind the children that they do not want to charge an excessive price for tickets but they must cover their costs.

Review

Find out which group has the most inventive party menu and the most reasonable ticket price. Ask questions such as: *Did you have to compromise in order to keep your costs down? How did you decide on your menu if individuals had strong views? What persuaded you to cut out _____? Tell me the calculation you had to do to work out the total cost of sausages. Tell me the calculation you used to decide the ticket price.*

Lessons 9-15

Preparation

Lesson 9: Make ratio cards (1:5; 1:6 and 1:4), one for each pair of children.

Lesson 11: Make an OHT or A3 copy of 'Cat food advertisments'. Write on the board some fractions to be ordered.

Lesson 12: Prepare a second ratio and proportion sheet similar to the 'Ratio and proportion' activity sheet.

Lesson 13: Provide some ratio and proportion questions that start with a percentage.

Lesson 14: Copy a newspaper table of exchange rates onto OHT. Prepare a chart with the headings 'Holiday destination', 'Local currency', '£ to exchange' and 'Amount received'.

Lesson 15: Write on the board the recipe for the starter. Display a fictional exchange rate chart.

You will need

Photocopiable pages
'Cat food advertisement' (page 220), copied to A3 or OHT; 'Ratio and proportion' (page 221), one for each child.

CD resources
Support and extension versions of 'Ratio and proportion'. General resource sheet: 'Number fan cards 0-9'.

Equipment
Calculators; disposable cups; squash; measuring jugs or cylinders; Multilink cubes; coloured pencils, card, scissors, adhesive, etc for game making.

Learning objectives

Starter

● Represent a puzzle or problem by identifying and recording the information or calculations needed to solve it; find possible solutions and confirm them in the context of the problem.

● Express a smaller whole number as a fraction of a larger one, eg recognise that 5 out of 8 is $\frac{5}{8}$; find equivalent fractions, eg $\frac{7}{10} = \frac{14}{20}$, or $\frac{19}{10} = 1\frac{9}{10}$; relate fractions to their decimal representations.

● Use sequences to scale numbers up or down; solve problems involving proportions of quantities, eg decrease quantities in a recipe designed to feed six people.

● Find fractions using division, eg $\frac{1}{100}$ of 5kg, and percentages of numbers and quantities, eg 10%, 5% and 15% of £80.

Main teaching activities

2006

● Represent a puzzle or problem by identifying and recording the information or calculations needed to solve it; find possible solutions and confirm them in the context of the problem.

● Understand percentage as the number of parts in every 100 and express tenths and hundredths as percentages.

● Use sequences to scale numbers up or down; solve problems involving proportions of quantities, eg decrease quantities in a recipe designed to feed six people.

1999

● Use all four operations to solve simple word problems involving numbers and quantities based on 'real life', money and measures (including time), using one or more steps, including finding simple percentages.

● Choose and use appropriate number operations to solve problems, and appropriate ways of calculating: mental, mental with jottings, written methods, calculator.

● Begin to understand percentage as the number of parts in every 100.

● Express one half, one quarter, three quarters, and tenths and hundredths, as percentages (eg know that $\frac{3}{4} = 75\%$).

● Solve problems involving ratio and proportion (Year 6).

Vocabulary

problem, solution, calculator, calculate, calculation, equation, operation,

symbol, inverse, answer, method, explain, predict, reason, reasoning, pattern, relationship, ratio, proportion, in every, for every, to every

Lesson 9 (Teach)

Starter
Rehearse: Shout out quick-fire percentage questions, and ask children to use number fans to show their answers: 10% of 60, 5% of 80, 25% of 36, 50% of 32, 20% of 50, and so on.

Main teaching activities
Whole class: Tell the children that they are going to make a drink of squash, since drinks during the day are said to rehydrate the brain and so will improve their concentration! However, they must make the drink in a particular ratio. Remind the children that ratio means 'for every': *if I make squash in the ratio 1:5, I will need five parts of water for every one part of squash.* Demonstrate this using coloured cubes. Explain that this ratio can be used to calculate amounts - for example: 5ml squash to 25ml water; 50ml squash to 250ml water; 10ml squash to 50ml water. Work through a number of these examples with the children to help them understand the relationship. Repeat with ratios of 1:4 and 1:3.

Paired work: Give each pair a ratio card and the equipment needed. Ask them to make up their drink in the ratio given on the card. Explain that they need to measure the capacity of their cup and mark the 'full' line (approximately 150–200ml) in order to calculate the correct amounts in millilitres. Then they should mark their cup with the level of squash needed before the water is added to fill up the cup. This will enable you to check the accuracy of their calculations. Once you have done this, they can make the squash and drink it. Expect to see improved concentration!

Review
Ask: *Were all the drinks the same strength? Which were stronger?* (The ones with more squash and less water.) *How many millilitres of squash did you use? How much water? Did you think your squash was too weak, too strong or just right?* Discuss how tastes differ and then take a vote on the children's preferences. *Is there a favourite ratio that makes the best squash drink?* Explain that this ratio could be expressed as a proportion - for example, 1:4 would mean that $\frac{1}{5}$ of the whole drink was squash. You can demonstrate this by creating a fraction from the amounts:
200ml in the ratio 1:4 means 40ml squash and 160ml water
Proportion of squash = $\frac{40}{200}$ = $\frac{4}{20}$ = $\frac{1}{5}$.

Differentiation
Differentiate by the level of support needed, particularly with measuring and calculation.

Lesson 10 (Teach and practise)

Starter
Revisit: Ask more complicated percentages than in Lesson 9, which need greater calculation, and ask the children to explain how they would calculate them: 30% may be found by adding 10% + 10% + 10%; 12% by finding 10% + 1% + 1% or 90% by subtracting 10% from the whole number. Discuss strategies.

Main teaching activities
Whole class: Explain that a ratio is a comparison of numbers or amounts. Work through some examples, such as adults to children or chairs to tables in the classroom. Use the latter context to show that sometimes ratios can be simplified in a similar way to fractions. If you have 32 chairs and 8 tables, this is a ratio of 4:1 (dividing both numbers by 8). Explain that some ratios cannot be reduced to *x*:1. For example, a mixture of pens and pencils might be in a ratio of 3:2.

Independent work: Ask the children to represent some ratios by drawing or writing. Discuss a first example: 10 cats in a ratio of 1:4 ginger to black.

The children must draw two ginger cats and eight black ones. Either provide some more examples or ask children to make up their own.

Review

Check the children's answers and understanding. Ask: *If I have a box of chocolates with a ratio 1:4 white chocolate to dark chocolate, how many chocolates could there be in the box?* (Any multiple of 5.) *Explain how you know.* (The ratio has 5 parts.)

Ask: *Can you explain in words what a proportion is? Can you explain what a ratio is?* Give 20 coloured cubes to each group: 10 in one colour and 10 in another. Explain that you are going to say a ratio or a proportion, and that you would like the children to represent it with coloured cubes. Say: *Show me a proportion of 7 out of 10...1/6... 6/7... 8 out of 11. Also show me a ratio of 1:6... 3:4... 6:7... 8:5.* Use this game to assess the children's understanding.

Lesson 11 (Teach and practise)

Starter

Revisit: Indicate the fractions written on the board, some of which need to be simplified for the children to order them:

$^3/_3$, $^2/_6$, $^3/_9$, $^1/_3$, $^1/_5$, $^1/_4$, $^2/_4$, $^1/_9$, $^1/_6$

Ask the children to order them, smallest first. Encourage them to explain how they know which is smaller.

Main teaching activities

Whole class: Display the A3 or OHT copy of 'Cat food advertisement'. Look at the statement. Ask the children: *What does this mean? How many cat owners did they ask?* Some children may answer '18', which will need to be corrected by explaining that a multiple of 10 must have been asked. 8 out of 10 can be expressed as the fraction $^8/_{10}$, which can be simplified to $^4/_5$ by dividing the top and bottom numbers by 2. Explain that this is a proportion. The ratio of cat owners who said their cats liked 'Yummy Kit' cat food to those who didn't is 8:2. This can be simplified to 4:1, which is less impressive-looking in advertising terms. So the ratio is 4:1 and the proportion of owners who said their cats liked the product is $^4/_5$.

Independent work: Distribute the 'Ratio and proportion' activity sheet. Explain that the children must convert these proportions to ratios in their simplest form.

Review

Explain that you are going to say ratios and proportions that the children need to simplify before making them out of cubes. For example, a ratio of 3:6 can be simplified to 1:2. Distribute the cubes and say: *Show me a ratio in its simplest form of 6:8... 8:4... 2:10... 3:9. Now show me a proportion in its simplest form of 3 out of 12... 5 out of 10... 2/6... 4/12.* Look out for errors in simplifying. Ask for a volunteer to show each arrangement of cubes and explain how he or she simplified the ratio or proportion.

Differentiation

Less confident learners: The children can use coloured cubes to help them visualise the ratios suggested by the teacher. They may need adult support.
More confident learners: The children could write and draw some ratios of their own.

Differentiation

Less confident learners: Provide the support version of the activity sheet. The children could use coloured cubes to help them visualise the proportions and ratios. They may need additional support.
More confident learners: Provide the extension version of the activity sheet. The children could create some similar proportion/ratio problems of their own, then swap with a friend to work out the answers.

Securing number facts, relationships and calculating

BLOCK E

Lesson 12 (Apply)

Starter
Reason: Ask the children to work out the following on their calculator. Say: *Which would you prefer to be given, 25% of £120 or 20% of £100?* Ask them to explain their answers and the keys they pressed to get there. Record these key presses on the board. Repeat for similar questions.

Main teaching activities
Whole class: Explain that we use ratio and proportion quite often in daily life for comparison, even if we don't realise it. Show the children the 'Cat food advertisement' sheet again; can they suggest any other examples? Every time we vote or express a preference, a ratio can be created. For example, say: *8 out of 32 children in our class want to stay in at playtime. What is the ratio of children who want to stay in to children who want to go out?* (8:24 or 1:3) *6 out of 24 children choose baked beans instead of spaghetti at lunchtime. What is the ratio of those who chose baked beans to those who chose spaghetti?* (6:18 or 1:3)
Independent work: Distribute your prepared ratio and proportion sheet. Explain that these are more ratio and proportion problems for the children to solve. Encourage them to show their working.

Review
Ask: *If 6 out of 30 children say they do not watch the TV news, what proportion do watch it?* ($^{24}/_{30}$ or $^4/_5$) Explain how you worked that out. *What is the ratio of children who watch the news to those who do not?* (1:4)

Explain that the order in which a ratio is expressed is important to the meaning. Demonstrate this by asking three children with brown hair and two with blond hair to stand up facing the class. Ask the rest of the class to express this as a ratio. They may say, correctly, that there is a ratio of 3:2 brown hair to blond. Write this on the board, then ask the volunteers to change places. Ask: *What is the ratio now? Can we simply say 'There is a ratio of 3:2 or 2:3', or do we have to explain what is in ratio with what? Who can tell me the proportion of children who do NOT have brown hair?* Repeat with other examples.

Differentiation
Less confident learners: As before, the children can use cubes to help them visualise the groups.
More confident learners: After completing the given problems, the children can go on to create their own scenarios and questions, then swap with a friend to work out the answers.

Lesson 13 (Teach and practise)

Starter
Reason: Ask the children to think about the following questions and to explain how they arrived at their answer. Say: *In a test Lee scored 40 out of 50. What percentage is that? I think 30% is the same as $^3/_{10}$ – am I right? Explain why 30% is not the same as $^1/_3$.*

Main teaching activities
Whole class: Explain that this lesson links proportion and ratio with percentages. Give an example: *if 80% of people asked are happy with their car, that means 80 out of 100 or $^{80}/_{100}$, which can be simplified to $^8/_{10}$ or $^4/_5$.* Ask: *What proportion is unhappy?* (20%, which means $^{20}/_{100}$, which can be simplified to $^2/_{10}$ or $^1/_5$.) *What is the ratio of unhappy to happy people?* (1:4) Explain that if you know the size of the sample, you can then work out the actual numbers involved. If 200 people were asked, how many were happy with their car? Demonstrate the calculation:
$^4/_5 × 200 = 800/5 = 1600/10 = 160$
Independent work: The children should be given some questions that begin with a percentage linked to proportion. They should use proportion out of 100 to find the answers, for example:
- 100 people were asked if they liked school; 25% said they did not. How many were happy at school?
- 40% of people questioned agreed that the climate is changing. If 200 people were asked, how many thought that the weather remained unchanged?

Differentiation
Less confident learners: Provide simpler calculations. As in the core activities, but only 100 people in each survey.
More confident learners: The children could devise their own percentage or proportion questions, then swap with a friend to work out the answers.

• 90% of people said their dogs loved walking. If 150 people were asked, how many dog owners had lazy pets?

Review

Share some of the children's answers. Invite some of the children who have made up their own questions to challenge the rest of the class to solve them. Ask: *How would you explain the difference between ratio and proportion to someone? How are they linked to percentages? Does it matter that the number in the sample is not 100 when you are converting to a percentage? How much is 100%?*

Lesson 14 (Teach)

Starter

Reason: Ask the children to explain how they would solve the following:
• A recipe gives an amount to feed two people. Explain how you would change the recipe to feed eight people.
• A packet of sweets contains two mints for every three toffees. How many toffees would be needed for a packet of sweets that contains 12 mints?
• I use three onions to make 0.5 litres of soup. How much soup could I make if I used nine onions?

Main teaching activities

Whole class: Ask the children if they can think of any currencies used in other countries: euro, US dollar, Australian dollar, Japanese yen, and so on. Explain that when you travel from one country to another it is necessary to convert your money from one currency to another. Ask where they could find out about exchange rates (banks, newspapers, internet). Use the current exchange rate to calculate simple conversions: if £1.00 = 1.5 euros, how many euros would I receive for £10.00 or £100.00 or £150.00?
Independent work: Choose six destinations to visit on your world tour and fill them in on the prepared chart. Ask the children to make a copy of the chart and use the exchange rates on your OHT to calculate how much local currency they would receive at the current exchange rate. They should complete the chart for all of the currencies chosen.

Review

Share as a class the results of the currency conversions. Ask: *Which currencies were the most difficult to convert? Did you have to use a calculator? If you were on holiday and trying to calculate the cost of things would you be as exact as this?* Also pose questions such as: *If I receive 1.5 euros for each £1.00, how do I calculate 50p? I want to buy a vase for 32 euros, how much is that in pounds sterling? A flight to New York costs £250 – how much is that in euros... US dollars... Japanese yen?*

Differentiation
Less confident learners: You might wish to round the exchange rates for simpler calculations.
More confident learners: Extend the number of currencies to calculate.

Lesson 15 (Apply)

Starter

Recall: Ask the children to alter the following recipe to make 51 cakes instead of 6.
Chocolate sponge cakes (makes 6)
50g sugar
50g butter
40g self raising flour
15g cocoa
1 teaspoon baking powder
1 egg
1 tablespoon milk
6 chocolate buttons
6 paper cake cases

Unit 3 ▭ 3 weeks

Ask: *What did you have to work out first before you could calculate? What number did you multiply all the ingredients by?*

Main teaching activities
Whole class: Display a fictional exchange rate such as 4 orbs = £1.00 sterling. Write up: 2 orbs, 6 orbs, 1 orb, 16 orbs, 18 orbs. Ask the children to convert the amounts to £ sterling and explain their strategies for doing so. Explain to the children that they are going to design a game based on exchange rates. This could be a board game, such as 'Snakes and ladders' but introducing a currency exchange or a card game such as 'Pairs' or 'Snap'. To simplify the fluctuating exchange rates, the game could use foreign currency to pounds sterling or some imaginary currencies. Advise against having too many currencies or the game will become unmanageable.

Paired work: Design a game using the concept of exchange rates. Plan the look of the game and the rules. Decide on the materials that will be needed to construct it.

Review
Invite each pair to explain the basis of their game, the rules and where the exchange rate element occurs.

Differentiation
Less confident learners: Encourage this group to plan a simple card game such as 'Snap'. This might simply feature different currency cards to match.
More confident learners: This group may be able to create a game requiring exchange calculations and penalties, or a 'Snap' type game where the equivalent sum of money is matched, eg 1.5 euros match with £1.00.

■SCHOLASTIC

Name _____   Date _____

Division word problems

1. Aunt Joan sent £152 to be divided equally between me and my two sisters. How much did we receive each?

   _____

2. In a marathon relay race, six people run a total of 159 miles. How far does each individual run?

   _____

3. There are 209 litres of fuel to be shared between five vans. How much fuel will each van receive?

   _____

4. I have 342cm of fabric to make four identical cushions. How much fabric can I use in each one?

   _____

5. I use 1265g of flour to make eight cakes. How much flour is used in each cake?

   _____

Now make up some division word problems of your own.

Securing number facts, relationships and calculating

BLOCK E

Name _____   Date _____

DIY at Number 32

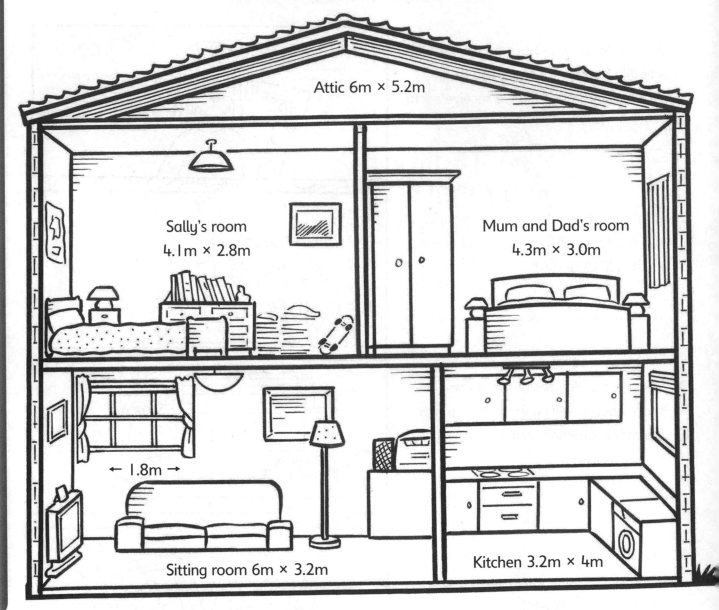

Attic 6m × 5.2m

Sally's room
4.1m × 2.8m

Mum and Dad's room
4.3m × 3.0m

← 1.8m →

Sitting room 6m × 3.2m

Kitchen 3.2m × 4m

1. Sally wants four shelves in her bedroom. The wall measures 2.8m wide. Shelving is sold in 300cm lengths costing £2.40 each or 10m lengths costing £9.00. Which is the best value for money? How much will be wasted?

_____

2. The sitting room curtains need replacing. The material chosen is £8.20 per metre. They need to buy 4 times the length of the window. How much do they have to buy? How much will it cost?

_____

3. The attic needs new floor boards. Floor boards can be bought in 6m lengths, each 20cm wide. How many are needed?

_____

4. The kitchen floor needs tiles. What is the area of the floor?

_____

Name _____   Date _____

Shopping list

Pack of 6 burger rolls	68p	Jar mayonnaise	£2.15
Pack of 6 burgers	£1.99	Baking potatoes (12)	£1.69
Pack 12 sausages	£2.19	Butter	69p
6 Hot dog rolls	72p	500g cheese	£4.58
Net of 4 onions	36p	Chicken kebabs (12)	£2.99
Roasted vegetable kebabs (12)	£1.99	Veggieburgers (6)	£1.49
Tomato ketchup	£1.19	1.5 litre water	99p
1 litre orange juice	£1.12	3 litre squash	£2.50
16 mini doughnuts	£1.67	6 fruit kebabs	£2.18

Securing number facts, relationships and calculating

BLOCK E

Name _____   Date _____

Cat food advertisement

Securing number facts, relationships and calculating

BLOCK E

100 MATHS FRAMEWORK LESSONS · YEAR 5

PHOTOCOPIABLE ■SCHOLASTIC

Name _____   Date _____

Ratio and proportion

Convert these proportions to ratios.
The first example has been done for you.

1. 8 out of 10 owners say their cats prefer 'Yummy Kit'.

   Ratio of Yummy Kit preferred to other brands is   **8:2**

2. $\frac{6}{9}$ dogs are brown.

   Ratio of brown dogs to other colours is

3. 7 out of 20 boys like football.

   Ratio of boys who like football to those who don't is

4. I out of 10 coins are 5p pieces.

   Ratio of 5p pieces to other coins is

5. 8 out of 12 birds are sparrows.

   Ratio of sparrows to other birds is

6. $\frac{7}{21}$ children love maths.

   Ratio of children who love maths to those who don't is

7. $\frac{90}{100}$ teachers need a holiday.

   Ratio of teachers who need a holiday to those who don't is

SCHOLASTIC PHOTOCOPIABLE

Securing number facts, relationships and calculating

BLOCK E

Comments

Year 5 End-of-year objectives	✓	Comments
Explain what each digit represents in whole numbers and decimals with up to two places, and partition, round and order these numbers.		
Use knowledge of place value and addition and subtraction of two-digit numbers to derive sums and differences and doubles and halves of decimals (eg 6.5 ± 2.7, half of 5.6, double 0.34).		
Use efficient written methods to add and subtract whole numbers and decimals with up to two places.		
Construct frequency tables, pictograms and bar and line graphs to represent the frequencies of events and changes over time.		
Draw and measure lines to the nearest millimetre; measure and calculate the perimeter of regular and irregular polygons; use the formula for the area of a rectangle to calculate the rectangle's area.		
Read and plot coordinates in the first quadrant; recognise parallel and perpendicular lines in grids and shapes; use a set-square and ruler to draw shapes with perpendicular or parallel sides.		

Pupil name _____   Class name _____

Year 5 End-of-year objectives						
Explain what each digit represents in whole numbers and decimals with up to two places, and partition, round and order these numbers.						
Use knowledge of place value and addition and subtraction of two-digit numbers to derive sums and differences and doubles and halves of decimals (eg 6.5 + 2.7, half of 5.6, double 0.34).						
Use efficient written methods to add and subtract whole numbers and decimals with up to two places.						
Construct frequency tables, pictograms and bar and line graphs to represent the frequencies of events and changes over time.						
Draw and measure lines to the nearest millimetre; measure and calculate the perimeter of regular and irregular polygons; use the formula for the area of a rectangle to calculate the rectangle's area.						
Read and plot coordinates in the first quadrant; recognise parallel and perpendicular lines in grids and shapes; use a set-square and ruler to draw shapes with perpendicular or parallel sides.						

Mainly level 4

Recording sheet

CLASS